Introduction to the Essay

HAYDEN GENRE SERIES

ROBERT W. BOYNTON, *Consulting Editor*

INTRODUCTION TO THE SHORT STORY (SECOND ED.)
Robert W. Boynton and Maynard Mack

INTRODUCTION TO THE POEM (SECOND ED.)
Robert W. Boynton and Maynard Mack

INTRODUCTION TO THE PLAY: IN THE THEATER OF THE MIND (SECOND ED.)
Robert W. Boynton and Maynard Mack

INTRODUCTION TO THE NOVEL (SECOND ED.)
O. B. Davis

INTRODUCTION TO THE ESSAY
Edmund Fuller and O. B. Davis

INTRODUCTION TO BIBLICAL LITERATURE
O. B. Davis

INTRODUCTION TO MYTH
Peter R. Stillman

INTRODUCTION TO TRAGEDY
Edward J. Gordon

INTRODUCTION TO FOLKLORE
David C. Laubach

EXPERIENCING BIOGRAPHY
Robert E. Beck

SOUNDS AND SILENCES: POEMS FOR PERFORMING
Robert W. Boynton and Maynard Mack

WHODUNITS, FARCES, AND FANTASIES: TEN SHORT PLAYS
Robert W. Boynton and Maynard Mack

STORIES IN PERSPECTIVE
Eric W. Johnson

Introduction to the Essay

EDMUND FULLER

Chairman, English Department
South Kent School

O. B. DAVIS

Chairman, English Department
Kent School

HAYDEN BOOK COMPANY, INC.
Rochelle Park, New Jersey

Acknowledgments

G. K. CHESTERTON. "On the Classics" reprinted by permission of Miss D. E. Collins and A. P. Watt & Son, London.

LOREN EISELEY. "Wolf" copyright © 1965 by Loren Eiseley. Reprinted from his volume *The Unexpected Universe* by permission of Harcourt Brace Jovanovich, Inc.

CLIFTON FADIMAN. "Faulkner, Extra-Special, Double-Distilled" copyright © 1936, 1964. The New Yorker Magazine, Inc. Reprinted by permission of Clifton Fadiman.

EDMUND FULLER. "Lord of the Hobbits: J. R. R. Tolkien" from *Books With Men Behind Them* by Edmund Fuller, copyright © 1962 by Edmund Fuller. Reprinted by permission of Random House, Inc.

WILLIAM GOLDING. "Fable" from *The Hot Gates and Other Occasional Pieces* copyright © 1965 by William Golding. Reprinted by permission of Harcourt Brace Jovanovich, Inc. and Faber and Faber Ltd.

ALFRED KAZIN. "Brownsville" from *A Walker in the City* copyright 1951 by Alfred Kazin. Reprinted by permission of Harcourt Brace Jovanovich, Inc.

 Library of Congress Catalog Number 71-169102.

Printed in the United States of America

6 7 8 9 PRINTING

79 YEAR

Preface

Any literate person who practices his literacy reads and writes more of the essay kind of prose than of any other. It follows that good essays are worth study, understanding, mulling over, and even imitating.

Our aim in this book is to introduce the essay as a living form, far more than what is left over when poetry, fiction, drama, and reportage have been subtracted from written experience. We make it clear in our brief introduction ("What is an Essay?") that we shun rigid definitions of either the form or the purpose of the essay. But we don't shun trying to define the parameters and perimeters of what has been for centuries a useful if elusive term.

What follows is a collection of excellent essays. Most of them are modern – William Hazlitt, Mark Twain and Lord Macaulay representing earlier examples of the tradition. All of them in some sense evaluate, though they deal with subjects as diverse as the hanging of a man and prizefighting, which are *actions*, to patriotism and the humanities, which are *ideas*. History, education, and literature, classical and modern, are discussed. One writer tells how he wrote a book. Another describes his own education. Three men look back at boyhood scenes and experiences and try to extract a meaning from them. For another, the physical activity of chopping wood is a medium for reflection.

Forewords and afterwords (essays about essays) are supplied where they seemed useful. Questions and topics for discussion and writing follow each essay. Their purpose is to direct close reading with attention to both content and method.

Contents

What Is an Essay? 1

1. REACTIONS TO A FINAL SCENE 5

foreword to *A Hanging*, 6

A Hanging by George Orwell 8

afterword to *A Hanging*, 12

The Presence of Mine Enemies by O. B. Davis 14

Danny Deever by Rudyard Kipling 18

afterword to *A Hanging, The Presence of Mine Enemies,* and *Danny Deever,* 19

2. THE SPORTING LIFE 21

foreword to *Boxing With the Naked Eye* and *The Fight,* 22

Boxing With the Naked Eye by A. J. Liebling 24

The Fight by William Hazlitt 34

afterword to *Boxing With the Naked Eye* and *The Fight,* 50

3. MEN AND HISTORY 53

foreword to *Charles II,* 54

Charles II by Thomas Babington Macaulay 55

foreword to *Of Mr. Booker T. Washington and Others,* 59

Of Mr. Booker T. Washington and Others by W. E. B. DuBois 60

foreword to *The Politician,* 71

The Politician by H. L. Mencken 72

4. PRO PATRIA 77

foreword to *The Idea of Patriotism* and *On Patriotism — A Fragment*, 78

The Idea of Patriotism by A. L. Rowse 79

On Patriotism — A Fragment by William Hazlitt 86

afterword to *The Idea of Patriotism* and *On Patriotism — A Fragment*, 87

foreword to *Wrong Ism*, 91

Wrong Ism by J. B. Priestley 92

foreword to *The War Prayer*, 96

The War Prayer by Mark Twain 97

5. BOOKS 101

foreword to *Fable*, 102

Fable by William Golding 103

afterword to *Fable*, 118

foreword to *The Lord of the Hobbits: J. R. R. Tolkien*, 119

The Lord of the Hobbits: J. R. R. Tolkien by Edmund Fuller .. 120

foreword to *Faulkner, Extra-Special, Double-Distilled*, 136

Faulkner, Extra-Special, Double-Distilled by Clifton Fadiman 137

6. EDUCATION 143

foreword to *New Eyes for Old*, 144

New Eyes for Old by Richard McKenna 145

foreword to *How Impractical Are the Humanities?*, 156

How Impractical Are the Humanities? by Louis B. Salomon ... 157

afterword to *New Eyes for Old* and *How Impractical Are the Humanities?*, 167 foreword to *On the Classics,* 168

On the Classics by G. K. Chesterton 169

7. CHILDHOOD REMEMBERED 173

foreword to *A Memory of Father, Brownsville,* and *Once More to the Lake,* 174

A Memory of Father by J. Saunders Redding 175

Brownsville by Alfred Kazin 180

Once More to the Lake by E. B. White 185

8. MAN AND NATURE 193

foreword to *Confessions of a Wood-Chopping Man,* 194

Confessions of a Wood-Chopping Man by Hugh MacLennan 195

foreword to *Wolf,* 200

Wolf by Loren Eiseley 201

foreword to *The Individual and the Species,* 203

The Individual and the Species by Joseph Wood Krutch 204

Essay: A loose sally of the mind; an irregular indigested piece; not a regular and orderly composition.

Samuel Johnson

What is an Essay?

In 1580, the French philosopher Montaigne published the first edition of his *Essais*, a collection of his personal reflections on various topics. When he did so, Montaigne made a substantial contribution to the mass of writing which is one of Western civilization's chief glories. He also supplied the world with a useful term, although the world has been uneasy about defining it. L'*essai* means the *attempt*. Montaigne chose his title to indicate that his brief prose discussions of such things as lies, cannibals, speech, certain works of classical literature, conversation, war, women, and hatred are tentative and personal rather than conclusive and objective. These short pieces are, he asserted, *attempts* to express how various things seem to him.

Of course essays in this sense were written centuries before Montaigne. Aristotle wrote them in the fourth century B. C., as did Plato. The Old Testament of the Bible contains them, notably the whole book of *Ecclesiastes* and a good part of the book of *Job*, which also happens to be a drama. Plutarch's brief *Lives*, which are the beginning of biography, are really biographical essays. Ever since human beings have made a practice of writing personal letters to their friends and families there have been essayists as Montaigne uses the term. Today, most of us who write at all write more brief prose discussions of matters toward which we have personal attitudes than anything else. Certainly most modern people read more of such material than they do of poetry, drama, or fiction. Consider the essential qualities of most magazine articles, newspaper editorials, a great deal of what passes for news reporting, advertising copy, political platforms, sermons, reviews, as well as the vast flow of nonfiction books which presume to instruct us about diet, religion, sex, getting into college, and who killed President Kennedy.

Although we might make a case for calling any short personal piece of nonfiction an essay, the fact is that since Montaigne's gift of a name, a somewhat more formal and slightly more restrictive description of the essay has developed. This has been largely a matter of self-conscious intention. In imitation of the inventor of the term, writers set themselves the task of writing prose discussions of things that interested them, not as letters to friends, practical instruction booklets, or for other incidental purposes, but simply and explicitly as essays — short, carefully constructed attempts to edify and entertain the public with their thoughts. In response, the literate public developed expectations about essayists and essays.

In some ways these expectations were and remain very broad. Essays have been written about individual people, historical events, historical theories, mathematics, science, and every sort of human relationship — indeed, virtually everything about which the human being is capable of having a personal attitude. Essays may be solemn, satiric, funny, melancholy, business-like — may take any tone of which the writer is capable. The technical form of an essay may be descriptive, expository (or explanatory), argumentative, or narrative. It is often a combination.

Alexander Pope, in the 18th Century, wrote *An Essay on Man* and *An Essay on Criticism* in rhymed couplets — both famous works and both undoubted essays. Other poets have done the same without using the word "essay." James Russell Lowell's *A Fable for Critics* is an example and so is Lord Byron's satirical poem, *English Bards and Scotch Reviewers.* Milton's "L'Allegro" and "Il Penseroso" are, in effect, poetical essays on joy and melancholy. Though commonly the essay expresses one person's view, even that may have exceptions. This Introduction is an essay expressing the shared opinions of two persons about essays. Yet in spite of, or rather together with, this accepted looseness of definition, the reader who picks up something labeled an "essay" written by one who acknowledges himself an "essayist," does expect certain things.

He expects, first of all, that the essay will be short, something to be read in one sitting. He expects that, whatever its topic or rhetorical techniques, the heart of the matter will be the personal attitude of the essayist and that this attitude will be revealed clearly. Finally, he expects that the essay will fulfill these expectations in a manner that holds his interest. Aware of these anticipations, the self-conscious essayist must work hardest for success on the last. The ability to interest readers who are strangers to him in a short presentation of his attitudes about something is not a natural gift (although some people are born with aptitudes which make it easier for them to achieve than it is for others). The essayist must *learn* to write an essay; he must learn what combinations of thoughts, words, examples, and other devices help to maintain interest in the sort of project he is undertaking. He learns, as we all do, from the examples of those who have attempted his task before him. The modern essay, granting changes in language and point of view, in form and manner is essentially what has been expected of essayists since Montaigne.

Most of the pieces in this book were written as essays by men aware of themselves as essayists. That is, you will not find letters, editorials, or advertising copy — a few of many kinds of material written for other purposes, but which may happen to fulfill Montaigne's general definition and the expectations of the modern reader. Here we will study pieces written to be essays and consequently composed in that particular tradition and exemplifying its most characteristic techniques and varieties.

There are three exceptions, all having precedent in collections of essays, which in themselves are worthwhile examples of the flexibility of the form: Macaulay's brief examination of the character of Charles II of England, and Alfred Kazin's and Saunders Redding's descriptions of the environments of their childhoods. All are taken from longer contexts, respectively a history and autobiographical memoirs. Yet the selections presented possess the qualities and fulfill the aims of the essay.

Some essays are written originally to be spoken. Not every speech is an essay, but an essay first written for the ear is no less truly an essay than one intended first for the eye. Those by A. L. Rowse and Richard McKenna are examples of this kind.

Two characteristics appear to be present in a society where the essay flourishes: intellectual curiosity and a strong feeling for personal liberty. Of course, in the most intellectually torpid of societies some few can be found who want to know the ideas of others and in the most tyrannical of worlds there are those who risk persecution to write what they think. The great times and places for the essay, however, have been those in which ideas and their free exchange have been valued. Partly "invented" and named by a Frenchman, the essay exists in the literatures of all languages, but it may be significant that writers in English have had a special affinity for it, possibly unmatched anywhere.

Dr. Vannevar Bush, a distinguished scientist who has also written excellent essays, remarks in the Preface to one of his collections, "Writing essays is a rugged experience." The "rugged" aspect of the task is the effort to achieve *focus* and *refinement*. Thought must be generated in the mind, clarified, and organized. What is set down on paper is the result of those processes, but in varying degrees it still requires a painful refining and revising before it is ready for the eyes of readers and is published. It is a discipline of mind and craft and, like all disciplines, is demanding. It is also often a pleasure, as any form of accomplished mastery may be.

Another fine modern essayist was Joseph Wood Krutch, who said, "One of the most gratifying privileges of the essayist is that of expressing opinions on subjects he doesn't know much about." This self-deprecating exaggeration by one of our best-stocked minds reflects Montaigne's concept which gives this literary form its name — the attempt to explore opinion, to push past the safely known or smugly assumed, and to speculate, challenge, propose, or to evaluate by a personal standard of principle or taste. It refuses to concede thought on any subject to specialists alone.

1

Reactions to a Final Scene

Eight O'Clock

He stood and heard the steeple
    Sprinkle the quarters on the morning town.
One, two, three, four, to market place and people
    It tossed them down.

Strapped, noosed, nighing his hour,
    He stood and counted them and cursed his luck;
And then the clock collected in the tower
    Its strength, and struck.

A. E. HOUSMAN

Foreword to *A Hanging*

To most people, George Orwell is the man who wrote *1984.* If he had done nothing else, that remarkable novel of warning or prophecy would ensure his fame. *1984,* however, was not published until 1949, the year before Orwell's death, and he had been writing and publishing for twenty years before that. He was a journalist, poet, autobiographer, novelist, literary critic, reviewer, and essayist.

Here we are primarily interested in Orwell as essayist. Certain characteristics of the man and his work suggest that this may have been the role for which he was best fitted. He had unusually strong personal convictions. Again and again the events of his life demonstrate that he would back his opinions at his own expense. He quit a secure career as a colonial administrator in Burma because he came to believe that British rule in the East was wrong in practice and even more so in principle. He subjected himself to absolute poverty in Paris and London because he felt it important to learn the life of the poor. He fought and bled for the Spanish Loyalists in the Spanish Civil War in the 1930's. Unlike many of his contemporaries, for whom talk was cheap, Orwell backed his opinions with his actions.

Accompanying this passionate devotion to his beliefs was a kind of moral objectivity which is rarely found in association with strong feelings. Orwell's personal commitments did not blind him to the weaknesses of his own side or the virtues of the other. About his own period as a colonial administrator, for example, he says:

> I did not even know that the British Empire is dying, still less did I know that it is a great deal better than the younger empires that are going to supplant it. All I knew was that I was stuck between my hatred of the empire I served and my rage against the evil-spirited little beasts who tried to make my job impossible.

A self-proclaimed socialist, he did not hesitate to infuriate the socialist establishment by noting that the working classes are *not* made up of downtrodden saints nor are the values of capitalist society entirely sinister and corrupt. His book about his experiences in the Spanish Civil War deals frankly with the weaknesses and corruptions of the side on which he fought. He left Spain with a Loyalist price on his head.

It is easy to disagree with George Orwell; often we find his general knowledge of his subject matter incomplete and his interpretations questionable. But in this man, "the conscience of his generation" as V. S. Pritchett called him, we encounter something like absolute sincerity of position and absolute honesty of perception.

These are qualities of the man; they are surely significant in, perhaps absolutely necessary to, the makeup of a great essayist. Yet obviously, such personal qualities are not enough in themselves to account for any sort of artist. The great essayist must be a skillful writer, who clearly recognizes what it is he wants to say and how he plans to go about saying it.

Orwell was an extremely self-aware writer. He talks directly of his approach to the art in his essay "Why I Write," and he sets forth his ideas about the technical aspects of good writing in "Politics and the English Language." The first of these essays lists what Orwell believes to be the four great motives for writing prose: (1) "sheer egoism," (2) "esthetic enthusiasm," (3) "historical impulse," and (4) "political purpose." The last of these motives, he says, is most important to his own work, but notice in what a broad sense he uses the word "political":

> What I have most wanted to do throughout the past ten years is to make political writing into an art. My starting point is always a feeling of partisanship, a sense of injustice. When I sit down to write a book, I do not say to myself, "I am going to produce a work of art." I write it because there is some lie that I want to expose, some fact to which I want to draw attention, and my initial concern is to get a hearing.

Such an attitude may have implicit disadvantages for the writer of novels, plays, or poems. The novelist, playwright, or poet who devotes himself to getting a hearing for his personal views on what is wrong (or right) with the world must usually do so by indirection or his work may be dismissed as polemics or sermonizing. However, getting a hearing is precisely what an essayist is expected to attempt directly.

In "Politics and the English Language," Orwell attaches his "political" motive to the actual craft of writing. If a writer wants his hearing he must write in precise terms of what he means and not be a purveyor of worn-out phrases and used-up figurative language which may give a tone of the familiar to his writing, but will take away his precise meaning. He must be economical and concrete. Here are the six rules for modern prose with which he concludes the essay:

1. Never use a metaphor, simile, or other figure of speech which you are used to seeing in print.
2. Never use a long word where a short one will do.
3. If it is possible to cut a word out, always cut it out.
4. Never use the passive where you can use the active.
5. Never use a foreign phrase, a scientific word, or jargon if you can think of an everyday English equivalent.
6. Break any of these rules sooner than say anything outright barbarous.

His essay "A Hanging" was first published in 1950, but its source is the much earlier Burmese period of his life.

A Hanging

by George Orwell (1903-1950)

It was in Burma, a sodden morning of the rains. A sickly light, like yellow tinfoil, was slanting over the high walls into the jail yard. We were waiting outside the condemned cells, a row of sheds fronted with double bars, like small animal cages. Each cell measured about ten feet by ten and was quite bare within except for a plank bed and a pot for drinking water. In some of them brown silent men were squatting at the inner bars, with their blankets draped round them. These were the condemned men, due to be hanged within the next week or two.

One prisoner had been brought out of his cell. He was a Hindu, a puny wisp of a man, with a shaven head and vague liquid eyes. He had a thick, sprouting moustache, absurdly too big for his body, rather like the moustache of a comic man on the films. Six tall Indian warders were guarding him and getting him ready for the gallows. Two of them stood by with rifles and fixed bayonets, while the others handcuffed him, passed a chain through his handcuffs and fixed it to their belts, and lashed his arms tight to his sides. They crowded very close about him, with their hands always on him in a careful, caressing grip, as though all the while feeling him to make sure he was there. It was like men handling a fish which is still alive and may jump back into the water. But he stood quite unresisting, yielding his arms limply to the ropes, as though he hardly noticed what was happening.

Eight o'clock struck and a bugle call, desolately thin in the wet air, floated from the distant barracks. The superintendent of the jail, who was standing apart from the rest of us, moodily prodding the gravel with his stick, raised his head at the sound. He was an army doctor, with a gray toothbrush moustache and a gruff voice. "For God's sake hurry up, Francis," he said irritably. "The man ought to have been dead by this time. Aren't you ready yet?"

Francis, the head jailer, a fat Dravidian in a white drill suit and gold spectacles, waved his black hand. "Yes sir, yes sir," he bubbled. "All iss satisfactorily prepared. The hangman iss waiting. We shall proceed."

"Well, quick march, then. The prisoners can't get their breakfast till this job's over."

We set out for the gallows. Two warders marched on either side of the prisoner, with their rifles at the slope; two others marched close against him, gripping him by arm and shoulder, as though at once pushing and supporting him. The rest of us, magistrates and the like, followed behind. Suddenly, when we had gone ten yards, the procession stopped short without any order or warning. A dreadful thing had happened — a dog, come goodness knows whence, had appeared in the yard. It came bounding among us with a loud volley of barks, and leapt round us wagging its whole body, wild with glee at finding so many human beings together. It was a large woolly dog, half Airedale, half pariah. For a moment it pranced round us, and then, before anyone could stop it, it had made a dash for the prisoner and, jumping up, tried to lick his face. Everyone stood aghast, too taken aback even to grab at the dog.

"Who let that bloody brute in here?" said the superintendent angrily. "Catch it, someone!"

A warder, detached from the escort, charged clumsily after the dog, but it danced and gamboled just out of his reach, taking everything as part of the game. A young Eurasian jailer picked up a handful of gravel and tried to stone the dog away, but it dodged the stones and came after us again. Its yaps echoed from the jail walls. The prisoner, in the grasp of the two warders, looked on incuriously, as though this was another formality of the hanging. It was several minutes before someone managed to catch the dog. Then we put my handkerchief[1] through its collar and moved off once more, with the dog still straining and whimpering.

It was about forty yards to the gallows. I watched the bare brown back of the prisoner marching in front of me. He walked clumsily with his bound arms, but quite steadily, with that bobbing gait of the Indian who never straightens his knees. At each step his muscles slid neatly into place, the lock of hair on his scalp danced up and down, his feet printed themselves on the wet gravel. And once, in spite of the men who gripped him

1. handkerchief: neck scarf.

by each shoulder, he stepped slightly aside to avoid a puddle on the path.

It is curious, but till that moment I had never realized what it means to destroy a healthy, conscious man. When I saw the prisoner step aside to avoid the puddle I saw the mystery, the unspeakable wrongness, of cutting a life short when it is in full tide. This man was not dying, he was alive just as we are alive. All the organs of his body were working — bowels digesting food, skin renewing itself, nails growing, tissues forming — all toiling away in solemn foolery. His nails would still be growing when he stood on the drop, when he was falling through the air with a tenth of a second to live. His eyes saw the yellow gravel and the gray walls, and his brain still remembered, foresaw, reasoned — reasoned even about puddles. He and we were a party of men walking together, seeing, hearing, feeling, understanding the same world; and in two minutes, with a sudden snap, one of us would be gone — one mind less, one world less.

The gallows stood in a small yard, separate from the main grounds of the prison, and overgrown with tall prickly weeds. It was a brick erection like three sides of a shed, with planking on top, and above that two beams and a crossbar with the rope dangling. The hangman, a gray-haired convict in the white uniform of the prison, was waiting beside his machine. He greeted us with a servile crouch as we entered. At a word from Francis the two warders, gripping the prisoner more closely than ever, half led half pushed him to the gallows and helped him clumsily up the ladder. Then the hangman climbed up and fixed the rope round the prisoner's neck.

We stood waiting, five yards away. The warders had formed in a rough circle round the gallows. And then, when the noose was fixed, the prisoner began crying out to his god. It was a high, reiterated cry of "Ram![2] Ram! Ram! Ram!" not urgent and fearful like a prayer or cry for help, but steady, rhythmical, almost like the tolling of a bell. The dog answered the sound with a whine. The hangman, still standing on the gallows, produced a small cotton bag like a flour bag and drew it down over the prisoner's face. But the sound, muffled by the cloth, still persisted, over and over again: "Ram! Ram! Ram! Ram! Ram!"

The hangman climbed down and stood ready, holding the lever. Minutes seemed to pass. The steady, muffled crying from the prisoner went on and on, "Ram! Ram! Ram!" never faltering for an instant. The superintendent, his head on his chest, was slowly poking the ground with his stick; perhaps he was counting the cries, allowing the prisoner a fixed number — fifty, perhaps, or a hundred. Everyone had changed color. The Indians had gone gray like bad coffee, and one or two of the bayonets were wavering.

---

2. Ram: Rama, Hindu epic hero worshipped as an incarnation of the god Vishnu.

We looked at the lashed, hooded man on the drop, and listened to his cries — each cry another second of life; the same thought was in all our minds: oh, kill him quickly, get it over, stop that abominable noise!

Suddenly the superintendent made up his mind. Throwing up his head he made a swift motion with his stick. "Chalo!" he shouted almost fiercely.

There was a clanking noise, and then dead silence. The prisoner had vanished, and the rope was twisting on itself. I let go of the dog, and it galloped immediately to the back of the gallows; but when it got there it stopped short, barked, and then retreated into a corner of the yard, where it stood among the weeds, looking timorously out at us. We went round the gallows to inspect the prisoner's body. He was dangling with his toes pointed straight downward, very slowly revolving, as dead as a stone.

The superintendent reached out with his stick and poked the bare brown body; it oscillated slightly. "*He's* all right," said the superintendent. He backed out from under the gallows, and blew out a deep breath. The moody look had gone out of his face quite suddenly. He glanced at his wrist watch. "Eight minutes past eight. Well, that's all for this morning, thank God."

The warders unfixed bayonets and marched away. The dog, sobered and conscious of having misbehaved itself, slipped after them. We walked out of the gallows yard, past the condemned cells with their waiting prisoners, into the big central yard of the prison. The convicts, under the command of warders armed with lathis,[3] were already receiving their breakfast. They squatted in long rows, each man holding a tin pannikin,[4] while two warders with buckets marched round ladling out rice; it seemed quite a homely, jolly scene, after the hanging. An enormous relief had come upon us now that the job was done. One felt an impulse to sing, to break into a run, to snigger. All at once everyone began chattering gaily.

The Eurasian boy walking beside me nodded toward the way we had come, with a knowing smile: "Do you know, sir, our friend [he meant the dead man] when he heard his appeal had been dismissed, he pissed on the floor of his cell. From fright. Kindly take one of my cigarettes, sir. Do you not admire my new silver case, sir? From the boxwalah,[5] two rupees eight annas. Classy European style."

Several people laughed — at what, nobody seemed certain.

Francis was walking by the superintendent, talking garrulously: "Well, sir, all hass passed off with the utmost satisfactoriness. It was all finished —

---

3. lathis: heavy bamboo sticks, bound with iron.
4. pannikin: a small pan or cup.
5. boxwalah: peddler.

flick! like that. It iss not always so — oah, no! I have known cases where the doctor wass obliged to go beneath the gallows and pull the prissoner's legs to ensure decease. Most disagreeable!"

"Wriggling about, eh? That's bad," said the superintendent.

"Ach, sir, it iss worse when they become refractory! One man, I recall, clung to the bars of hiss cage when we went to take him out. You will scarcely credit, sir, that it took six warders to dislodge him, three pulling at each leg. We reasoned with him. 'My dear fellow,' we said, think of all the pain and trouble you are causing to us!' But no, he would not listen! Ach, he wass very troublesome!"

I found that I was laughing quite loudly. Everyone was laughing. Even the superintendent grinned in a tolerant way. "You'd better all come out and have a drink," he said quite genially. "I've got a bottle of whisky in the car. We could do with it."

We went through the big double gates of the prison into the road. "Pulling at his legs!" exclaimed a Burmese magistrate suddenly, and burst into a loud chuckling. We all began laughing again. At that moment Francis' anecdote seemed extraordinarily funny. We all had a drink together, native and European alike, quite amicably. The dead man was a hundred yards away.

Questions

1. To what extent does Orwell describe each of the people who appear in "A Hanging"? What descriptive methods does he use?
2. What exactly does the dog do?
3. To what reflection does the prisoner's avoiding a puddle lead Orwell?
4. What do the various witnesses do after the death of the condemned?
5. What details of time and place does Orwell include in "A Hanging"? What details of time and place *might* Orwell have included which he apparently does not choose to include? Why is the inclusion or exclusion of such details important?

Afterword to *A Hanging*

A good deal is said these days about capital punishment, the penalty of death under the law. Nations and states have considered and debated it;

some have abolished and others have sustained the right or duty of the community to execute people convicted of certain kinds of crimes. Once it was not uncommon in the civilized world to hang a man for stealing a loaf of bread; today the hanging of a man for murder is challenged by many morally sensitive people. The trend appears to be against capital punishment, against the idea that society should deliberately deprive any human being of his life. Whatever the merits of the various arguments may be, and the weight of the evidence marshalled in support of them, it is surely true that capital punishment is cruel and that it contains the possibility of error that cannot be corrected.

Orwell's "A Hanging" is more effective than any direct argument in its impact upon the sensibilities of the reader. With a minimum of explanation, we are forced to share an experience and to contemplate ironic elements in it, which give more than a debater's force to the author's convictions against executions.

Consider the first paragraph of the essay. The author does not theorize that to kill men legally is to treat them like animals; he suggests by means of concrete detail that the cells of condemned men are like a wretched zoo.

As the essay continues we encounter other ironies, most of them evoked in visual images. The guards who escort the condemned man to the gallows are large, armed men, visibly dangerous; he, on the other hand, is small and harmless-looking. Yet if he is to be executed, must he not be the dangerous one in the eyes of the executing society? Their actions are careful and solicitous; they handle him as though he were a fish who might get away. He seems unconscious of what is going on until he calls tonelessly on his god. Yet *he* is the one to whom the hanging is ultimately important. The dog picks out the condemned man for affection; the others have come to pick him out for death. Afterwards, the dog shows shame at having misbehaved — but has he misbehaved, in spite of the disapproval that has abashed him? Who are the innocent and who the guilty? The guards, magistrates, and jailors are the forces of "righteousness" and law. They are supposed to regard the hanging as a proper routine duty, but watch the little details of how they behave before and after the death of the condemned one.

As we observe how Orwell uses narrative and descriptive detail here, we may feel that "A Hanging" is just as much a short story as an essay — a short story with a moral. Consider the following short story about a similar circumstance. In turn, it is followed by Kipling's ballad, "Danny Deever." Can we arrive at any distinctions between narrative essays, short stories. and even narrative poems?

The Presence of Mine Enemies

by O. B. Davis (1924-)

More than fifty of us were waiting in the rain. Most of us leaned against the wall, as far back from the platform as we could be. Apart stood only four or five men who broke up the empty space between the other witnesses and the gallows. One of them suddenly threw down his cigarette and came back next to me. At first he didn't lean, but stood as he had before, wide-legged, his hands behind him. After a minute he lit another cigarette. With it in his mouth he turned to me. "Most time they let us out of here," he said.

Then he said, "You ever seen one of these things before?"

"Not just this kind."

"Christ," he said, "I never seen anything like this before." Then he said, "It ought to be interesting."

A door in the big stone farmhouse that made the opposite side of the enclosure opened. Four enlisted men came out and walked over to the platform. By the time they were climbing up the steps two more men, without raincoats, came through the door. These were followed by a colonel and a first lieutenant wearing forty-fives over their field coats. We all got our shoulders off the wall, we shuffled our feet a little, and a lot put out their cigarettes. The one who had spoken to me snapped his down fast and looked as though he might be going to stand at attention.

One of the two men without raincoats was a chaplain. He had a white cross painted on the front of his helmet, and he kept talking to the man beside him. I couldn't even hear his voice, but his face was working hard as they walked slowly towards the middle of the yard. The prisoner was a small man with black curly hair. He held himself straight and he looked straight ahead of him to where he was going. He stopped at the foot of the steps and glanced, past the chaplain's nose, to his left and then to his right. Then he went up. When he got there he stood facing us witnesses, his hands at his sides. I thought he was staring right at me. Beside him, the chaplain fumbled with a pack of cigarettes, still talking in a voice we couldn't hear. When he got a couple sticking out he put one hand on the prisoner's shoulder and offered him the pack with the other. Still looking right at me, the man just shook his head. I wished he'd look at the men in the empty place between where the rest of us were and the platform. They stood there shining in their raincoats.

The chaplain stopped talking and stood looking at the cigarettes in his hand. They must have been getting soggy in the steady rain. He handed them to one of the soldiers working around with the things on the platform. Then the chaplain knelt down with his arms on the low railing. He looked up sideways at the prisoner, but that one shook his head again. The chaplain got up.

The man with me turned his back on everything and leaned the front rim of his helmet against the wall. The scraping ring it made wasn't loud, but it made the other men turn to look. As soon as he had made the noise he spun around again and showed his teeth. His eyes were way back in his head and his breath sounded harsh and quick through his teeth.

One of the men who had first arrived at the platform took off his raincoat and hung it over the rail. He was the only one there wearing an overseas cap. He was big and tall, a little fat, and maybe forty-five or fifty years old. On the arms of his shirt were master sergeant's chevrons. He came up behind the prisoner and touched him on the elbow. The prisoner, still standing straight, nodded and faced about, raising his hands a little and, I guess, he held them out to be locked together. The master sergeant bent down and said something to him. Then, taking the smaller man gently by the arms, he turned him around so that he faced us again. The big hands, handcuffs dangling from one, slipped down to the prisoner's wrists and eased them behind his back. The catch on the cuffs clicked.

One of the lone men standing between the platform and the rest of us began to fish something out of his raincoat pocket. It was a stethoscope. One of the hooks that go in the doctor's ears caught on the edge of the pocket. The man didn't look down to see what was the matter; he just tugged at it. Then he stopped, crammed the thing back into the pocket, and clasped his hands behind him.

The master sergeant, standing directly behind the prisoner, began to bring a black cloth bag down over his head. The prisoner stepped aside quickly and began to shake his head. I could see his lips moving, but the big man moved smoothly behind him again and fitted the black bag over him anyway. When it was on, the master sergeant tied it just below the point of the prisoner's chin.

The frame of the gallows stood about seven feet above the deck of the platform. It looked like what it was, all right, but not just how I had thought about it. I had always thought that it would be like an illustration from a book about pirates that I had once. It was a picture of Captain Kidd hanging in chains, and it showed the pirate suspended from a horizontal beam which was supported by a single vertical post and a brace. Here there were two upright posts, about five feet apart, and a horizontal beam on top of them. In the middle of the horizontal there was a big pulley. A rope ran through that.

The master sergeant spoke to the chaplain, and the two of them guided the prisoner backwards until he was standing under the horizontal. The two parts of the rope rubbed across his covered face until the master sergeant snatched them away. He frowned and said in a loud voice to one of the other men, "What you think you're doing, Lonigan?" The man said jeeze he was sorry and reached out a hand to take one of the ropes. The colonel was standing near the steps and he looked at his watch and cleared his throat. The master sergeant nodded and his man pulled one end of the rope through the pulley until he was told to stop. Then he tied his end to something down near the deck and put his weight against the knot a couple of times. The master sergeant then had about six feet of free rope looping and rising from the big noose that he held in both hands. His uniform was black-wet like the prisoner's and the chaplain's. You could see the rain-water running down his face as he turned toward the prisoner. On the other side, the chaplain tilted his face up and I knew that he was going to start reciting the 23rd psalm. No book would have lasted in that wet.

But he didn't recite the 23rd psalm, or anything else. A new group of men appeared in the courtyard. In the lead was one of those tall, young-looking brigadier generals that you don't usually find anywhere but at corps or army headquarters. "Hold it, Colonel," he commanded.

The colonel and the first lieutenant came clattering down the steps. The master sergeant, the prisoner, the chaplain, and the other men on the platform stood right where they were, without moving so much as their heads. The rest of us began to rustle around and murmur. The man with me said, "You think they're going to let him off? How long we been here anyway? You think they're going to let him off?"

The colonel turned around from the brigadier general and yelled at us, "Okay, okay, it's all off. Sorry to take your time, gentlemen. It's all off." He waved his arm at us as though maybe he could make us disappear.

Up on the platform, when the colonel yelled, the chaplain started trying to untie the string that held the bag close under the prisoner's chin. He couldn't do much with it, but the master sergeant got the handcuffs off behind and the prisoner untied the thing himself. Then he slowly pulled it up off his face. His mouth was wide open with the lower lip tight so that the corners were drawn down. His eyes were tight shut. You wouldn't have recognized him as the same man that the master sergeant had covered up. The lines around his cheeks and eyes were terrible and deep.

The chaplain grabbed his hand, and the master sergeant started to pat his shoulder, but he tore away from them and backed, blind, to the far corner of the platform. Nobody was behind him. Only the rail at the corner kept him from stepping off backwards. Then he opened his eyes. Then he screamed. He screamed to all of us, to everybody there, the brigadier general and all, "You bastards. You dirty bastards. You wanted to kill me."

Danny Deever

by Rudyard Kipling (1865-1936)

"What are the bugles blowin' for?" said Files-on-Parade.[1]
"To turn you out, to turn you out," the Color-Sergeant[2] said.
"What makes you look so white, so white?" said Files-on-Parade.
"I'm dreadin' what I've got to watch," the Color-Sergeant said.
For they're hangin' Danny Deever, you can hear the Dead March play,
The regiment's in 'ollow square[3] — they're hangin' him to-day;
They've taken of his buttons off an' cut his stripes away,
An' they're hangin' Danny Deever in the mornin'.

"What makes the rear-rank breathe so 'ard?" said Files-on-Parade.
"It's bitter cold, it's bitter cold," the Color-Sergeant said.
"What makes that front-rank man fall down?" said Files-on-Parade.
"A touch o' sun, a touch o' sun," the Color-Sergeant said.
They are hangin' Danny Deever, they are marchin' of 'im round,
They 'ave 'alted Danny Deever by 'is coffin on the ground;
An' 'e'll swing in 'arf a minute for a sneakin' shootin' hound —
O they're hangin' Danny Deever in the mornin'!

" 'Is cot was right-'and cot to mine," said Files-on-Parade.
" 'E's sleepin' out an' far to-night," the Color-Sergeant said.
"I've drunk 'is beer a score o' times," said Files-on-Parade.
" 'E's drinkin' bitter beer alone," the Color-Sergeant said.
They are hangin' Danny Deever, you must mark 'im to 'is place,
For 'e shot a comrade sleepin' — you must look 'im in the face;
Nine 'undred of 'is county an' the regiment's disgrace,
While they're hangin' Danny Deever in the mornin'.

1. Files-on-Parade: average, ordinary soldier, one of the "file." In the U.S. today it would be "G.I. Joe."
2. Color-Sergeant: in British Army, Company, First, or "Top" Sergeant.
3. 'ollow square: lined up in formation in the form of a square.

"What's that so black agin the sun?" said Files-on-Parade.
"It's Danny fightin' 'ard for life," the Color-Sergeant said.
"What's that that whimpers over'ead?" said Files-on-Parade.
"It's Danny's soul that's passin' now," the Color-Sergeant said.
For they're done with Danny Deever, you can 'ear the quickstep play,
The regiment's in column, an' they're marchin' us away;
Ho! the young recruits are shakin', an' they'll want their beer to-day,
After hangin' Danny Deever in the mornin'!

Afterword to *A Hanging*, *The Presence of Mine Enemies*, and *Danny Deever*

A good deal of insight into form and its effects may be gained by comparing "A Hanging," "The Presence of Mine Enemies," and "Danny Deever." They differ in form, place, time, and circumstance, although the context of all three is military. What unites them is that the governing words of each are the verb "hanging" and the noun "man," and that all the persons in each are preoccupied with the emotions and reactions generated by that verb and noun.

We see that the difference between a narrative essay and a short story can be slight, though individual devices and emphases, especially those of the writer of fiction, could make the difference greater than it is in this case. For a classic example of how far beyond the literal a short-story writer may carry the situation of a military hanging, read "Incident at Owl Creek Bridge," by Ambrose Bierce.

In "Danny Deever" the narrative poet, the ballad maker, compresses all the elements of the action to the utmost. The effect is stark. A few carefully chosen elemental images and repetitive lines carry the burden of what is spelled out in much more detail by both prose narrations. The dramatic impact of the poem is heightened in direct proportion to the reader's ability to fill in the skeletal framework from his own imagination.

General Discussion Questions

1. "Danny Deever," "The Presence of Mine Enemies," and "A Hanging" are observations of the process of execution, each from the point of view of an official witness. Do you find significant differences, however, among the three points of view – perhaps in the immediate attitude of each witness to his condemned man? Discuss.
2. To what extent do the poem and the short story present their authors' evaluation of capital punishment? Do you agree to the proposition that only in the essay is this personal reaction the main end of the work? Why or why not? What seem to you to be the purposes of the poet and the short story writer in "Danny Deever" and "The Presence of Mine Enemies"?

2

The Sporting Life

To those, Sir, who prefer *effeminacy* to hardihood . . .
assumed *refinement* to rough *nature* . . . and whom a
shower of rain can terrify, under the alarm of their
polite frames, suffering from the unruly elements . . . or
would not mind Pugilism, if BOXING was not so shockingly
vulgar . . . the following work can create no interest
whatsoever; but to those persons who feel that Englishmen are
not automatons . . . *Boxiana* will convey amusement, if not
information . . .

from the Dedication to the first volume
of *Boxiana* by PIERCE EGAN

Foreword to *Boxing With the Naked Eye* and *The Fight*

As this book goes to press, professional boxing is in one of its periodic times of relative public disfavor. Articles on the subject these days generally condemn the sport as sadistic and corrupt, except for those appearing in *Sports Illustrated* or other special-interest publications. Our inclination is to agree with the present trend: boxing is, we think, essentially a brutal and brutalizing affair.

Nevertheless, we must also remember that professional combat of one kind or another, as a spectator sport, has survived centuries of disapproval, sometimes mild, sometimes bitter and enforced by law. That this is so, and that the fight game is still with us, are simply facts — like them or not. Prizefighting is certain to continue in some form after today's critics are long gone. Even in its least-popular or most-suppressed eras, boxing has always had enthusiastic proponents. The American journalist and essayist, A. J. Liebling, was one such faithful, expert proponent; the English journalist and essayist, William Hazlitt (1778-1830), was another.

What these two men, separated by more than a hundred years, have in common besides an enthusiasm for the "fancy," the "ring," or "the fight game," is significant. Both are essayists of the first rank, skillful writers who want, and know how, to get a hearing. Liebling and Hazlitt have wide, varied interests and enthusiasms, many of them held in common. As professional journalists both had opportunities to witness news events of their respective times and to talk with people involved in such events. They are both interested in sports, politics, crime, literature, and good food. Their interest in such things is not theoretical, but practical and personal. Characteristically they *talk* with politicians, athletes, or policemen; they relish the details of a meal at a good restaurant as they do the details of a good fight. Liebling and Hazlitt draw their conclusions from experience and set them forth so vividly that we share the experiences vicariously.

At the same time, both essayists are well-read and draw on the written past for references to clarify, enliven, and support their positions. Their learning, impressive as it sometimes appears, is not the general learning of conventionally educated men; it, too, is a form of personal experience. Each reference Liebling or Hazlitt makes to other literature has the stamp of individual enthusiasm or humor on it.

Although some acquaintance with the achievements of Joe Louis is picked up by readers of Liebling's essay, it may be interesting for those who grew up after Joe's ring days were over to start with a few facts about this great fighter. Joseph Louis Barrow was the child of desperately poor Negro sharecroppers in the deep South. He held the world heavyweight championship longer than any other man: from 1937 until 1949, when he retired. During the time of his championship, in spite of years off for wartime service in the army, Joe defended his title twenty-five times. Twenty of these victories were by knockouts. Most informed opinion holds that either Joe Louis or the earlier Jack Dempsey was the greatest heavyweight of modern times. The record seems to support Louis.

In "Boxing With the Naked Eye" Joe appears well after his prime, in the course of one of the unsuccessful comeback attempts into which financial difficulties forced him after he had retired as champion. Joe was, and is, widely admired not only for his amazing speed and strength as a boxer, but for his integrity, sportsmanship, and moral courage.

Boxing With the Naked Eye

by A. J. Liebling (1904-1963)

Watching a fight on television has always seemed to me a poor substitute for being there. For one thing, you can't tell the fighters what to do. When I watch a fight, I like to study one boxer's problem, solve it, and then communicate my solution vocally. On occasion my advice is disregarded, as when I tell a man to stay away from the other fellow's left and he doesn't, but in such cases I assume that he hasn't heard my counsel, or that his opponent has, and has acted on it. Some fighters hear better and are more suggestible than others — for example, the pre-television Joe Louis. "Let him have it, Joe!" I would yell whenever I saw him fight, and sooner or later he would let the other fellow have it. Another fighter like that was the late Marcel Cerdan, whom I would coach in his own language, to prevent opposition seconds from picking up our signals. "*Vas-y, Marcel!*"[1] I used to shout, and Marcel always *y allait*.[2] I get a feeling of participation that way that I don't in front of a television screen. I could yell, of course, but I would know that if my suggestion was adopted, it would be by the merest coincidence.

Besides, when you go to a fight, the boxers aren't the only ones you want to be heard by. You are surrounded by people whose ignorance of the ring is exceeded only by their unwillingness to face facts — the sharp-

1. *"Vas-y, Marcel!":* Go get him Marcel!" (French).
2. *y allait:* went after him.

ness of your boxer's punching, for instance. Such people may take it upon themselves to disparage the principal you are advising. This disparagement is less generally addressed to the man himself (as "Gavilan, you're a bum!") than to his opponent, whom they have wrong-headedly picked to win. ("He's a cream puff, Miceli!" they may typically cry. "He can't hurt you. He can't hurt nobody. Look — slaps! Ha, ha!") They thus get at your man — and, by indirection, at you. To put them in their place, you address neither them nor their man but your man. ("Get the other eye, Gavilan!" you cry.) This throws them off balance, because they haven't noticed anything the matter with either eye. Then, before they can think of anything to say, you thunder, "Look at that eye!" It doesn't much matter whether or not the man has been hit in the eye; he will be. Addressing yourself to the fighter when you want somebody else to hear you is a parliamentary device, like "Mr. Chairman . . ." Before television, a prize-fight was to a New Yorker the nearest equivalent to the New England town meeting. It taught a man to think on his seat.

Less malignant than rooters for the wrong man, but almost as disquieting, are those who are on the right side but tactically unsound. At a moment when you have steered your boxer to a safe lead on points but can see the other fellow is still dangerous, one of these maniacs will encourage recklessness. "Finish the jerk, Harry!" he will sing out. "Stop holding him up! Don't lose him!" But you, knowing the enemy is a puncher, protect your client's interest. "Move to your left, Harry!" you call. "Keep moving! Keep moving! Don't let him set!" I sometimes finish a fight like that in a cold sweat.

If you go to a fight with a friend, you can keep up unilateral conversations on two vocal levels — one at the top of your voice, directed at your fighter, and the other a running *expertise* nominally aimed at your companion but loud enough to reach a modest fifteen feet in each direction. "Reminds me of Panama Al Brown," you may say as a new fighter enters the ring. "He was five feet eleven and weighed a hundred and eighteen pounds. This fellow may be about forty pounds heavier and a couple of inches shorter, but he's got the same kind of neck. I saw Brown box a fellow named Mascart in Paris in 1927. A guy stood up in the top gallery and threw an apple and hit Brown right on the top of the head. The whole house started yelling, 'Finish him, Mascart! He's groggy!' " Then, as the bout begins, "Boxes like Al, too, except this fellow's a southpaw." If he wins, you say, "I told you he reminded me of Al Brown," and if he loses, "Well, well, I guess he's no Al Brown. They don't make fighters like Al any more." This identifies you as a man who (a) has been in Paris, (b) has been going to fights for a long time, and (c) therefore enjoys what the fellows who write for quarterlies call a frame of reference.

It may be argued that this doesn't get you anywhere, but it at least constitutes what a man I once met named Thomas S. Matthews called communication. Mr. Matthews, who was the editor of *Time*, said that the most important thing in journalism is not reporting but communication. "What are you going to communicate?" I asked him. "The most important thing," he said, "is the man on one end of the circuit saying 'My God, I'm alive! You're alive!' and the fellow on the other end, receiving his message, saying 'My God, you're right! We're both alive!' " I still think it is a hell of a way to run a news magazine, but it is a good reason for going to fights in person. Television, if unchecked, may carry us back to a pre-tribal state of social development, when the family was the largest conversational unit.

Fights are also a great place for adding to your repertory of witty sayings. I shall not forget my adolescent delight when I first heard a fight fan yell, "I hope youse bot' gets knocked out!" I thought he had made it up, although I found out later it was a cliché. It is a formula adaptable to an endless variety of situations outside the ring. The only trouble with it is it never works out. The place where I first heard the line was Bill Brown's, a fight club in a big shed behind a trolley station in Far Rockaway.

On another night there, the time for the main bout arrived and one of the principals hadn't. The other fighter sat in the ring, a bantamweight with a face like a well-worn coin, and the fans stamped in cadence and whistled and yelled for their money back. It was thirty years before television, but there were only a couple of hundred men on hand. The preliminary fights had been terrible. The little fighter kept looking at his hands, which were resting on his knees in cracked boxing gloves, and every now and then he would spit on the mat and rub the spittle into the canvas with one of his scuffed ring shoes. The longer he waited, the more frequently he spat, and I presumed he was worrying about the money he was supposed to get; it wouldn't be more than fifty dollars with a house that size, even if the other man turned up. He had come there from some remote place like West or East New York, and he may have been thinking about the last train home on the Long Island Railroad, too. Finally, the other bantamweight got there, looking out of breath and flustered. He had lost his way on the railroad — changed to the wrong train at Jamaica and had to go back there and start over. The crowd booed so loud that he looked embarrassed. When the fight began, the fellow who had been waiting walked right into the new boy and knocked him down. He acted impatient. The tardy fellow got up and fought back gamely, but the one who had been waiting nailed him again, and the latecomer just about pulled up to one knee at the count of seven. He had been hit pretty hard, and you could see from his face that he was wondering whether to chuck it. Somebody in the crowd yelled out, "Hey, Hickey! You kept us all waiting! Why don't you stay around awhile?" So the fellow got up and caught for ten rounds and probably made the one who had come early miss his train. It's another formula with multiple applications, and I think the man who said it that night in Far Rockaway did make it up.

Because of the way I feel about watching fights on television, I was highly pleased when I read, back in June, 1951, that the fifteen-round match between Joe Louis and Lee Savold, scheduled for June thirteenth at the Polo Grounds, was to be neither televised, except to eight theater audiences in places like Pittsburgh and Albany, nor broadcast over the radio. I hadn't seen Louis with the naked eye since we shook hands in a pub in London in 1944. He had fought often since then, and I had seen his two bouts with Jersey Joe Walcott on television, but there hadn't been any fun in it. Those had been held in public places, naturally, and I could have gone, but television gives you so plausible an adumbration[3] of a fight, for nothing, that you feel it would be extravagant to pay your way in. It is like the potato, which is only a succedaneum[4] for something decent to eat but which, once introduced into Ireland, proved so cheap that the peasants gave up their grain-and-meat diet in favor of it. After that, the landlords let them keep just enough money to buy potatoes. William Cobbett,[5] a great Englishman, said that he would sack any workmen of his he caught eating one of the cursed things, because as soon as potatoes appeared anywhere they brought down the standard of eating. I sometimes think of Cobbett on my way home from the races, looking at the television aerials on all the little houses between here and Belmont Park. As soon as I heard that the fight wouldn't be on the air, I determined to buy a ticket.

On the night of the thirteenth, a Wednesday, it rained, and on the next night it rained again, so on the evening of June fifteenth the promoters, the International Boxing Club, confronted by a night game at the Polo Grounds, transferred the fight to Madison Square Garden. The postponements upset a plan I had had to go to the fight with a friend, who had another date for the third night. But alone is a good way to go to a fight or the races, because you have more time to look around you, and you always get all the conversation you can use anyway. I went to the Garden box office early Friday afternoon and bought a ten-dollar seat in the side arena — the first tiers rising in back of the boxes, midway between Eighth and Ninth Avenues on the 49th Street side of the house. There was only a scat-

3. adumbration: faint outline or sketch.
4. succedaneum: substitute.
5. William Cobbett, (1763-1835), English journalist, politician, radical, and progressive farmer.

tering of ticket buyers in the lobby, and the man at the ticket window was polite — a bad omen for the gate. After buying the ticket, I got into a cab in front of the Garden, and the driver naturally asked me if I was going to see the fight. I said I was, and he said, "He's all through."

I knew he meant Louis, and I said, "I know, and that's why it may be a good fight. If he weren't through, he might kill this guy."

The driver said, "Savold is a hooker. He breaks noses."

I said, "He couldn't break his own nose, even," and then began to wonder how a man would go about trying to do that. "It's a shame he's so hard up he had to fight at all at his age," I said, knowing the driver would understand I meant Louis. I was surprised that the driver was against Louis, and I was appealing to his better feelings.

"He must have plenty socked away," said the driver. "Playing golf for a hundred dollars a hole."

"Maybe that helped him go broke," I said. "And anyway, what does that prove? There's many a man with a small salary who bets more than he can afford." I had seen a scratch sheet[6] on the seat next to the hackie.[7] I was glad I was riding only as far as Brentano's with him.

The driver I had on the long ride home was a better type. As soon as I told him I was going to the fight, which was at about the same time that he dropped the flag, he said, "I guess the old guy can still sock."

I said, "I saw him murder Max Baer sixteen years ago. He was a sweet fighter then."

The driver said, "Sixteen years is a long time for a fighter. I don't remember anybody lasted sixteen years in the big money. Still, Savold is almost as old as he is. When you're a bum, nobody notices how old you get."

We had a pleasant time on the West Side Highway, talking about how Harry Greb had gone on fighting when he was blind in one eye, only nobody knew it but his manager, and how Pete Herman had been the best infighter in the world, because he had been practically blind in both eyes, so he couldn't afford to fool around outside. "What Herman did, you couldn't learn a boy now," the driver said. "They got no patience."

The fellow who drove me from my house to the Garden after dinner was also a man of good will, but rather different. He knew I was going to the fight as soon as I told him my destination, and once we had got under way, he said, "It is a pity that a man like Louis should be exploited to such a degree that he has to fight again." It was only nine-fifteen, and he agreed

6. scratch sheet: a publication giving information on a day's horse races for betting purposes.
7. hackie: cabdriver.

with me that I had plenty of time to get to the Garden for the main bout, which was scheduled to begin at ten, but when we got caught in unexpectedly heavy traffic on Eleventh Avenue he grew impatient. "Come on, Jersey!" he said, giving a station wagon in front of us the horn. "In the last analysis, we have got to get to the Garden sometime." But it didn't help much because most of the other cars were heading for the Garden, too. The traffic was so slow going toward Eighth Avenue on Fiftieth Street that I asked him to let me out near the Garden corner, and joined the people hurrying from the Independent Subway exit toward the Garden marquee. A high percentage of them were from Harlem, and they were dressed as if for a levee,[8] the men in shimmering gabardines and felt hats the color of freshly unwrapped chewing gum, the women in spring suits and fur pieces — it was a cool night — and what seemed to me the prettiest hats of the season. They seemed to me the prettiest lot of women I had seen in a long time, too, and I reflected that if the fight had been televised, I would have missed them. "Step out," I heard one beau say as his group swept past me, "or we won't maybe get in. It's just like I told you — he's still one hell of a draw." As I made my way through the now crowded lobby, I could hear the special cop next to the ticket window chanting, "Six-, eight-, ten-, and fifteen-dollar tickets only," which meant that the two-and-a-half-dollar general-admission and the twenty-dollar ringside seats were sold out. It made me feel good, because it showed there were still some gregarious people left in the world.

Inside the Garden there was the same old happy drone of voices as when Jimmy McLarnin was fighting and Jimmy Walker[9] was at the ringside. There was only one small patch of bare seats, in a particularly bad part of the ringside section. I wondered what sort of occupant I would find in my seat; I knew from experience that there would be somebody in it. It turned out to be a small, frail colored man in wine-red livery. He sat up straight and pressed his shoulder blades against the back of the chair, so I couldn't see the number. When I showed him my ticket, he said, "I don't know nothing about that. You better see the usher." He was offering this token resistance, I knew, only to protect his self-esteem — to maintain the shadowy fiction that he was in the seat by error. When an usher wandered within hailing distance of us, I called him, and the little man left, to drift to some other part of the Garden, where he had no reputation as a ten-dollar-seat holder to lose, and there to squat contentedly on a step.

---

8. levee: a formal reception.
9. Jimmy Walker: James J. Walker (1881-1946), ebullient and sports-loving Mayor of New York City (1925-32), who resigned his office following disclosures of municipal corruption.

My seat was midway between the east and west ends of the ring, and about fifteen feet above it. Two not very skillful colored boys were finishing a four-rounder that the man in the next seat told me was an emergency bout, put on because there had been several knockouts in the earlier preliminaries. It gave me a chance to settle down and look around. It was ten o'clock by the time the colored boys finished and the man with the microphone announced the decision, but there was no sign of Louis or Savold. The fight wasn't on the air, so there was no need of the punctuality required by the radio business. (Later I read in the newspapers that the bout had been delayed in deference to the hundreds of people who were still in line to buy tickets and who wanted to be sure of seeing the whole fight.) Nobody made any spiel about beer, as on the home screen, although a good volume of it was being drunk all around. Miss Gladys Gooding, an organist, played the national anthem and a tenor sang it, and we all applauded. After that, the announcer introduced a number of less than illustrious prizefighters from the ring, but nobody whistled or acted restless. It was a good-natured crowd.

Then Louis and his seconds — what the author of *Boxiana*[10] would have called his faction — appeared from a runway under the north stands and headed toward the ring. The first thing I noticed, from where I sat, was that the top of Louis's head was bald. He looked taller than I had remembered him, although surely he couldn't have grown after the age of thirty, and his face was puffy and impassive. It has always been so. In the days of his greatness, the press read menace in it. He walked stiff-legged, as was natural for a heavy man of thirty-seven, but when his seconds pulled off his dressing robe, his body looked all right. He had never been a lean man; his muscles had always been well buried beneath his smooth beige skin. I recalled the first time I had seen him fight — against Baer. That was at the Yankee Stadium, in September, 1935, and not only the great ball park but the roofs of all the apartment houses around were crowded with spectators, and hundreds of people were getting out of trains at the elevated I.R.T. station, which overlooks the field, and trying to loiter long enough to catch a few moments of action. Louis had come East that summer, after a single year as a professional, and had knocked out Primo Carnera in a few rounds. Carnera had been the heavyweight champion of the world in 1934, when Baer knocked him out. Baer, when he fought Louis, was the most powerful and gifted heavyweight of the day, although he had already fumbled away his title. But this mature Baer, who had fought everybody, was frightened

10. the author of *Boxiana:* Pierce Egan (1772-1849), English sportswriter, one of Liebling's favorites; he calls him "the greatest writer about the ring who ever lived."

stiff by the twenty-one-year-old mulatto boy. Louis outclassed him. The whole thing went only four rounds. There hadn't been anybody remotely like Louis since Dempsey in the early twenties.

The week of the Louis-Baer fight, a man I know wrote in a magazine: "With half an eye, one can observe that the town is more full of stir than it has been in many moons. It is hard to find a place to park, hard to get a table in a restaurant, hard to answer all the phone calls. . . . Economic seers can explain it, if you care to listen. We prefer to remember that a sudden inflation of the town's spirit can be just as much psychological or accidental as economic." I figured it was Louis.

Savold had now come up into the other corner, a jutty-jawed man with a fair skin but a red back, probably sunburned at his training camp. He was twenty pounds lighter than Louis, but that isn't considered a crushing handicap among heavyweights; Ezzard Charles, who beat Louis the previous year, was ten pounds lighter than Savold. Savold was thirty-five, and there didn't seem to be much bounce in him. I had seen him fight twice in the winter of 1946, and I knew he wasn't much. Both bouts had been against a young Negro heavyweight named Al Hoosman, a tall, skinny fellow just out of the Army. Hoosman had started well the first time, but Savold had hurt him with body punches and won the decision. The second time, Hoosman had stayed away and jabbed him silly. An old third-rater like Savold, I knew, doesn't improve with five more years on him. But an old third-rater doesn't rattle easily, either, and I was sure he'd do his best. It made me more apprehensive, in one way, than if he'd been any good. I wouldn't have liked to see Louis beaten by a good young fighter, but it would be awful to see him beaten by a clown. Not that I have anything against Savold; I just think it's immoral for a fellow without talent to get too far. A lot of others in the crowd must have felt the same way, because the house was quiet when the fight started — as if the Louis rooters didn't want to ask too much of Joe. There weren't any audible rooters for Savold, though, of course, there would have been if he had landed one good punch.

I remembered reading in a newspaper that Savold had said he would walk right out and bang Louis in the temple with a right, which would scramble his thinking. But all he did was come forward as he had against Hoosman, with his left low. A fellow like that never changes. Louis walked out straight and stiff-legged, and jabbed his left into Savold's face. He did it again and again, and Savold didn't seem to know what to do about it. And Louis jabs a lot harder than a fellow like Hoosman. Louis didn't have to chase Savold, and he had no reason to run away from him, either, so the stiff legs were all right. When the two men came close together, Louis jarred Savold with short punches, and Savold couldn't push him around, so that was all right, too. After the first round, the crowd knew Louis would win if his legs would hold him.

In the second round Louis began hitting Savold with combinations — quick sequences of punches, like a right under the heart and a left hook to the right side of the head. A sports writer I know had told me that Louis hadn't been putting combinations together for several fights back. Combinations demand a superior kind of coordination, but a fighter who has once had that can partly regain it by hard work. A couple of times it looked as if Louis was trying for a knockout, but when Savold didn't come apart, Louis returned to jabbing. A man somewhere behind me kept saying to a companion, "I read Savold was a tricky fighter. He's got to do something!" But Savold didn't, until late in the fifth round, by which time his head must have felt like a sick music box. Then he threw a right to Louis's head and it landed. I thought I could see Louis shrink, as if he feared trouble. His response ten years ago would have been to tear right back into the man. Savold threw another right, exactly the same kind, and that hit Louis, too. No good fighter should have been hit twice in succession with that kind of foolish punch. But the punches weren't hard enough to slow Louis down, and that was the end of that. In the third minute of the sixth round, he hit Savold with a couple of combinations no harder than those that had gone before, but Savold was weak now. His legs were going limp, and Louis was pursuing him as he backed toward my side of the ring. Then Louis swung like an axman with his right (he wasn't snapping it as he used to), and his left dropped over Savold's guard and against his jaw, and the fellow was rolling over and over on the mat, rolling the way football players do when they fall on a fumbled ball. The referee was counting and Savold was rolling, and he got up on either nine or ten, I couldn't tell which (later, I read that it was ten, so he was out officially), but you could see he was knocked silly, and the referee had his arms around him, and it was over.

The newspapermen, acres of them near the ring, were banging out the leads for the running stories they had already telegraphed, and I felt sorry for them, because they never have time to enjoy boxing matches. Since the fight was not broadcast, there was no oily-voiced chap to drag Louis over to a microphone and ask him stupid questions. He shook hands with Savold twice, once right after the knockout and again a few minutes later, when Savold was ready to leave the ring, as if he feared Savold wouldn't remember the first handshake.

I drifted toward the lobby with the crowd. The chic Harlem people were saying to one another, "It was terrific, darling! It was terrific!" I could see that an element of continuity had been restored to their world. But there wasn't any of the wild exultation that had followed those first Louis victories in 1935. These people had celebrated so many times — except, of course, the younger ones, who were small children when Louis knocked out Baer. I recognized one of the Garden promoters, usually a sour fellow, looking happy. The bout had brought in receipts of $94,684, including my ten dollars, but, what was more important to the Garden, Louis was sure to draw a lot more the next time, and at a higher scale of prices.

I walked downtown on Eighth Avenue to a point where the crowd began to thin out, and climbed into a taxi that had been stopped by the light on a cross street. This one had a Negro driver.

"The old fellow looked pretty good tonight," I said. "Had those combinations going."

"Fight over?" the driver asked. If there had been television, or even radio, he would have known about everything, and I wouldn't have had the fun of telling him.

"Sure," I said. "He knocked the guy out in the sixth."

"I was afraid he wouldn't," said the driver. "You know, it's a funny thing," he said, after we had gone on a way, "but I been twenty-five years in New York now and never seen Joe Louis in the flesh."

"You've seen him on television, haven't you?"

"Yeah," he said. "But that don't count." After a while he said, "I remember when he fought Carnera. The celebration in Harlem. They poisoned his mind before that fight, his managers and Jack Blackburn did. They told him Carnera was Mussolini's man and Mussolini started the Ethiopian War. He cut that man down like he was a tree."

Questions

1. What is the first reason Liebling offers for preferring to attend boxing matches rather than to see them on TV? To what extent is he both joking and serious as he develops this reason? By what means does he make his distinction between the serious and the jocular evident to the reader?
2. What are Liebling's reactions to the four cabdrivers? Why? How does Liebling indicate these reactions to the reader?
3. How does Liebling express his pleasure and his familiarity with the circumstance as he enters Madison Square Garden for the Louis-Savold fight?
4. What does Liebling note about Louis's appearance as the former champion enters the ring? Why does he center on those particular details? What are Liebling's reactions to Savold? How does he express them?
5. During the fight, what suggests that Louis is no longer a great boxer?
6. What reactions does Liebling note in the crowd directly after the fight? How does he explain these reactions? To what extent do you think he shares them?
7. What are your reactions to the last sentence of the essay: "He cut that man down like he was a tree."

The Fight

by William Hazlitt (1778-1830)

"—— The *fight*, the *fight*'s the thing,
Wherein I'll catch the conscience of the king."[1]

Where there's a will there's a way. — I said so to myself, as I walked down Chancery Lane, about half-past six o'clock on Monday, the 10th of December, to inquire at Jack Randall's where the fight the next day was to be; and I found the proverb nothing "musty" in the present instance. I was determined to see this fight, come what would, and see it I did, in great style. It was my *first fight*, yet it more than answered my expectations. Ladies! it is to you I dedicate this description; nor let it seem out of character for the fair to notice the exploits of the brave. Courage and modesty are the old English virtues; and may they never look cold and askance on one another! Think, ye fairest of the fair, loveliest of the lovely kind, ye practisers of soft enchantment, how many more ye kill with poisoned baits than ever fell in the ring; and listen with subdued air and without shuddering, to a tale tragic only in appearance, and sacred to the FANCY!

I was going down Chancery Lane, thinking to ask at Jack Randall's where the fight was to be, when looking through the glass-door of the

1. "______ The fight, the fight's the thing,/Wherein I'll catch the conscience of the king." : see Shakespeare's *Hamlet*, Act II, ii, 633-4.

Hole in the Wall, I heard a gentleman asking the same question *at* Mrs. Randall, as the author of *Waverley*[2] would express it. Now Mrs. Randall stood answering the gentleman's question, with all the authenticity of the lady of the Champion of the Light Weights.[3] Thinks I, I'll wait till this person comes out, and learn from him how it is. For to say a truth, I was not fond of going into this house of call for heroes and philosophers, ever since the owner of it (for Jack is no gentleman) threatened once upon a time to kick me out of doors for wanting a mutton-chop at his hospitable board, when the conqueror in thirteen battles was more full of *blue ruin*[4] than of good manners. I was the more mortified at this repulse, inasmuch as I had heard Mr. James Simpkins, hosier in the Strand, one day when the character of the *Hole in the Wall* was brought in question, observe — "The house is a very good house, and the company quite genteel: I have been there myself!" Remembering this unkind treatment of mine host, to which mine hostess was also a party, and not wishing to put her in unquiet thoughts at a time jubilant like the present, I waited at the door, when, who should issue forth but my friend Joe P____s, and, seeing him turn suddenly up Chancery Lane with that quick jerk and impatient stride which distinguish a lover of the FANCY, I said, "I'll be hanged if that fellow is not going to the fight, and is on his way to get me to go with him." So it proved in effect, and we agreed to adjourn to my lodgings to discuss measures with that cordiality which makes old friends like new, and new friends like old, on great occasions. We are cold to others only when we are dull in ourselves, and have neither thoughts nor feelings to impart to them. Give a man a topic in his head, a throb of pleasure in his heart, and he will be glad to share it with the first person he meets. Joe and I, though we seldom meet, were an *alter idem*[5] on this memorable occasion, and had not an idea that we did not candidly impart; and "so carelessly did we fleet the time,"[6] that I wish no better, when there is another fight, than to have him for a companion on my journey down, and to return with my friend Jack Pigott, talking of what was to happen or of what did happen, with a noble subject always at hand, and liberty to digress to others whenever they offered. Indeed, on my repeating the lines from Spenser[7] in an involuntary fit of enthusiasm,

---

2. author of *Waverly:* Sir Walter Scott (a contemporary of Hazlitt's).
3. lady of the Champion of the Light Weights: wife of the best of the lightweights, Jack Randall, owner of the *Hole in the Wall.*
4. blue ruin: gin.
5. alter idem: "each other's self"; the same man.
6. "so carelessly did we fleet the time": based on a quotation from Shakespeare's *As You Like It* (I, i, 126).
7. Spenser: Edmund Spenser, English poet (1552-1599).

"What more felicity can fall to creature,
Than to enjoy delight with liberty?"

my last-named ingenious friend stopped me by saying that this, translated into the vulgate, meant *"Going to see a fight."*

Joe and I could not settle about the method of going down. He said there was a caravan, he understood, to start from Tom Belcher's at two, which would go there *right out* and back again the next day. Now, I never travel all night, and said I should get a cast[8] to Newbury by one of the mails.[9] Joe swore the thing was impossible, and I could only answer that I had made up my mind to it. In short, he seemed to me to waver, said he only came to see if I was going, had letters to write, a cause coming on the day after, and faintly said at parting (for I was bent on setting out that moment) — "Well, we meet at Philippi?"[10] I made the best of my way to Piccadilly. The mail-coach stand was bare. "They are all gone," said I — "this is always the way with me — in the instant I lose the future — if I had not stayed to pour out that last cup of tea, I should have been just in time;" — and cursing my folly and ill-luck together, without inquiring at the coach-office whether the mails were gone or not, I walked on in despite,[11] and to punish my own dilatoriness and want of determination. At any rate, I would not turn back: I might get to Hounslow, or perhaps farther, to be on my road the next morning. I passed Hyde Park corner (my Rubicon[12]), and trusted to fortune. Suddenly I heard the clattering of a Brentford stage,[13] and the fight rushed full upon my fancy. I argued (not unwisely) that even a Brentford coachman was better company than my own thoughts (such as they were just then), and at his invitation mounted the box with him. I immediately stated my case to him — namely, my quarrel with myself for missing the Bath or Bristol mail, and my determination to get on in consequence as well as I could, without any disparagement or insulting comparison between longer or shorter stages. It is a maxim with me that stagecoaches, and consequently stage-coachmen, are respectable in proportion to the distance they have to travel: so I said nothing on that subject to my Brentford friend. Any incipient tendency to an abstract proposition, or (as he might have construed it) to a personal reflection of this kind, was

---

8. cast: a lift, a ride.
9. mails: stagecoaches.
10. "Well, we meet at Philippi?": in Shakespeare's *Julius Caesar,* the forces of Brutus and Cassius met those of Octavius and Antony in battle at Philippi.
11. despite: ill humor.
12. Rubicon: the river in northern Italy whose crossing by Julius Caesar was regarded as an act of war.
13. Brentford stage: a local and much slower coach than a mail.

however nipped in the bud; for I had no sooner declared indignantly that I had missed the mails, than he flatly denied that they were gone along, and lo! at the instant three of them drove by in rapid, provoking, orderly succession, as if they would devour the ground before them. Here again I seemed in the contradictory situation of the man in Dryden[14] who exclaims,

"I follow Fate, which does too hard pursue!"

If I had stopped to inquire at the White Horse Cellar, which would not have taken me a minute, I should now have been driving down the road in all the dignified unconcern and *ideal* perfection of mechanical conveyance. The Bath mail I had set my mind upon, and I had missed it, as I miss everything else, by my own absurdity, in putting the will for the deed, and aiming at ends without employing means. "Sir," said he of the Brentford, "the Bath mail will be up presently, my brother-in-law drives it, and I will engage to stop him if there is a place empty." I almost doubted my good genius[15]; but, sure enough, up it drove like lightning, and stopped directly at the call of the Brentford Jehu.[16] I would not have believed this possible, but the brother-in-law of a mail-coach driver is himself no mean man. I was transferred without loss of time from the top of one coach to that of the other, desired the guard to pay my fare to the Brentford coachman for me as I had no change, was accommodated with a great coat, put up my umbrella to keep off a drizzling mist, and we began to cut through the air like an arrow. The mile-stones disappeared one after another, the rain kept off; Tom Turtle[17] the trainer sat before me on the coach-box, with whom I exchanged civilities as a gentleman going to the fight; the passion that had transported me an hour before was subdued to pensive regret and conjectural musing on the next day's battle; I was promised a place inside at Reading, and upon the whole, I thought myself a lucky fellow. Such is the force of imagination! On the outside of any other coach on the 10th of December, with a Scotch mist drizzling through the cloudy moonlight air, I should have been cold, comfortless, impatient, and, no doubt, wet through; but seated on the Royal mail, I felt warm and comfortable, the air did me good, the ride did me good, I was pleased with the progress we had made, and confident that all would go well through the journey. When I got inside at Reading, I found Turtle and a stout valetudinarian,[18] whose

---

14. Dryden: John Dryden, English poet (1631-1700).
15. good genius: helpful spirit, i.e. the Brentford coachman.
16. Brentford Jehu: a humorous term suggesting a fast and reckless driver. Jehu was a king of Israel (II Kings 9:6 and 20) famed as a furious charioteer.
17. Tom Turtle: John Thurtell, to wit [Hazlitt's footnote].
18. valetudinarian: a sickly person.

costume bespoke him one of the FANCY, and who had risen from a three months' sick bed to get into the mail to see the fight. They were intimate, and we fell into a lively discourse. My friend the trainer was confined in his topics to fighting dogs and men, to bears and badgers; beyond this he was "quite chap-fallen,"[19] had not a word to throw at a dog, or indeed very wisely fell asleep, when any other game was started. The whole art of training (I, however, learnt from him) consists in two things, exercise and abstinence, abstinence and exercise, repeated alternately and without end. A yolk of an egg with a spoonful of rum in it is the first thing in a morning, and then a walk of six miles till breakfast. This meal consists of a plentiful supply of tea and toast and beef-steaks. Then another six or seven miles till dinner-time, and another supply of solid beef or mutton with a pint of porter, and perhaps, at the utmost, a couple of glasses of sherry. Martin trains on water, but this increases his infirmity on another very dangerous side. The Gasman[20] takes now and then a chirping glass (under the rose)[21] to console him, during a six weeks' probation, for the absence of Mrs. Hickman — an agreeable woman, with (I understand) a pretty fortune of two hundred pounds. How matter presses on me! What stubborn things are facts! How inexhaustible is nature and art! "It is well," as I once heard Mr. Richmond observe, "to see a variety." He was speaking of cock-fighting as an edifying spectacle. I cannot deny but that one learns more of what *is* (I do not say of what *ought to be*) in this desultory mode of practical study, than from reading the same book twice over, even though it should be a moral treatise. Where was I? I was sitting at dinner with the candidate for the honours of the ring, "where good digestion waits on appetite, and health on both."[22] Then follows an hour of social chat and native glee; and afterwards, to another breathing over healthy hill or dale. Back to supper, and then to bed, and up by six again — our hero

> "Follows so the ever-running sun,
> With profitable *ardour*" —

to the day that brings him victory or defeat in the green fairy circle. Is not this life more sweet than mine? I was going to say; but I will not libel any

---

19. "quite chap-fallen": glum, down in the mouth (see *Hamlet*, V, i, 190).
20. the Gasman: Tom Hickman, one of the fighters Hazlitt is going to see.
21. a chirping glass (under the rose): a drink of liquor (quietly).
22. "where good digestion waits on appetite, and health on both": see *Macbeth* (III, iv, 39-40).

life by comparing it to mine, which is (at the date of these presents[23]) bitter as coloquintida[24] and the dregs of aconitum![25]

The invalid in the Bath mail soared a pitch above the trainer, and did not sleep so sound, because he had "more figures and more fantasies." We talked the hours away merrily. He had faith in surgery, for he had three ribs set right, that had been broken in a *turn-up*[26] at Belcher's, but thought physicians old women, for they had no antidote in their catalogue for brandy. An indigestion is an excellent commonplace for two people that never met before. By way of ingratiating myself, I told him the story of my doctor, who, on my earnestly representing to him that I thought his regimen had done me harm, assured me that the whole pharmacopeia[27] contained nothing comparable to the prescription he had given me; and, as a proof of its undoubted efficacy, said, that "he had had one gentleman with my complaint under his hands for the last fifteen years." This anecdote made my companion shake the rough sides of his three greatcoats with boisterous laughter; and Turtle, starting out of his sleep, swore he knew how the fight would go, for he had had a dream about it. Sure enough the rascal told us how the three first rounds went off, but "his dream" like others, "denoted a foregone conclusion."[28] He knew his men. The moon now rose in silver state, and I ventured, with some hesitation, to point out this object of placid beauty, with the blue serene beyond, to the man of science, to which his ear he "seriously inclined,"[29] the more as it gave promise *d'un beau jour*[30] for the morrow, and showed the ring undrenched by envious showers, arrayed in sunny smiles. Just then, all going on well, I thought on my friend Joe, whom I had left behind, and said innocently, "There was a blockhead of a fellow I left in town, who said there was no possibility of getting down by the mail, and talked of going by a caravan from Belcher's at two in the morning, after he had written some letters." "Why," said he of the lapels, "I should not wonder if that was the very person we saw running about like mad from one coach-door to another, and asking if any one had seen a friend of his, a gentleman going to the fight, whom he had missed stupidly enough by staying to write a note." "Pray, sir," said my

---

23. these presents: the present time.
24. coloquintida: colocynth; an herbaceous vine from which a powerful cathartic is made.
25. aconitum: a poisonous herb.
26. turn-up: brawl.
27. pharmacopeia: a book describing drugs, chemicals, and medicinal preparations.
28. "his dream . . . denoted a foregone conclusion": adapted from Shakespeare's *Othello* (III, iii, 432-33).
29. "seriously inclined": adapted from *Othello* (I, iii, 146).
30. d'un beau jour: of a beautiful day (French).

fellow-traveller, "had he a plaid-cloak on?" "Why, no," said I, "not at the time I left him, but he very well might afterwards, for he offered to lend me one." The plaid-cloak and the letter decided the thing. Joe, sure enough, was in the Bristol mail, which preceded us by about fifty yards. This was droll enough. We had now but a few miles to our place of destination, and the first thing I did on alighting at Newbury, both coaches stopping at the same time, was to call out, "Pray is there a gentleman in that mail of the name of P——s?" "No," said Joe, borrowing something of the vein of Gilpin,[31] "for I have just got out." "Well!" says he, "this is lucky; but you don't know how vexed I was to miss you; for," added he, lowering his voice, "do you know when I left you I went to Belcher's to ask about the caravan, and Mrs. Belcher said very obligingly, she couldn't tell about that, but there were two gentlemen who had taken places by the mail and were gone on in a landau,[32] and she could frank us.[33] It's a pity I didn't meet with you; we could then have got down for nothing. But *mum's the word.*"[34] It's the devil for any one to tell me a secret, for it is sure to come out in print. I do not care so much to gratify a friend, but the public ear is too great a temptation to me.

Our present business was to get beds and supper at an inn; but this was no easy task. The public-houses were full, and where you saw a light at a private house, and people poking their heads out of the casement to see what was going on, they instantly put them in and shut the window, the moment you seemed advancing with a suspicious overture for accommodation. Our guard and coachman thundered away at the outer gate of the Crown[35] for some time without effect — such was the greater noise within; and when the doors were unbarred, and we got admittance, we found a party assembled in the kitchen round a good hospitable fire, some sleeping, others drinking, others talking on politics and on the fight. A tall English yeoman (something like Matthews in the face, and quite as great a wag) —

"A lusty man to ben an abbot able" —[36]

was making such a prodigious noise about rent and taxes, and the price of corn now and formerly, that he had prevented us from being heard at the gate. The first thing I heard him say was to a shuffling fellow who wanted

---

31. Gilpin: see William Cowper's poem, "The Diverting History of John Gilpin."
32. landau: a type of four-wheel carriage.
33. frank us: let us ride free.
34. "mum's the word": keep it quiet.
35. the Crown: name of an inn.
36. "A lusty man to ben an abbot able": part of Chaucer's description of the sporting monk in *Canterbury Tales.*

to be off a bet[37] for a shilling glass of brandy and water — "Confound it, man, don't be *insipid!*" Thinks I, that is a good phrase. It was a good omen. He kept it up so all night, nor flinched with the approach of morning. He was a fine fellow, with sense, wit, and spirit, a hearty body and a joyous mind, free-spoken, frank, convivial — one of that true English breed that went with Harry the Fifth[38] to the siege of Harfleur — "standing like greyhounds in the slips," etc. We ordered tea and eggs (beds were soon found to be out of the question), and this fellow's conversation was *sauce piquante*.[39] It did one's heart good to see him brandish his oaken towel[40] and to hear him talk. He made mince-meat of a drunken, stupid, red-faced, quarrelsome, *frowsy* farmer, whose nose "he moralised into a thousand similes," making it out a firebrand like Bardolph's.[41] "I'll tell you what, my friend," says he, "the landlady has only to keep you here to save fire and candle. If one was to touch your nose, it would go off like a piece of charcoal." At this the other only grinned like an idiot, the sole variety in his purple face being his little peering grey eyes and yellow teeth, called for another glass, swore he would not stand it, and after many attempts to provoke his humorous antagonist to single combat, which the other turned off (after working him up to a ludicrous pitch of choler[42]) with great adroitness, he fell quietly asleep with a glass of liquor in his hand, which he could not lift to his head. His laughing persecutor made a speech over him, and turning to the opposite side of the room, where they were all sleeping in the midst of this "loud and furious fun," said — "There's a scene, by G—d, for Hogarth[43] to paint. I think he and Shakespeare were our two best men at copying life." This confirmed me in my good opinion of him. Hogarth, Shakespeare, and Nature, were just enough for him (indeed for any man) to know. I said, "You read Cobbett,[44] don't you? At least," says I, "you talk just as well as he writes." He seemed to doubt this. But I said, "We have an hour to spare: if you'll get pen, ink, and paper, and keep on talking, I'll write down what you say; and if it doesn't make a capital *Political Register*,[45] I'll forfeit my head. You have kept me alive to-night, however. I don't know what I should have done without you." He did not

37. be off a bet: call off a bet.
38. Harry the Fifth: King Henry V of England. The following words are from Shakespeare's *Henry V* (III, i, 31).
39. sauce piquante: a spicy sauce or gravy.
40. oaken towel: his stick or cudgel (he can dry off with it).
41. Bardolph: Falstaff's flaming-nosed henchman in Shakespeare's *Henry IV*.
42. choler: hot temper.
43. Hogarth: William Hogarth (1697-1764), a famous engraver and painter whose satirical studies of the everyday life of his time are still well known.
44. Cobbett: political journalist of early 19th century England.
45. *Political Register:* popular journal of the time.

dislike this view of the thing, nor my asking if he was not about the size of Jem Belcher; and told me soon afterwards, in the confidence of friendship, that "the circumstance which had given him nearly the greatest concern in his life, was Cribb's[46] beating Jem after he had lost his eye by racket-playing." — The morning dawns; that dim but yet clear light appears, which weighs like solid bars of metal on the sleepless eyelids; the guests dropped down from their chambers one by one — but it was too late to think of going to bed now (the clock was on the stroke of seven), we had nothing for it but to find a barber's (the pole that glittered in the morning sun lighted us to his shop), and then a nine miles' march to Hungerford. The day was fine, the sky was blue, the mists were retiring from the marshy ground, the path was tolerably dry, the sitting-up all night had not done us much harm — at least the cause was good; we talked of this and that with amicable difference, roving and sipping of many subjects, but still invariably we returned to the fight. At length, a mile to the left of Hungerford, on a gentle eminence, we saw the ring surrounded by covered carts, gigs, and carriages, of which hundreds had passed us on the road; Joe gave a youthful shout, and we hastened down a narrow lane to the scene of action.

Reader, have you ever seen a fight? If not, you have a pleasure to come, at least if it is a fight like that between the Gasman and Bill Neate. The crowd was very great when we arrived on the spot; open carriages were coming up, with streamers flying and music playing, and the country-people were pouring in over hedge and ditch in all directions, to see their hero beat or be beaten. The odds were still on Gas, but only about five to four. Gully had been down to try Neate, and had backed him considerably, which was a damper to the sanguine confidence of the adverse party. About £200,000 were pending.[47] Gas says he has lost £3000, which were promised him by different gentlemen if he had won. He had presumed too much on himself, which had made others presume on him. This spirited and formidable young fellow seems to have taken for his motto, the old maxim, that "there are three things necessary to success in life — *Impudence! Impudence! Impudence!*" It is so in matters of opinion, but not in the *Fancy*, which is the most practical of all things, though even here confidence is half the battle, but only half. Our friend had vapoured[48] and swaggered too much, as if he wanted to grin and bully his adversary out of the fight. "Alas! the Bristol man[49] was not so tamed!" — This is the *grave-digger*"

46. Jem Belcher and Tom Cribb were two prominent champions among the fancy.
47. pending: bet, "hanging in the balance."
48. vapoured: blustered, bragged.
49. the Bristol man: Bill Neate.

(would Tom Hickman exclaim in the moments of intoxication from gin and success, showing his tremendous right hand), "this will send many of them to their long homes; I haven't done with them yet!" Why should he — though he had licked four of the best men within the hour — why should he threaten to inflict dishonorable chastisement on my old master Richmond, a veteran going off the stage, and who has borne his sable honours[50] meekly? Magnanimity, my dear Tom, and bravery, should be inseparable. Or why should he go up to his antagonist, the first time he ever saw him at the Fives Court,[51] and measuring him from head to foot with a glance of contempt, as Achilles surveyed Hector, say to him, "what, are you Bill Neate? I'll knock more blood out of that great carcase of thine, this day fortnight, than you ever knock'd out of a bullock's!" It was not manly — 'twas not fighter-like. If he was sure of the victory (as he was not), the less said about it the better. Modesty should accompany the *Fancy* as its shadow. The best men were always the best behaved. Jem Belcher, the Game Chicken[52] (before whom the Gasman could not have lived) were civil, silent men. So is Cribb; so is Tom Belcher, the most elegant of sparrers, and not a man for every one to take by the nose.[53] I enlarged on this topic in the mail (while Turtle was asleep), and said very wisely (as I thought) that impertinence was a part of no profession. A boxer was bound to beat his man, but not to thrust his fist, either actually or by implication, in every one's face. Even a highwayman, in the way of trade, may blow out your brains, but if he uses foul language at the same time, I should say he was no gentleman. A boxer, I would infer, need not be a blackguard[54] or a coxcomb,[55] more than another. Perhaps I press this point too much on a fallen man — Mr. Thomas Hickman has by this time learnt that first of all lessons, "That man was made to mourn."[56] He has lost nothing by the late fight but his presumption; and that every man may do as well without! By an over display of this quality, however, the public had been prejudiced against him, and the *knowing ones* were taken in. Few but those who had bet on him wished Gas to win. With my own prepossessions on the subject, the result of the 11th of December appeared to me as fine a piece of poetical justice as I had ever witnessed. The difference of weight between the

---

50. sable honours: dark glories (the great fighter Richmond was black).
51. Fives Court: a court for an English ball game also commonly used for smaller boxing matches and sparring.
52. the Game Chicken: nickname for another small, fancy, and valorous fighter of the time.
53. take by the nose: treat scornfully.
54. blackguard: a rude brute or hoodlum.
55. coxcomb: fool.
56. "That man was made to mourn": line from a poem by the same name by Robert Burns, Scottish poet (1759-1796).

two combatants (14 stones to 12)[57] was nothing to the sporting men. Great, heavy, clumsy, long-armed Bill Neate kicked the beam in the scale of the Gasman's vanity.[58] The amateurs were frightened at his big words, and thought they would make up for the difference of six feet and five feet nine. Truly, the *Fancy* are not men of imagination. They judge of what has been, and cannot conceive of anything that is to be. The Gasman had won hitherto; therefore he must beat a man half as big again as himself — and that to a certainty. Besides, there are as many feuds, factions, prejudices, pedantic notions in the *Fancy* as in the state or in the schools. Mr. Gully is almost the only cool, sensible man among them, who exercises an unbiased discretion, and is not a slave to his passions in these matters. But enough of reflections, and to our tale. The day, as I have said, was fine for a December morning. The grass was wet, and the ground miry, and ploughed up with multitudinous feet, except that, within the ring itself, there was a spot of virgin-green, closed in and unprofaned by vulgar tread, that shone with dazzling brightness in the mid-day sun. For it was now noon, and we had an hour to wait. This is the trying time. It is then the heart sickens, as you think what the two champions are about, and how short a time will determine their fate. After the first blow is struck, there is no opportunity for nervous apprehensions; you are swallowed up in the immediate interest of the scene — but

> "Between the acting of a dreadful thing
> And the first motion, all the interim is
> Like a phantasma, or a hideous dream."[59]

I found it so as I felt the sun's rays climbing to my back, and saw the white wintry clouds sink below the verge of the horizon. "So," I thought, "my fairest hopes have faded from my sight! — so will the Gasman's glory, or that of his adversary, vanish in an hour." The *swells*[60] were parading in their white box-coats, the outer ring was cleared with some bruises on the heads and shins of the rustic assembly (for the *cockneys*[61] had been distanced by the sixty-six miles); the time drew near; I had got a good stand; a bustle, a buzz, ran through the crowd; and from the opposite side

57. 14 stones to 12: in England, human weight was measured by the *stone* which equals 14 pounds. Bill Neate, then, weighed 196 pounds as opposed to the Gasman at 168.
58. kicked the beam in the scale of the Gasman's vanity: made his pride seem the heavier or greater.
59. *Julius Caesar* (II, i, 63-5).
60. swells: dandies.
61. cockneys: Londoners; city fellows.

entered Neate, between his second and bottleholder. He rolled along, swathed in his loose greatcoat, his knock-knees bending under his huge bulk; and, with a modest, cheerful air, threw his hat into the ring. He then just looked round, and begun quietly to undress; when from the other side there was a similar rush and an opening made, and the Gasman came forward with a conscious air of anticipated triumph, too much like the cock-of-the-walk. He strutted about more than became a hero, sucked oranges with a supercilious air, and threw away the skin with a toss of his head, and went up and looked at Neate, which was an act of supererogation.[62] The only sensible thing he did was, as he strode away from the modern Ajax,[63] to fling out his arms, as if he wanted to try whether they would do their work that day. By this time they had stripped, and presented a strong contrast in appearance. If Neate was like Ajax, "with Atlantean shoulders, fit to bear"[64] the pugilistic reputation of all Bristol, Hickman might be compared to Diomed,[65] light, vigorous, elastic, and his back glistened in the sun, as he moved about, like a panther's hide. There was now a dead pause — attention was awe-struck. Who at that moment, big with a great event, did not draw his breath short — did not feel his heart throb? All was ready. They tossed up for the sun,[66] and the Gasman won. They were led up to the *scratch*[67] — shook hands, and went at it.

In the first round every one thought it was all over. After making play a short time, the Gasman flew at his adversary like a tiger, struck five blows in as many seconds, three, first, and then following him as he staggered back, two more, right and left, and down he fell, a mighty ruin. There was a shout, and I said, "There is no standing this." Neate seemed like a lifeless lump of flesh and bone, round which the Gasman's blows played with the rapidity of electricity or lightning, and you imagined he would only be lifted up to be knocked down again. It was as if Hickman held a sword or a fire in that right hand of his, and directed it against an unarmed body. They met again, and Neate seemed, not cowed, but particularly cautious. I saw his teeth clenched together and his brows knit close against the sun. He held out both arms at full length straight before him, like two sledge

---

62. superogation: uncalled-for insolence.
63. Ajax: one of the Greek heroes in Homer's *Iliad,* possessed of great stature and strength.
64. "with Atlantean shoulders, fit to bear": see Milton's *Paradise Lost* Book II, line 306.
65. Diomed: legendary Greek warrior.
66. tossed up for the sun: flipped a coin to see which would start with the sun in his eyes.
67. scratch: literally a line scratched in the middle of the ring. If a fighter could not or would not come to it unassisted he was declared the loser. Note our common expression, "up to scratch".

hammers, and raised his left an inch or two higher. The Gasman could not get over this guard — they struck mutually and fell, but without advantage on either side. It was the same in the next round; but the balance of power was thus restored — the fate of the battle was suspended. No one could tell how it would end. This was the only moment in which opinion was divided; for, in the next, the Gasman aiming a mortal blow at his adversary's neck, with his right hand, and failing from the length he had to reach, the other returned it with his left at full swing, planted a tremendous blow on his cheek-bone and eyebrow, and made a red ruin on that side of his face. The Gasman went down, and there was another shout — a roar of triumph as the waves of fortune rolled tumultuously from side to side. This was a settler. Hickman got up, and "grinned horrible a ghastly smile," yet he was evidently dashed in his opinion of himself; it was the first time he had ever been so punished; all one side of his face was perfect scarlet, and his right eye was closed in dingy blackness, as he advanced to the fight, less confident, but still determined. After one or two rounds, not receiving another such remembrancer, he rallied and went at it with his former impetuosity. But in vain. His strength had been weakened — his blows could not tell at such a distance — he was obliged to fling himself at his adversary, and could not strike from his feet; and almost as regularly as he flew at him with his right hand, Neate warded the blow, or drew back out of its reach, and felled him with the return of his left. There was little cautious sparring — no half-hits — no tapping and trifling, none of the *petit-maitreship*[68] of the art — they were almost all knock-down blows: — the fight was a good stand-up fight. The wonder was the half-minute time. If there had been a minute or more allowed between each round, it would have been intelligible how they should by degrees recover strength and resolution; but to see two men smashed to the ground, smeared with gore, stunned, senseless, the breath beaten out of their bodies; and then, before you recover from the shock, to see them rise up with new strength and courage, stand ready to inflict or receive mortal offence, and rush upon each other "like two clouds over the Caspian" — this is the most astonishing thing of all: — this is the high and heroic state of man! From this time forward the event became more certain every round; and about the twelfth it seemed as if it must have been over. Hickman generally stood with his back to me; but in the scuffle, he had changed positions, and Neate just then made a tremendous lunge at him, and hit him full in the face. It was doubtful whether he would fall backwards or forwards; he hung suspended for a minute or two, and then fell back, throwing his hands in the air, and with his face

---

68. petit-maitreship: little refinements.

lifted up to the sky. I never saw anything more terrific[69] than his aspect just before he fell. All traces of life, of natural expression, were gone from him. His face was like a human skull, a death's head spouting blood. The eyes were filled with blood, the nose streamed with blood, the mouth gaped blood. He was not like an actual man, but like a preternatural, spectral appearance, or like one of the figures in Dante's *Inferno*. Yet he fought on after this for several rounds, still striking the first desperate blow, and Neate standing on the defensive, and using the same cautious guard to the last, as if he had still all his work to do; and it was not till the Gasman was so stunned in the seventeenth or eighteenth round, that his senses forsook him, and he could not come to time,[70] that the battle was declared over.[71] Ye who despise the Fancy, do something to show as much *pluck*, or as much self-possession as this, before you assume a superiority which you have never given a single proof of by any one action in the whole course of your lives! — When the Gasman came to himself, the first words he uttered were, "Where am I? What is the matter?" "Nothing is the matter, Tom, — you have lost the battle, but you are the bravest man alive." And Jackson whispered to him, "I am collecting a purse for you, Tom." — Vain sounds, and unheard at that moment! Neate instantly went up and shook him cordially by the hand, and seeing some old acquaintance, began to flourish with his fists, calling out, "Ah! you always said I couldn't fight — what do you think now?" But all in good humour, and without any appearance of arrogance; only it was evident Bill Neate was pleased that he had won the fight. When it was over, I asked Cribb if he did not think it was a good one? He said, "*Pretty well!*" The carrier-pigeons now mounted into the air, and one of them flew with the news of her husband's victory to the bosom of Mrs. Neate. Alas, for Mrs. Hickman!

Mais au revoir,[72] as Sir Fopling Flutter says. I went down with Joe P——s; I returned with Jack Pigott, whom I met on the ground. Toms is a rattle-brain; Pigott is a sentimentalist. Now, under favour, I am a sentimentalist too — therefore I say nothing, but that the interest of the excursion did not flag as I came back. Pigott and I marched along the causeway

---

69. terrific: frightful.
70. come to time: he would not "answer the bell" by coming out to fight when time for rest and recovery was up.
71. Scroggins said of the Gasman, that he thought he was a man of that courage, that if his hands were cut off he would still fight on with the stumps – like that of Widdrington–

   – "In doleful dumps,
   Who, when his legs were smitten off,
   still fought upon his stumps." [Hazlitt's footnote]

72. *Mais au revoir:* but until we meet again (French). Sir Fopling Flutter is a pretentious dandy and mock hero of a comedy by Sir George Etherege.

leading from Hungerford to Newbury, now observing the effect of a brilliant sun on the tawny meads or moss-coloured cottages, now exulting in the fight, now digressing to some topic of general and elegant literature. My friend was dressed in character for the occasion, or like one of the Fancy; that is, with a double portion of greatcoats, clogs, and overhauls: and just as we had agreed with a couple of country-lads to carry his superfluous wearing-apparel to the next town, we were overtaken by a return post-chaise,[73] into which I got, Pigott preferring a seat on the bar. There were two strangers already in the chaise, and on their observing they supposed I had been to the fight, I said I had, and concluded they had done the same. They appeared, however, a little shy and sore on the subject; and it was not till after several hints dropped, and questions put, that it turned out that they had missed it. One of these friends had undertaken to drive the other there in his gig: they had set out, to make sure work, the day before at three in the afternoon. The owner of the one-horse vehicle scorned to ask his way, and drove right on to Bagshot, instead of turning off at Hounslow: there they stopped all night, and set off the next day across the country to Reading, from whence they took coach, and got down within a mile or two of Hungerford, just half-an-hour after the fight was over. This might be safely set down as one of the miseries of human life. We parted with these two gentlemen who had been to see the fight, but had returned as they went, at Wolhampton, where we were promised beds (an irresistible temptation, for Pigott had passed the preceding night at Hungerford as we had done at Newbury), and we turned into an old bow-windowed parlour with a carpet and a snug fire; and after devouring a quantity of tea, toast, and eggs, sat down to consider, during an hour of philosophic leisure, what we should have for supper. In the midst of an Epicurean deliberation between a roasted fowl and mutton chops with mashed potatoes, we were interrupted by an inroad of Goths and Vandals — *O procul este profani*[74] — not real flash-men,[75] but interlopers, noisy pretenders, builders from Tothill Fields, brokers from Whitechapel,[76] who called immediately for pipes and tobacco, hoping it would not be disagreeable to the gentlemen, and began to insist that it was *a cross*[77] Pigott withdrew from the smoke and noise into another room, and left me to dispute the point with them for a couple of hours *sans intermission*[78] by the dial.

---

73. post-chaise: small fast coach or carriage available for hire for special trips.
74. O procul este profani: "O hence, ye are uninitiated" (Virgil, *Aeneid,* vi, 258).
75. flash-men: sporting types, fellows "in the know".
76. Tothill Fields and Whitechapel: lower middle class districts of greater London.
77. a cross: a "fixed" fight.
78. sans intermission: without pause (French). In context here the line is suggested by one from Shakespeare's *As You Like It* (II, vii, 139).

The next morning we rose refreshed; and on observing that Jack had a pocket volume in his hand, in which he read in the intervals of our discourse, I inquired what it was, and learned to my particular satisfaction that it was a volume of the *New Eloise*.[79] Ladies, after this, you will contend that a love for the Fancy is incompatible with the cultivation of sentiment? — We jogged on as before, my friend setting me up in a genteel drab great coat and green silk handkerchief (which I must say became me exceedingly), and after stretching our legs for a few miles, and seeing Jack Randall, Ned Turner, and Scroggins pass on the top of one of the Bath coaches, we engaged with the driver of the second to take us to London for the usual fee. I got inside, and found three other passengers. One of them was an old gentleman with an aquiline nose, powdered hair, and a pig-tail, and who looked as if he had played many a rubber[80] at the Bath rooms. I said to myself, he is very like Mr. Windham; I wish he would enter into conversation, that I might hear what fine observations would come from those finely-turned features. However, nothing passed, till, stopping to dine at Reading, some inquiry was made by the company about the fight, and I gave (as the reader may believe) an eloquent and animated description of it. When we got into the coach again, the old gentleman, after a graceful exordium,[81] said he had, when a boy, been to a fight between the famous Broughton and George Stevenson, who was called the *Fighting Coachman,* in the year 1770, with the late Mr. Windham. This beginning flattered the spirit of prophecy with me, and riveted my attention. He went on — "George Stevenson was coachman to a friend of my father's. He was an old man when I saw him, some years afterwards. He took hold of his own arm and said, 'there was muscle here once, but now it is no more than this young gentleman's.' He added, 'well, no matter; I have been here long, I am willing to go hence, and I hope I have done no more harm than another man.' Once," said my unknown companion, "I asked him if he had ever beat Broughton? He said Yes; that he had fought with him three times, and the last time he fairly beat him, though the world did not allow it. 'I'll tell you how it was, master. When the seconds lifted us up in the last round, we were so exhausted that neither of us could stand, and we fell upon one another, and as Master Broughton fell uppermost, the mob gave it in his favour, and he was said to have won the battle. But the fact was, that as his second (John Cuthbert) lifted him up, he said to him, "I'll fight no more, I've had enough;" which,' says Stevenson, 'you know gave me the victory. And to prove to you that this was the case,

79. *New Eloise:* Publication of sentimental fiction popular at the time.
80. rubber: a sequence in the game of whist — as now in bridge.
81. exordium: beginning.

when John Cuthbert was on his death-bed, and they asked him if there was anything on his mind which he wished to confess, he answered, "Yes, that there was one thing he wished to set right, for that certainly Master Stevenson won that last fight with Master Broughton; for he whispered him as he lifted him up in the last round of all, that he had had enough." ' "This," said the Bath gentleman, "was a bit of human nature;" and I have written this account of the fight on purpose that it might not be lost to the world. He also stated as a proof of the candour of mind in this class of men, that Stevenson acknowledged that Broughton could have beat him in his best day; but that he (Broughton) was getting old in their last encounter. When we stopped in Piccadilly, I wanted to ask the gentleman some questions about the late Mr. Windham, but had not courage. I got out, resigned my coat and green silk handkerchief to Pigott (loth to part with these ornaments of life), and walked home in high spirits.

P.S. — Joe called upon me the next day, to ask me if I did not think the fight was a complete thing? I said I thought it was. I hope he will relish my account of it.

Questions

1. Although Hazlitt does not say so directly, prizefighting was illegal in England at the time he writes of. What indications of this fact do you find in the essay?
2. With what details of description or incident does Hazlitt create a "character" of himself as narrator of the essay? Why do you think he does so?
3. What various sorts of people does Hazlitt encounter on his journey to and from the fight? How does he suggest that the interest in prizefighting in his society was not confined to a particular group? What does he suggest that those interested in prizefighting had in common?
4. How does Hazlitt compare and contrast the Gasman (Tom Hickman) with Bill Neate?
5. What explanation does Hazlitt offer for preferring to travel to the fight with one friend and home from it with another?
6. What details of the fight itself impress the essayist most?

Afterword to *Boxing With the Naked Eye* and *The Fight*

Until this point we have treated "Boxing With the Naked Eye" as though it were simply about boxing, and about Liebling's interest in the sport and his preference for attending fights over watching them on television. These things are, of course, the immediate terms of the essay, but they are not everything, and indeed they are not ultimately what is most interesting and important in it. Liebling has nothing good to say about television in "Boxing with the Naked Eye," but we would be superficial to conclude that the central target of his piece is TV's deleterious effect on modern life, although we are getting closer to the center as we consider this as a possibility.

In his characteristically personal and informal essay, A. J. Liebling is really approaching one of the most universal and pressing questions of all places and all times: how to live. His answer appears to be: "gregariously." From the beginning to end of "Boxing with the Naked Eye" the essayist stresses personal involvement with other people, and he deplores the isolation of those who think in statistics (like the first cab driver) or of those who are content to study in silence the selected offerings of the television screen. T. S. Matthews' version of communication ("My God, I'm alive! You're alive!") is, Liebling says, a hell of a way to run a news magazine, but it is perfectly clear that it is the way he wants to do most of everything else.

Perhaps this is the key to Liebling's interest in the ring, for whatever may be said about the encounter of two strong fellows with the gloves on, such an encounter is personal . . . they are really involved with one another. A good crowd at a good fight is also "involved," insists Liebling. They talk to each other (through the fighters), they speculate freely, they are, he would have us believe . . . *alive* together. Liebling develops this sense of being alive with other people throughout the essay, and it is interesting to note how similar in this respect is the essay of the earlier fight fan, William Hazlitt. Both men represent themselves as chatty fellows who fall immediately into talk with cab drivers and coach drivers and who eagerly overhear and retell the remarks and conversations of anyone around them. Both are witty and give their readers that impression of comic vitality that comes with Hazlitt's: "Even a highwayman, in the way of trade, may blow out your brains, but if he uses foul language at the same time, I should say he was no gentleman," or Liebling: "He [Panama Al Brown] was five feet eleven and weighed a hundred and eighteen pounds. This fellow may be about forty pounds heavier and a couple of inches shorter, but he's got the same kind of neck."

Hazlitt, like Liebling, gives a good deal of space to the matter of getting to a fight, as well as to the movement and disposition of the audience before and after the match. Note the gusto with which these essayists approach each detail of their projects. Liebling enjoys the pretty women and the gay sentimentality of the Harlem Louis fans; Hazlitt obviously relishes the spectacle of the *swells* parading in their white boxcoats and the bustle and buzz of the crowd. Consider, too, how both essayists use casual references to current events, past events, and their own reading and gain the effect of putting their experience with *boxiana* in the main stream of human life. By such means and many others Liebling and Hazlitt insist on the vital humanity of what is so often represented as an inhumane occasion.

Do they do so for the same ends? It has been suggested that Liebling's essay is centrally concerned with being personally involved (with the naked eye) as a better way to live than most people do these days (isolated by the television screen). He puts his genuine enthusiasm for the ring at the service of his philosophy. (We should note in passing that he appears a much more experienced fight fan than does Hazlitt.) Is, on the other hand, the English essayist of "The Fight" doing any more than what he claims for his piece in its postscript: giving an account, to be relished, of a "complete" fight? How serious are his direct defenses of pugilism addressed to the Ladies and "Ye who despise the Fancy"?

As you consider this question, recall the story Hazlitt reports from the old gentleman on the Bath coach at the end of the essay. Remember, too, Hazlitt's description of the once-impudent Gasman as that fighter meets defeat. Do you suppose that the Fancy represents some ideal of valor and honor to Hazlitt which he does not find at large elsewhere in his world?

General Discussion Questions

1. As modern publicists know very well, famous athletes, like other celebrities, attract particular attention if they are presented to the public as human beings with individual traits and virtues, past histories, and present problems. Great athletic skill in itself is apparently only part of what captures and holds popular enthusiasm for the star. How do Liebling and Hazlitt apply this principle to their treatment of Joe Louis and the Gasman? What particular personal details does each essayist select? To what extent are they the same sorts of details in each essay?
2. It is a fairly frequent practice in some intellectual and academic circles to dismiss spectator sports as irrelevant to real life. By what means do Liebling and Hazlitt emphasize that they find boxing both part of "real life" and a significant analogy to it?
3. What kinds of readers are Liebling and Hazlitt writing for? What sort of reference does each essayist assume that his audience will recognize without explanation? For example, are these essayists writing for readers who are in some sense "intellectual" or "academic"? Explain.

3

Men and History

The history of the world is but the biography of great men.

THOMAS CARLYLE

History is little else than a picture of human crimes and misfortunes.

VOLTAIRE

Foreword to *Charles II*

Charles I, King of England from 1625 to 1649, was defeated in a Civil War fought over a combination of political and religious issues. The leaders of the anti-royalist faction, a Puritan majority in Parliament, sentenced and beheaded him. This shocking event marked the zenith of the power of seventeenth-century radical Puritanism, and clearly illustrated, for anyone who still needed illustration, that the role of the King as God's unassailable deputy was no longer an idea on which society could depend for security and order.

After the execution of King Charles I, the great Puritan leader, Oliver Cromwell, became dictator of England with the title of Lord Protector. The period of Cromwell's "protectorate," and the few years before and after it, gave the general populace of England rather more than they wanted of discipline, austerity, and local government by major-generals, and in 1660 the exiled son of the dead king was called home by popular mandate to take the throne. During the Protectorate, Charles II had led an uneasy existence in France and Holland, barely supported by contributions from his scattered loyalist followers. His "Restoration" brought strong general reactions against the dourness of the Puritan domination, and he, who quickly earned the nickname of "the Merry Monarch," proved a more than adequate symbol of that reaction. If the King of England no longer represented in his person divine authority, he seemed to represent in his person (of Charles II, at least) the authority of pleasure.

Lord Macaulay's short piece on Charles II combines the elements of biography, history, and political theory. Perhaps political theory is uppermost, for Macaulay's positive opinions on what the head of a government ought to be and ought not to be, should be clear even to a reader who knows nothing about Charles or about the Civil War or the Restoration.

For any but the most careless reader, the essayist's real feelings are emphasized rather than masked by the pose of judicious detachment with which Macaulay considers Charles's good qualities and makes justification for his bad ones. Indeed, Macaulay skillfully condemns with praise; he underlines King Charles's tolerance in order to demonstrate his irresponsibility.

At the same time, although Macaulay is unlikely to have anything like personal sympathy for Charles II, he is too clever to put his attack on an apparently personal level; the Merry Monarch is an engaging personality in history romantically imagined. Macaulay is a practical, hard-headed sort of essayist who put popular sentiments to his own uses.

Frequently printed alone as an essay, this piece is part of Macaulay's *History of England.*

Charles II

by Thomas Babington Macaulay (1800-1859)

The restored king was at this time more loved by the people than any of his predecessors had ever been. The calamities of his house, the heroic death of his father, his own long sufferings and romantic adventures, made him an object of tender interest. His return had delivered the country from an intolerable bondage. Recalled by the voice of both the contending factions, he was the very man to arbitrate between them; and in some respects he was well qualified for the task. He had received from nature excellent parts and a happy temper. His education had been such as might have been expected to develop his understanding, and to form him to the practice of every public and private virtue. He had passed through all varieties of fortune and had seen both sides of human nature. He had, while very young, been driven forth from a palace to a life of exile, penury, and danger. He had, at the age when the mind and body are in their highest perfection, and when the first effervescence of boyish passions should have subsided, been recalled from his wanderings to wear a crown. He had been taught by bitter experience how much baseness, perfidy, and ingratitude may lie hid under the obsequious demeanor of courtiers. He had found, on the other hand, in the huts of the poorest, true nobility of soul. When wealth was offered to any who would betray him, when death was denounced against all who should shelter him, cottagers and serving-men had kept his secret truly, and had kissed his hand under his mean disguises with as much reverence as if he had been seated on his ancestral throne. From such a school it might have been expected that a young man who wanted[1] neither abilities nor amiable qualities would have come forth a great and good king. Charles came forth from that school with social habits, with polite and engaging manners, and with some talent for lively conversation, addicted beyond measure to sensual indulgence, fond of sauntering and of frivolous amusements, incapable of self-denial and of exertion, without faith in human virtue or in human attachment, without desire of renown, and without sensibility to reproach. According to him, every person was to be bought. But some people haggled more about their price than others; and when this haggling was very obstinate and very skilful, it was called by some fine name. The chief trick by which clever men kept up the price of their abilities was called integrity. The chief trick by which handsome women kept up the price of their beauty was called modesty. The love of God, the love of country, the love of family, the love of friends, were phrases of the same sort, delicate and convenient synonyms for the love of self. Thinking thus of mankind, Charles naturally cared very little for what they thought of him. Honor and shame were scarcely more to him than light and darkness to the blind. His contempt for flattery has been highly commended, but seems, when viewed in connection with the rest of his character, to deserve no commendation. It is possible to be below flattery as well as above it. One who trusts nobody will not trust sycophants. One who does not value real glory will not value its counterfeit.

It is creditable to Charles's temper that, ill as he thought of his species, he never became a misanthrope. He saw little in men but what was hateful. Yet he did not hate them; nay, he was so far humane that it was highly disagreeable to him to see their sufferings or to hear their complaints. This, however, is a sort of humanity which, though amiable and laudable in a private man whose power to help or hurt is bounded by a narrow circle, has in princes often been rather a vice than a virtue. More than one well-disposed ruler has given up whole provinces to rapine and oppression, merely from a wish to see none but happy faces round his own board and in his own walks. No man is fit to govern great societies who hesitates disobliging the few who have access to him for the sake of the many whom he will never see. The facility of Charles was such as has, perhaps, never been found in any man of equal sense. He was a slave without being a dupe. Worthless men and women, to the very bottom of whose hearts he saw, and whom he knew to be destitute of affection for him, and undeserving of his confidence, could easily wheedle him out of titles, places, domains, state secrets, and pardons. He bestowed much; yet he neither enjoyed the

1. wanted: lacked.

pleasure nor acquired the fame of beneficence. He never gave spontaneously; but it was painful to him to refuse. The consequence was that his bounty generally went, not to those who deserved it best, nor even to those whom he liked best, but to the most shameless and importunate suitor who obtain an audience.

The motives which governed the political conduct of Charles the Second differed widely from those by which his predecessor and his successor were actuated. He was not a man to be imposed upon by the patriarchal theory of government and the doctrine of divine right. He was utterly without ambition. He detested business, and would sooner have abdicated his crown than have undergone the trouble of really directing the administration. Such was his aversion to toil, and such his ignorance of affairs, that the very clerks who attended him when he sat in council could not refrain from sneering at his frivolous remarks and at his childish impatience. Neither gratitude nor revenge had any share in determining his course, for never was there a mind on which both services and injuries left such faint and transitory impressions. He wished merely to be a king such as Louis the Fifteenth of France afterwards was; a king who could draw without limit on the treasury for the gratification of his private tastes, who could hire with wealth and honors persons capable of assisting him to kill the time, and who, even when the state was brought by maladministration to the depths of humiliation and to the brink of ruin, could still exclude unwelcome truth from the purlieus[2] of his own seraglio,[3] and refuse to see and hear whatever might disturb his luxurious repose. For these ends, and for these ends alone, he wished to obtain arbitrary power, if it could be obtained without risk or trouble. In the religious disputes which divided his Protestant subjects, his conscience was not at all interested, for his opinions oscillated in a state of contented suspense between infidelity and popery. But though his conscience was neutral in the quarrel between the Episcopalians and the Presbyterians, his taste was by no means so. His favorite vices were precisely those to which the Puritans were least indulgent. He could not get through the day without the help of diversions which the Puritans regarded as sinful. As a man eminently well bred, and keenly sensible of the ridiculous, he was moved to contemptous mirth by the Puritan oddities. He had, indeed, some reason to dislike the rigid sect. He had, at the age when passions are most impetuous, and when levity is most pardonable, spent some months in Scotland, a king in name, but in fact a state prisoner in the hands of austere Presbyterians. Not content with requiring

2. purlieus: confines.
3. seraglio: harem.

him to conform to their worship and to subscribe to their Covenant, they had watched all his motions, and lectured him on all his youthful follies. He had been compelled to give reluctant attendance at endless prayers and sermons, and might think himself fortunate when he was not insolently reminded from the pulpit of his own frailties, of his father's tyranny, and of his mother's idolatry. Indeed, he had been so miserable during this part of his life, that the defeat which made him again a wanderer might be regarded as a deliverance rather than as a calamity. Under the influence of such feelings as these, Charles was desirous to depress the party which had resisted his father.

Questions

1. This essay is entitled "Charles II", and it is dependent on a good deal of biographical material. Yet it is not a biography, nor even in the strict sense, perhaps, a biographical essay. What facts about the life of Charles II does Macaulay choose to report? (Be sure to distinguish between fact and opinion.) What is missing in this essay which would otherwise make it a biographical work?
2. Macaulay is critical of Charles II. What specific faults does Macaulay find with Charles *as a king?* To what weakness in Charles *as a man* does Macaulay appear to attribute these faults?
3. What strengths or abilities does Macaulay attribute to Charles II? With what advantages and recommendations for success did he start his reign? What relationships does Macaulay make between his strengths and weaknesses?
4. John Wilmot, Earl of Rochester, one of Charles II's companions in disreputable adventures, wrote the following "Epitaph on Charles II" (while Charles was still alive and well). Would Macaulay find it accurate and apt? Explain why or why not.

   Here lies one Sovereign Lord the King,
   Whose word no man relies on,
   Who never said a foolish thing,
   Nor ever did a wise one.

Foreword to *Of Mr. Booker T. Washington and Others*

Like Macaulay, DuBois writes, in this essay, of a famous man whom he sees as both a result and a cause of significant historical conditions. Although Macaulay's Charles is a frivolous cynic and DuBois's Washington is a misguided idealist, you may find more to compare in the two treatments than your first glance perhaps suggests.

Yet, first, certain superficial and perhaps important differences between the two essays merit some of our consideration. Macaulay is a white Englishman writing about another white Englishman, but he is also a subject writing about a king, and he is writing about a king who has been dead for more than a century and a half at the time he writes. DuBois is a black American leader who is writing about another black American leader, a man older than himself but still alive and active as he writes. Like Lord Macaulay, Dr. Du Bois was a man of vast scholarly ability and interests, but much more than the Englishman he was himself a political activist of fame and talent.

Of Mr. Booker T. Washington and Others

by W. E. B. Du Bois (1868-1963)

Easily the most striking thing in the history of the American Negro since 1876[1] is the ascendancy of Mr. Booker T. Washington. It began at the time when war memories and ideals were rapidly passing; a day of astonishing commercial development was dawning; a sense of doubt and hesitation overtook the freedmen's sons, — then it was that his leading began. Mr. Washington came, with a single definite programme, at the psychological moment when the nation was a little ashamed of having bestowed so much sentiment on Negroes, and was concentrating its energies on Dollars. His programme of industrial education, conciliation of the South, and submission and silence as to civil and political rights, was not wholly original; the Free Negroes from 1830 up to war-time had striven to build industrial schools, and the American Missionary Association had from the first taught various trades; and Price and others had sought a way of honorable alliance with the best of the Southerners. But Mr. Washington first indissolubly linked these things; he put enthusiasm, unlimited energy, and perfect faith into his programme, and changed it from a by-path into a veritable Way of Life. And the tale of the methods by which he did this is a fascinating study of human life.

1. 1876: the year of the election of President Rutherford B. Hayes, which marked the end of "Reconstruction" in the South.

It startled the nation to hear a Negro advocating such a programme after many decades of bitter complaint; it startled and won the applause of the South, it interested and won the admiration of the North; and after a confused murmur of protest, it silenced if it did not convert the Negroes themselves.

To gain the sympathy and cooperation of the various elements comprising the white South was Mr. Washington's first task; and this, at the time Tuskegee[2] was founded, seemed, for a black man, well-nigh impossible. And yet ten years later it was done in the word spoken at Atlanta: "In all things purely social we can be as separate as the five fingers, and yet one as the hand in all things essential to mutual progress." This "Atlanta Compromise" is by all odds the most notable thing in Mr. Washington's career. The South interpreted it in different ways: the radicals received it as a complete surrender of the demand for civil and political equality; the conservatives, as a generously conceived working basis for mutual understanding. So both approved it, and to-day its author is certainly the most distinguished Southerner since Jefferson Davis,[3] and the one with the largest personal following.

Next to this achievement comes Mr. Washington's work in gaining place and consideration in the North. Others less shrewd and tactful had formerly essayed to sit on these two stools and had fallen between them; but as Mr. Washington knew the heart of the South from birth and training, so by singular insight he intuitively grasped the spirit of the age which was dominating the North. And so thoroughly did he learn the speech and thought of triumphant commercialism, and the ideals of material prosperity, that the picture of a lone black boy poring over a French grammar amid the weeds and dirt of a neglected home soon seemed to him the acme of absurdities. One wonders what Socrates and St. Francis of Assisi would say to this.

And yet this very singleness of vision and thorough oneness with his age is a mark of the successful man. It is as though Nature must needs make men narrow in order to give them force. So Mr. Washington's cult has gained unquestioning followers, his work has wonderfully prospered, his friends are legion, and his enemies are confounded. To-day he stands as the one recognized spokesman of his ten million fellows, and one of the most notable figures in a nation of seventy millions. One hesitates, therefore, to criticise a life which, beginning with so little, has done so much. And yet the time is come when one may speak in all sincerity and utter courtesy of

---

2. Tuskegee: Tuskegee Institute in Alabama, founded by Booker T. Washington in 1881.
3. Jefferson Davis: President of the Confederate States of America (1861-1865).

the mistakes and shortcomings of Mr. Washington's career, as well as of his triumphs, without being thought captious or envious, and without forgetting that it is easier to do ill than well in the world.

The criticism that has hitherto met Mr. Washington has not always been of this broad character. In the South especially has he had to walk warily to avoid the harshest judgments, — and naturally so, for he is dealing with the one subject of deepest sensitiveness to that section. Twice — once at the Chicago celebration of the Spanish-American War he alluded to the color-prejudice that is "eating away the vitals of the South," and once when he dined with President Roosevelt — has the resulting Southern criticism been violent enough to threaten seriously his popularity. In the North the feeling has several times forced itself into words, that Mr. Washington's counsels of submission overlooked certain elements of true manhood, and that his educational programme was unnecessarily narrow. Usually, however, such criticism has not found open expression, although, too, the spiritual sons of the Abolitionists have not been prepared to acknowledge that the schools founded before Tuskegee, by men of broad ideals and self-sacrificing spirit, were wholly failures or worthy of ridicule. While, then, criticism has not failed to follow Mr. Washington, yet the prevailing public opinion of the land has been but too willing to deliver the solution of a wearisome problem into his hands, and say, "If that is all you and your race ask, take it."

Among his own people, however, Mr. Washington has encountered the strongest and most lasting opposition, amounting at times to bitterness, and even today continuing strong and insistent even though largely silenced in outward expression by the public opinion of the nation. Some of this opposition is, of course, mere envy; the disappointment of displaced demagogues and the spite of narrow minds. But aside from this, there is among educated and thoughtful colored men in all parts of the land a feeling of deep regret, sorrow, and apprehension at the wide currency and ascendancy which some of Mr. Washington's theories have gained. These same men admire his sincerity of purpose, and are willing to forgive much to honest endeavor which is doing something worth the doing. They cooperate with Mr. Washington as far as they conscientiously can; and, indeed, it is no ordinary tribute to this man's tact and power that, steering as he must between so many diverse interests and opinions, he so largely retains the respect of all.

But the hushing of the criticism of honest opponents is a dangerous thing. It leads some of the best of the critics to unfortunate silence and paralysis of effort, and others to burst into speech so passionately and intemperately as to lose listeners. Honest and earnest criticism from those whose interests are most nearly touched, — criticism of writers by readers, of government by those governed, of leaders by those led, — this is the soul of democracy and the safeguard of modern society. If the best of the American Negroes receive by outer pressure a leader whom they had not recognized before, manifestly there is here a certain palpable gain. Yet there is also irreparable loss, — a loss of that peculiarly valuable education which a group receives when by search and criticism it finds and commissions its own leaders. The way in which this is done is at once the most elementary and the nicest problem of social growth. History is but the record of such group-leadership; and yet how infinitely changeful is its type and character! And of all types and kinds, what can be more instructive than the leadership of a group within a group? — that curious double movement where real progress may be negative and actual advance be relative retrogression. All this is the social student's inspiration and despair.

Now in the past the American Negro has had instructive experience in the choosing of group leaders, founding thus a peculiar dynasty which in the light of present conditions is worth while studying. When sticks and stones and beasts form the sole environment of a people, their attitude is largely one of determined opposition to and conquest of natural forces. But when to earth and brute is added an environment of men and ideas, then the attitude of the imprisoned group may take three main forms, — a feeling of revolt and revenge; an attempt to adjust all thought and action to the will of the greater group; or finally, a determined effort at self-realization and self-development despite environing opinion. The influence of all of these attitudes at various times can be traced in the history of the American Negro, and in the evolution of his successive leaders.

Before 1750, while the fire of African freedom still burned in the veins of the slaves, there was in all leadership or attempted leadership but the one motive of revolt and revenge, — typified in the terrible Maroons, the Danish blacks, and Cato of Stono, and veiling all the Americas in fear of insurrection. The liberalizing tendencies of the latter half of the eighteenth century brought, along with kindlier relations between black and white, thoughts of ultimate adjustment and assimilation. Such aspiration was especially voiced in the earnest songs of Phyllis, in the martyrdom of Attucks, the fighting of Salem and Poor, the intellectual accomplishments of Banneker and Derham, and the political demands of the Cuffes.

Stern financial and social stress after the war cooled much of the previous humanitarian ardor. The disappointment and impatience of the Negroes at the persistence of slavery and serfdom voiced itself in two movements. The slaves in the South, aroused undoubtedly by vague rumors of the Haytian revolt, made three fierce attempts at insurrection, — in 1800 under Gabriel in Virginia, in 1822 under Vesey in Carolina, and in 1831 again in Virginia under the terrible Nat Turner. In the Free States, on the other hand, a new and curious attempt at self-development was made. In Philadelphia and New York color-prescription led to a withdrawal of Negro communicants from white churches and the formation of a peculiar socio-religious institution among the Negroes known as the African Church, — an organization still living and controlling in its various branches over a million of men.

Walker's wild appeal against the trend of the times showed how the world was changing after the coming of the cotton-gin. By 1830 slavery seemed hopelessly fastened on the South, and the slaves thoroughly cowed into submission. The free Negroes of the North, inspired by the mulatto immigrants from the West Indies, began to change the basis of their demands; they recognized the slavery of slaves, but insisted that they themselves were freemen, and sought assimilation and amalgamation with the nation on the same terms with other men. Thus, Forten and Purvis of Philadelphia, Shad of Wilmington, Du Bois of New Haven, Barbadoes of Boston, and others, strove singly and together as men, they said, not as slaves; as "people of color," not as "Negroes." The trend of the times, however, refused them recognition save in individual and exceptional cases, considered them as one with all the despised blacks, and they soon found themselves striving to keep even the rights they formerly had of voting and working and moving as freemen. Schemes of migration and colonization arose among them; but these they refused to entertain, and they eventually turned to the Abolition movement as a final refuge.

Here, led by Remond, Nell, Wells-Brown, and Douglass, a new period of self-assertion and self-development dawned. To be sure, ultimate freedom and assimilation was the ideal before the leaders, but the assertion of the manhood rights of the Negro by himself was the main reliance, and John Brown's raid was the extreme of its logic. After the war and emancipation, the great form of Frederick Douglass, the greatest of American Negro leaders, still led the host. Self-assertion, especially in political lines, was the main programme, and behind Douglass came Elliot, Bruce, and Langston, and the Reconstruction politicians, and, less conspicuous but of greater social significance, Alexander Crummell and Bishop Daniel Payne.

Then came the Revolution of 1876, the suppression of the Negro votes, the changing and shifting of ideals, and the seeking of new lights in the great night. Douglass, in his old age, still bravely stood for the ideals of his early manhood, — ultimate assimilation *through* self-assertion, and on no other terms. For a time Price arose as a new leader, destined, it seemed, not to give up, but to re-state the old ideals in a form less repugnant to the white South. But he passed away in his prime. Then came the new leader. Nearly all the former ones had become leaders by the silent suffrage of their fellows, had sought to lead their own people alone, and were usually, save Douglas, little known outside their race. But Booker T. Washington arose as essentially the leader not of one race but of two, — a compromiser between the South, the North, and the Negro. Naturally the Negroes resented, at first bitterly, signs of compromise which surrendered their civil and political rights, even though this was to be exchanged for larger chances of economic development. The rich and dominating North, however, was not only weary of the race problem, but was investing largely in Southern enterprises, and welcomed any method of peaceful cooperation. Thus, by national opinion, the Negroes began to recognize Mr. Washington's leadership; and the voice of criticism was hushed.

Mr. Washington represents in Negro thought the old attitude of adjustment and submission; but adjustment at such a peculiar time as to make his programme unique. This is an age of unusual economic development, and Mr. Washington's programme naturally takes an economic cast, becoming a gospel of Work and Money to such an extent as apparently almost completely to overshadow the higher aims of life. Moreover, this is an age when the more advanced races are coming in closer contact with the less developed races, and the race-feeling is therefore intensified; and Mr. Washington's programme practically accepts the alleged inferiority of the Negro races. Again, in our own land, the reaction from the sentiment of war time has given impetus to race-prejudice against Negroes, and Mr. Washington withdraws many of the high demands of Negroes as men and American citizens. In other periods of intensified prejudice all the Negro's tendency to self-assertion has been called forth; at this period a policy of submission is advocated. In the history of nearly all other races and peoples the doctrine preached at such crises has been that manly self-respect is worth more than lands and houses, and that a people who voluntarily surrender such respect, or cease striving for it, are not worth civilizing.

In answer to this, it has been claimed that the Negro can survive only through submission. Mr. Washington distinctly asks that black people give up, at least for the present, three things, —

First, political power,

Second, insistence on civil rights,

Third, higher education of Negro youth, —

and concentrate all their energies on industrial education, and accumulation of wealth, and the conciliation of the South. This policy has been courageously and insistently advocated for over fifteen years, and has been triumphant for perhaps ten years. As a result of this tender of the palm-branch, what has been the return? In these years there have occurred:

1. The disfranchisement of the Negro.

2. The legal creation of a distinct status of civil inferiority for the Negro.

3. The steady withdrawal of aid from institutions for the higher training of the Negro.

These movements are not, to be sure, direct results of Mr. Washington's teachings; but his propaganda has, without a shadow of doubt, helped their speedier accomplishment. The question then comes: Is it possible, and probable, that nine millions of men can make effective progress in economic lines if they are deprived of political rights, made a servile caste, and allowed only the most meagre chance for developing their exceptional men? If history and reason give any distinct answer to these questions, it is an emphatic *No.* And Mr. Washington thus faces the triple paradox of his career:

1. He is striving nobly to make Negro artisans business men and property-owners; but it is utterly impossible, under modern competitive methods, for workingmen and property-owners to defend their rights and exist without the right of suffrage.

2. He insists on thrift and self-respect, but at the same time counsels a silent submission to civic inferiority such as is bound to sap the manhood of any race in the long run.

3. He advocates common-school and industrial training, and depreciates institutions of higher learning; but neither the Negro common-schools, nor Tuskegee itself, could remain open a day were it not for teachers trained in Negro colleges, or trained by their graduates.

This triple paradox in Mr. Washington's position is the object of criticism by two classes of colored Americans. One class is spiritually descended from Toussaint the Savior, through Gabriel, Vesey, and Turner, and they represent the attitude of revolt and revenge; they hate the white South blindly and distrust the white race generally, and so far as they agree on definite action, think that the Negro's only hope lies in emigration beyond the borders of the United States. And yet, by the irony of fate, nothing has more effectually made this programme seem hopeless than the recent course of the United States toward weaker and darker peoples in the West Indies, Hawaii, and the Philippines, — for where in the world may we go and be safe from lying and brute force?

The other class of Negroes who cannot agree with Mr. Washington has hitherto said little aloud. They deprecate the sight of scattered counsels, of internal disagreement; and especially they dislike making their just criticism of a useful and earnest man an excuse for a general discharge of venom from small-minded opponents. Nevertheless, the questions involved are so fundamental and serious that it is difficult to see how men like the Grimkes, Kelly Miller, J. W. E. Bowen, and other representatives of this group, can much longer be silent. Such men feel in conscience bound to ask of this nation three things:

1. The right to vote.
2. Civic equality.
3. The education of youth according to ability.

They acknowledge Mr. Washington's invaluable service in counselling patience and courtesy in such demands; they do not ask that ignorant black men vote when ignorant whites are debarred, or that any reasonable restrictions in the suffrage should not be applied; they know that the low social level of the mass of the race is responsible for much discrimination against it, but they also know, and the nation knows, that relentless color-prejudice is more often a cause than a result of the Negro's degradation; they seek the abatement of this relic of barbarism, and not its systematic encouragement and pampering by all agencies of social power from the Associated Press to the Church of Christ. They advocate, with Mr. Washington, a broad system of Negro common schools supplemented by thorough industrial training; but they are surprised that a man of Mr. Washington's insight cannot see that no such educational system ever has rested or can rest on any other basis than that of the well-equipped college and university, and they insist that there is a demand for a few such institutions throughout the South to train the best of the Negro youth as teachers, professional men, and leaders.

This group of men honor Mr. Washington for attitudes of conciliation toward the white South; they accept the "Atlanta Compromise" in its broadest interpretation; they recognize, with him, many signs of promise, many men of high purpose and fair judgment, in this section; they know that no easy task has been laid upon a region already tottering under heavy burdens. But, nevertheless, they insist that the way to truth and right lies in straightforward honesty, not in indiscriminate flattery; in praising those of the South who do well and criticising uncompromisingly those who do ill; in taking advantage of the opportunities at hand and urging their fellows to do the same, but at the same time in remembering that only a firm adherence to their higher ideals and aspirations will ever keep those ideals within the realm of possibility. They do not expect that the free right to vote, to enjoy civic rights, and to be educated, will come in a moment; they do not expect to see the bias and prejudices of years disappear at the blast of a trumpet; but they are absolutely certain that the way for a people to gain their reasonable rights is not by voluntarily throwing them away and insisting that they do not want them; that the way for a people to gain respect is not by continually belittling and ridiculing themselves; that, on the contrary, Negroes must insist continually, in season and out of season, that voting is necessary to modern manhood, that color discrimination is barbarism, and that black boys need education as well as white boys.

In failing thus to state plainly and unequivocally the legitimate demands of their people, even at the cost of opposing an honored leader, the thinking classes of American Negroes would shirk a heavy responsibility, — a responsibility to themselves, a responsibility to the struggling masses, a responsibility to the darker races of men whose future depends so largely on this American experiment, but especially a responsibility to this nation, — this common Fatherland. It is wrong to encourage a man or a people in evil-doing; it is wrong to aid and abet a national crime simply because it is unpopular not to do so. The growing spirit of kindliness and reconciliation between the North and South after the frightful difference of a generation ago ought to be a source of deep congratulation to all, and especially to those whose mistreatment caused the war; but if that reconciliation is to be marked by the industrial slavery and civic death of those same black men, with permanent legislation into a position of inferiority, then those black men, if they are really men, are called upon by every consideration of patriotism and loyalty to oppose such a course by all civilized methods, even though such opposition involves disagreement with Mr. Booker T. Washington. We have no right to sit silently by while the inevitable seeds are sown for a harvest of disaster to our children, black and white.

First, it is the duty of black men to judge the South discriminatingly. The present generation of Southerners are not responsible for the past, and they should not be blindly hated or blamed for it. Furthermore, to no class is the indiscriminate endorsement of the recent course of the South toward Negroes more nauseating than to the best thought of the South. The South is not "solid"; it is a land in the ferment of social change, wherein forces of all kinds are fighting for supremacy; and to praise the ill the South is today perpetrating is just as wrong as to condemn the good. Discriminating and broad-minded criticism is what the South needs, — needs it for the sake of her own white sons and daughters, and for the insurance of robust, healthy, mental and moral development.

Today even the attitude of the Southern whites toward the blacks is not, as so many assume, in all cases the same; the ignorant Southerner hates the Negro, the workingmen fear his competition, the money-makers wish to use him as a laborer, some of the educated see a menace in his upward development, while others — usually the sons of the masters — wish to help him to rise. National opinion has enabled this last class to maintain the Negro common schools, and to protect the Negro partially in property, life, and limb. Through the pressure of the money-makers, the Negro is in danger of being reduced to semi-slavery, especially in the country districts; the workingmen, and those of the educated who fear the Negro, have united to disfranchise him, and some have urged his deportation; while the passions of the ignorant are easily aroused to lynch and abuse any black man. To praise this intricate whirl of thought and prejudice is nonsense; to inveigh indiscriminately against "the South" is unjust; but to use the same breath in praising Governor Aycock, exposing Senator Morgan, arguing with Mr. Thomas Nelson Page, and denouncing Senator Ben Tillman, is not only sane, but the imperative duty of thinking black men.

It would be unjust to Mr. Washington not to acknowledge that in several instances he has opposed movements in the South which were unjust to the Negro; he sent memorials to the Louisiana and Alabama constitutional conventions, he has spoken against lynching, and in other ways has openly or silently set his influence against sinister schemes and unfortunate happenings. Notwithstanding this, it is equally true to assert that on the whole the distinct impression left by Mr. Washington's propaganda is, first, that the South is justified in its present attitude toward the Negro because of the Negro's degradation; secondly, that the prime cause of the Negro's failure to rise more quickly is his wrong education in the past; and, thirdly, that his future rise depends primarily on his own efforts. Each of these propositions is a dangerous half-truth. The supplementary truths must never be lost sight of: first, slavery and race-prejudice are potent if not sufficient causes of the Negro's position; second, industrial and common-school training were necessarily slow in planting because they had to await the black teachers trained by higher institutions, — it being extremely doubtful if any essentially different development was possible, and certainly a Tuskegee was unthinkable before 1880; and, third, while it is a great truth to say that the Negro must strive mightily to help himself, it is equally true that unless his striving be not simply seconded, but rather aroused and encouraged, by the initiative of the richer and wiser environing group, he cannot hope for great success.

In his failure to realize and impress this last point, Mr. Washington is especially to be criticised. His doctrine has tended to make the whites, North and South, shift the burden of the Negro problem to the Negro's shoulders and stand aside as critical and rather pessimistic spectators; when in fact the burden belongs to the nation, and the hands of none of us are clean if we bend not our energies to righting these great wrongs.

The South ought to be led, by candid and honest criticism, to assert her better self and do her full duty to the race she has cruelly wronged and is still wronging. The North — her co-partner in guilt — cannot salve her conscience by plastering it with gold. We cannot settle this problem by diplomacy and suaveness, by "policy" alone. If worse comes to worst, can the moral fibre of this country survive the slow throttling and murder of nine millions of men?

The black men of America have a duty to perform, a duty stern and delicate, — a forward movement to oppose a part of the work of their greatest leader. So far as Mr. Washington preaches Thrift, Patience, and

Industrial Training for the masses, we must hold up his hands and strive with him, rejoicing in his honors and glorying in the strength of this Joshua called of God and of man to lead the headless host. But so far as Mr. Washington apologizes for injustice, North or South, does not rightly value the privilege and duty of voting, belittles the emasculating effects of caste distinctions, and opposes the higher training and ambition of our brighter minds, — so far as he, the South, or the Nation, does this, — we must unceasingly and firmly oppose them. By every civilized and peaceful method we must strive for the rights which the world accords to men, clinging unwaveringly to those great words which the sons of the Fathers would fain forget: "We hold these truths to be self-evident: That all men are created equal; that they are endowed by their Creator with certain unalienable rights; that among these are life, liberty, and the pursuit of happiness."

Questions

1. At what point in your reading of "Of Mr. Booker T. Washington and Others" do you first realize that the author is in fact critical of his subject? Does the title suggest that he will be? Discuss.
2. How much of the objective facts of Booker T. Washington's life is the uninformed reader given in this essay? Is Du Bois more interested in the man or in the ideas and attitudes he represents? Discuss.
3. For what qualities or actions does the essayist apparently admire Booker T. Washington? What qualities does he not admire?
4. How does Du Bois fit the life and work of Washington into the history of the African races in America?
5. What exactly is "the triple paradox," as Du Bois calls it, of Washington's career?
6. With what projections into the future, that is, into history after 1903, does Du Bois conclude his essay?

Foreword to *The Politician*

The previous two essays in our "Men and History" section are directed towards specific famous men. In "The Politician," H. L. Mencken puts together his personal reactions to a composite man of his time (and ours) whom he names only in the general term of his title. This difference predicates other differences in the nature of Mencken's essay as opposed to those by Macaulay and Du Bois. For one thing, we readers cannot check on specific biographical facts — like Charles's exile or Washington's birth as a slave. An essay on a general personality or public type is less apt to be intensely controversial than is an essay on a certain important figure. In a way, the essayist can get away with more at the price of convincing us less.

Yet a basic similarity remains among the three treatments. Mencken, like Macaulay and Du Bois, shows us a public man as both the product and the producer of the world in which he lives and pursues his particular destiny.

The Politician

by H. L. Mencken (1880-1956)

After damning politicians up hill and down dale for many years, as rogues and vagabonds, frauds and scoundrels, I sometimes suspect that, like everyone else, I often expect too much of them. Though faith and confidence are surely more or less foreign to my nature, I not infrequently find myself looking to them to be able, diligent, candid, and even honest. Plainly enough, that is too large an order, as anyone must realize who reflects upon the manner in which they reach public office. They seldom if ever get there by merit alone, at least in democratic states. Sometimes, to be sure, it happens, but only by a kind of miracle. They are chosen normally for quite different reasons, the chief of which is simply their power to impress and enchant the intellectually underprivileged. It is a talent like any other, and when it is exercised by a radio crooner, a movie actor or a bishop, it even takes on a certain austere and sorry respectability. But it is obviously not identical with a capacity for the intricate problems of statecraft.

Those problems demand for their solution — when they are soluble at all, which is not often — a high degree of technical proficiency, and with it there should go an adamantine kind of integrity, for the temptations of a public official are almost as cruel as those of a glamor girl or a dipsomaniac. But we train a man for facing them, not by locking him up in a monastery and stuffing him with wisdom and virtue, but by turning him loose on the stump. If he is a smart and enterprising fellow, which he usually is, he quickly discovers there that hooey pleases the boobs a great deal more than sense. Indeed, he finds that sense really disquiets and alarms them — that it makes them, at best, intolerably uncomfortable, just as a tight collar makes them uncomfortable, or a speck of dust in the eye, or the thought of Hell. The truth, to the overwhelming majority of mankind, is indistinguishable from a headache. After trying a few shots of it on his customers, the larval statesman concludes sadly that it must hurt them, and after that he taps a more humane keg, and in a little while the whole audience is singing "Glory, glory hallelujah," and when the returns come in the candidate is on his way to the White House.

I hope no one will mistake this brief account of the political process under democracy for exaggeration. It is almost literally true. I do not mean to argue, remember, that all politicians are villains in the sense that a burglar, a child-stealer, or a Darwinian are villains. Far from it. Many of them in their private characters, are very charming persons, and I have known plenty that I'd trust with my diamonds, my daughter or my liberty, if I had any such things. I happen to be acquainted to some extent with nearly all the gentlemen, both Democrats and Republicans, who are currently itching for the Presidency, including the present incumbent, and I testify freely that they are all pleasant fellows, with qualities above rather than below the common. The worst of them is a great deal better company than most generals in the army, or writers of murder mysteries, or astrophysicists, and the best is a really superior and wholly delightful man — full of sound knowledge, competent and prudent, frank and enterprising, and quite as honest as any American can be without being clapped into a madhouse. Don't ask me what his name is, for I am not in politics. I can only tell you that he has been in public a long while, and has not been caught yet.

But will this prodigy, or any of his rivals, ever unload any appreciable amount of sagacity on the stump? Will any of them venture to tell the plain truth, the whole truth and nothing but the truth about the situation of the country, foreign or domestic? Will any of them refrain from promises that he knows he can't fulfill — that no human being *could* fulfill? Will any of them utter a word, however obvious, that will alarm and alienate any of the huge packs of morons who now cluster at the public trough, wallowing in the pap that grows thinner and thinner, hoping against hope? Answer: maybe for a few weeks at the start. Maybe before the campaign really begins. Maybe behind the door. But not after the issue is fairly joined, and the struggle is on in earnest. From that moment they will all resort to demagogy, and by the middle of June of election year the only choice among them will be a choice between amateurs of that science and professionals.

They will all promise every man, woman and child in the country whatever he, she or it wants. They'll all be roving the land looking for chances to make the rich poor, to remedy the irremediable, to succor the unsuccorable, to unscramble the unscrambleable, to dephlogisticate the undephlogisticable. They will all be curing warts by saying words over them, and paying off the national debt with money that no one will have to earn. When one of them demonstrates that twice two is five, another will prove that it is six, six and a half, ten, twenty, *n*. In brief, they will divest themselves of their character as sensible, candid and truthful men, and become simply candidates for office, bent only on collaring votes. They will all know by then, even supposing that some of them don't know it now, that votes are collared under democracy, not by talking sense but by talking nonsense, and they will apply themselves to the job with a hearty yo-heave-ho. Most of them, before the uproar is over, will actually convince themselves. The winner will be whoever promises the most with the least probability of delivering anything.

Some years ago I accompanied a candidate for the Presidency on his campaign-tour. He was, like all such rascals, an amusing fellow, and I came to like him very much. His speeches, at the start, were full of fire. He was going to save the country from all the stupendous frauds and false pretenses of his rival. Every time that rival offered to rescue another million of poor fish from the neglects and oversights of God he howled his derision from the back platform of his train. I noticed at once that these blasts of common sense got very little applause, and after a while the candidate began to notice it too. Worse, he began to get word from his spies on the train of his rival that the rival was wowing them, panicking them, laying them in the aisles. They threw flowers, hot dogs and five-cent cigars at him. In places where the times were especially hard they tried to unhook the locomotive from his train, so that he'd have to stay with them awhile longer, and promise them some more. There were no Gallup polls in those innocent days, but the local politicians had ways of their own for finding out how the cat was jumping, and they began to join my candidate's train in the middle of the night, and wake him up to tell him that all was lost, including honor. This had some effect upon him — in truth, an effect almost as powerful as that of sitting in the electric chair. He lost his intelligent manner, and became something you could hardly distinguish from an idealist. Instead of mocking he began to promise, and in a little while he was promising everything that his rival was promising, and a good deal more.

One night out in the Bible country, after the hullabaloo of the day was over, I went into his private car along with another newspaper reporter, and we sat down to gabble with him. This other reporter, a faithful member of the candidate's own party, began to upbraid him, at first very gently, for letting off so much hokum. What did he mean by making promises that no human being on this earth, and not many of the angels in Heaven, could ever hope to carry out? In particular, what was his idea in trying to work off all those preposterous bile-beans and snake-oils on the poor farmers, a class of men who had been fooled and rooked by every fresh wave of politicians since Apostolic times? Did he really believe that the Utopia he had begun so fervently to preach would ever come to pass? Did he honestly think that farmers, as a body, would ever see all their rosy dreams come true, or that the share-croppers in their lower ranks would ever be more than a hop, skip and jump from starvation? The candidate thought awhile, took a long swallow of the coffin-varnish he carried with him, and then replied that the answer in every case was no. He was well aware, he said, that the plight of the farmers was intrinsically hopeless, and would probably continue so, despite doles from the treasury, for centuries to come. He had no notion that anything could be done about it by merely human means, and certainly not by political means: it would take a new Moses, and a whole series of miracles. "But you forget, Mr. Blank," he concluded sadly, "that our agreement in the premises must remain purely personal. You are not a candidate for President of the United States. *I am.*" As we left him his interlocutor, a gentleman grown gray in Washington and long ago lost to every decency, pointed the moral of the episode. "In politics," he said, "man must learn to rise above principle." Then he drove it in with another: "When the water reaches the upper deck," he said, "follow the rats."

Questions

1. What basic premises does the reader of this essay have to accept, temporarily at least, about mankind and about successful leaders in order to accept Mencken's view of politics in the American democracy?
2. The position Mencken takes about the politician and his historical implications is cynical and cheerless indeed. What gives the essay itself, however, a rather easy, good-natured tone?
3. On what grounds, in spite of all, does Mencken indicate that he rather likes the politician?
4. Is there anything in this essay that is constructive? Does Mencken tell us that the thing to do is to have the politician stop giving hooey to the boobs and serve up the truth?

General Discussion Questions

1. These three essays provide a particularly clear view of the importance of the essayist as an individual with a unique perspective from which he goes about his work. How does each writer indicate his particular place in time, society, and public affairs? How does each reveal his own personality, his prejudices, his interests, his temperament? (Perhaps a good way to deal with this question is to suppose that one of the subjects was being handled by another of the authors.)
2. To what extent do the three essayists of this section share a particular attitude about the various effects of a man's private life on his public life?
3. Each of these essays is persuasive; that is, each invites us to share a position with its author. What differences do you find in the methods by which Macaulay, Du Bois, and Mencken go about winning the reader's agreement? To what extent does each author order historical fact towards a logical conclusion? depend on ridicule? employ certain moral presuppositions? adopt a judicious attitude?

4

Pro Patria

Hats off, boys, here comes the flag.

ANONYMOUS

To take the jingoism out of patriotism, we have not only destroyed the icon of manifest destiny but gratitude for the land that has blest us and pride that its people made it bright beyond compare.

VERMONT ROYSTER

Foreword to *The Idea of Patriotism* and *On Patriotism—A Fragment*

These are two related essays of which the common subject is an *idea*, an *abstraction*. In each case, the writer's aim is "to pin down" (as explicitly expressed by Rowse) what this idea — patriotism — really means. "Pin down" is a metaphor, and a good one, deriving from the idea of pinning a butterfly, or a scrap of parchment, to a board for the purpose of close scrutiny. The metaphor thus suggests bringing substance, touchability, to the abstract, which is precisely what both essayists here attempt. As almost always, this is done for a dual purpose: to think it out for the essayist himself, and to pass on the thought to others. In the case of the longer, more complete essay, A. L. Rowse is trying to reach others by the most direct medium of all, the spoken word, for he wrote the essay for a BBC broadcast to schools, in October, 1940. England was then in the early stages of World War II. These are thoughts in a time of crisis when the meaning of any man's relationship to his country has to be determined by each of us in a manner which, in normal times, we are seldom called upon to do. A Fellow of All Souls College, Oxford, by profession a historian and biographer, A. L. Rowse possesses special insights into such questions and a depth of perspective. "The Idea of Patriotism" comes from *The English Spirit, Essays in History and Literature* (1945).

William Hazlitt's essay is quite different in tone and scale. It is a self-sufficient statement, yet the fact that he appends the words, "A Fragment," to his title indicates that he has not said all that he might on the subject, whether or not he thought seriously of saying any more. In any case, the essay is a form in which a man seldom if ever intends, or pretends, to exhaust a subject.

"On Patriotism — A Fragment" comes from Hazlitt's first volume of essays, *The Round Table,* which also included twelve essays by his friend and literary associate, the essayist and poet, Leigh Hunt. Hazlitt had been dividing his energies between writing and portrait painting. Reaching the conclusion that as a painter he would never attain the excellence he demanded of himself, he gave up that art and came up to London, in 1812, to concentrate entirely upon literature. He began to write essays for a newspaper, the *Morning Chronicle,* and also became its drama critic. In 1815 he transferred these activities to the *Examiner,* of which Leigh Hunt was an editor. The essays in *The Round Table* appeared in one or another of those papers.

You may already have read the much longer essay by Hazlitt, altogether different in kind, "The Fight," found on p. 34.

The Idea of Patriotism

by A. L. Rowse (1903-   )

What is it that we mean by "patriotism"? We know the word so well, we have heard it so often, that we are apt to take for granted what it means without inquiring further. If we go into it together we shall find that it is by no means so simple as you might think, but a great deal more complex and subtle. We shall want to know what other people have meant by patriotism — what it has meant to other forms of society at other times than our own.

And first, a word about the word itself, before we come to the thing it describes. The word "patriot" came to us through the French from late Latin, and ultimately derives from the Greek word *patrios*, meaning "of one's fathers." Its stem is that very elemental word that runs through all the Aryan languages, cognate with "father." That already tells you a good deal. It suggests two things: (1) that the idea of patriotism hinges on to something very fundamental in social life; but (2) that in itself it is a comparatively late development in society, an emotion or feeling which has been built up out of more primitive ones. It is, in fact, a complex construction of emotions and sentiments and associations, more sophisticated and abstract than the simpler emotions like fear, anger, love (though the last is perhaps complex enough!).

But that is not to deny its strength and power. Professors Julian Huxley and Haddon tell us in their book *We Europeans* that "patriotism has proved itself one of the strongest forces known to history, second perhaps to religion alone."

Now we can come to the definition of patriotism: the Oxford Dictionary defines it as "love of or zealous devotion to one's own country." That fixes for us a further point in the exact pinning-down of the idea. Patriotism, to be exact, implies a *patria:* it is that particular kind of loyalty which is directed to the nation, and without which the nation could not exist. It did not come into existence, therefore, in the full sense until the development of the modern nation-state. We owe it, like so many other things, to the Renaissance. It is significant that we do not come across the word "patriot" in French until the fifteenth century: that period of prolonged war between the French and the English out of which the modern states, France and England, with their feeling of nationality, of distinctiveness, of a character of their own, developed. And the word does not appear in English until the end of the sixteenth century. I do not think that it appears in Shakespeare at all.

Patriotism is a form of group-feeling. Every kind of group — a cricket club, a church, a trade union, a university, a school — counts on the loyalty of its members and could not exist without it. Patriotism is that particular group-feeling called forth by the nation.

The most highly developed states of antiquity, the city-states of Greece, and Rome, had a very recognisable spirit of patriotism akin to our own. They had something to be proud about, and they were proud of their cities' achievements. It was Athens that was the beacon-light of the ancient world; and the highest expression of their patriotism is to be found in that wonderful oration which Pericles made over the bodies of the Athenians who fell in the first year of the Peloponnesian War. It was a conscious celebration of the particular qualities that made Athens what it was, as against Sparta — the Nazi-state of the ancient world:

> "They toil from early boyhood in a laborious pursuit after courage, while we, free to live and wander as we please, march out none the less to face the selfsame dangers. Indeed, if we choose to face danger with an easy mind rather than after a rigorous training, and to trust rather in native manliness than in state-made courage, the advantage lies with us; for we are spared all the weariness of practising for future hardships, and when we find ourselves amongst them we are as brave as our plodding rivals. . . . In a word I claim that our city as a whole is an education to Greece, and that her members yield to none, man by man, for independence of spirit, many-sidedness of attainment, and complete self-reliance in limbs and brain. . . . Our pioneers have forced a way into every sea and every land, establishing among all mankind, in punishment or beneficence, eternal memorials of their settlement."

That is magnificent; but what is even more important, Pericles was justified in his claims for Athens. It will not have escaped your notice what a parallel there is between Athens and Sparta, and what England stands for as against Nazi Germany. When you think of the great achievements and the great men whom this country has produced — Shakespeare, Newton, Milton, Darwin, Cromwell, Nelson, the Pitts — our tradition of political freedom, the triumphs of modern industry, the British Commonwealth of Nations — I think we are not unjustified in saying that when Pericles spoke for Athens two thousand years ago he spoke also for us today.

Sparta too had her patriotism; but it was a gloomy, repressive, and ultimately a sterile creed, like the Moloch[1]-worship of the state which we see incarnate in Nazi Germany. Everything was sacrificed to the pursuit of power; and when they had achieved power they found they had never faced the question — Power to what end? to what purpose? The whole thing crumbled, leaving nothing but a name to signify the cult of rigour and hardship for its own sake — Spartanism. While Athens was the creator, the seed-bed of western civilisation.

The Roman Republic exhibited the spirit of Sparta, and with it something of the same sombre, gloomy, exclusive patriotism. To me — and I think really to all of us — Rome begins to be much more interesting when she developed an empire, became more receptive of outside influences and developed the idea of universal citiznship based upon common allegiance to Rome, a sharing of her civilisation that was open to all peoples and languages and creeds. That was Rome's greatest contribution to the world, a common pride open to all in being able to say, as St. Paul was able to claim, "*Civis Romanus sum.*"[2] That was a kind of patriotism, though a very different one from any that we have yet mentioned, or from what we are accustomed to in the modern world. Perhaps the nearest thing to it yet achieved is the free citizenship, the unforced allegiance that runs through the British Empire; and who knows, before we are through our present trials, whether the greatest of English-speaking countries, the United States, may not come to be included in a wider unity? Of the older civilisations, probably the Chinese came closest to Rome in its spirit of a quasi-universal loyalty. At any rate I am clear that it is this aspect of Rome — its ability to hold diverse peoples and tongues in a spirit of common allegiance — a sort of universal patriotism, that has most to say to us in the modern world.

Then came the break-down of the Roman Empire: the inrush of the barbarians, the Goths, the Vandals, the Huns: the oncoming of the Dark Ages. All these primitive peoples in that miserable, confused era — where "ignorant armies clash by night" — had their folk-loyalties. Read Tacitus

---

1. Moloch: an ancient Semitic god to whom children were sacrificed; hence, any worship demanding great and cruel sacrifice.
2. *Civis Romanus sum:* I am a Roman citizen.

on the Germans, Caesar on the Gauls: pretty dreary reading I find it, with all their squabbles and quarrels, and incessant internecine strife. Like the Anglo-Saxon Heptarchy. No wonder a civilised eighteenth-century gentleman like Gibbon thought its history the "battles of kites and crows." But their tribal loyalties were not what we mean by patriotism.

That brings me to a further point. For patriotism to be true patriotism, it must attach itself to a really significant entity, a nation or a state that has achieved some greatness, that possesses a tradition and a record that means something to civilisation. We can all recognise French or German or Dutch patriotism — but then we get to a border-line with the smaller indeterminate nationalities which are really agglomerations of tribes with very little conscious corporate existence. I appreciate the point well as a Cornishman: devoted as I am to Cornwall and its history, is there such a thing as Cornish patriotism? It comes, I think, under the heading of what we call "local patriotism": not a bad thing — a good thing rather, provided it is kept in proper perspective.

Nor did the Middle Ages develop patriotism as we know it. The way they found out of the confusion of the Dark Ages was in a shadow-version of the Roman Empire, in which loyalty to the universal Church took the place of the Roman citizenship. On one side you had the universal claims of the Church — a great deal more real and effective than those of the Holy Roman Emperor — and on the other the localism which went with feudalism. No place, no need, for patriotism there. You had a society which was ruled by a cosmopolitan upper class, speaking for the most part French in Western Europe, like the Anglo-Norman baronage or the English kings right up to Henry VI. It was with the break-up of that feudal, cosmopolitan society that the modern nations as we know them came into existence, and with them, patriotism.

First and most important were France and England, whose national consciousness was heightened by their long struggle with each other. For France that struggle produced a national hero, imbued with the purest spirit of patriotism, whose personality stands for all time as the symbol of national regeneration: Joan of Arc. She was a patriot, if ever there was one. (Read what Bernard Shaw has to say on the subject.) I doubt if our Henry V was: he was much more a conqueror, an imperialist, a medieval Napoleon. Shakespeare was reading back from his own time when he made Henry V say before Agincourt:

> "This day is called the feast of Crispian:
> He that outlives this day, and comes safe home,
> Will stand a-tiptoe when this day is named,
> And rouse him at the name of Crispian.

He that shall live this day, and see old age,
Will yearly on the vigil feast his neighbours,
And say, 'Tomorrow is Saint Crispian':
Then will he strip his sleeve and show his scars,
And say, 'These wounds I had on Crispian's day'."

Yet that is medieval enough in feeling, for it is just human, a natural human reaction of almost any time or place.

One English reaction in the long struggle with France, it is said, was the development of the University of Oxford, so that English students should not have to go to the University of Paris as in the earlier Middle Ages. But it was the French who in their poetry first expressed this new-found feeling of love for their native land as such, the foundation of all patriotism. Do you know that charming pathetic ballad of Charles D'Orléans, who was prisoner in England, and how one day upon the cliffs of Dover the desire to see France again overcame him?

"En regardant vers le pais de France,
Un jour m'avint, à Dovre sur la mer,
Qu'il me souvint de la douce plaisance
Que je souloye oùdit pais trouver."[3]

I suppose the most famous expression of all of this sentiment are the sonnets of Joachim du Bellay, the French Renaissance poet, written about France when he was an exile in Rome:

"Quand revoirai-je, hélas, de mon petit village
Fumer la cheminée: en quelle saison
Revoirai-je le clos de ma pauvre maison,
Qui m'est une province, et beaucoup d'avantage?"[4]

You see the poet thinking of France in terms of his own Anjou, his own little village, his small house there with the smoke coming from its chimney. I dare say at bottom we all think of our native country, see it in the mind's eye, in little imaginative glimpses like that. I know when I have been very ill before now, away from home, in London, I found myself taking refuge in images of home, little Cornish coves where one bathed in summer, a

3. While looking towards the coast of France
One day there came to me, at Dover on the sea,
Something recalled of the sweet happiness
That I was used to find in that same country.
Charles d'Orleans, 1391-1465

4. When will I see again, alas, from my little town
The chimney smoke; in what season
Will I see again the yard of my little home
Which is a province to me, and more than plenty?
Joachim du Bellay, 1522-1560

stream running down a moorland valley, the cool interior of a church, the sun printed on the wall. At the same time it was Joachim du Bellay who wrote the proudest of all patriotic lines:

"France, mère des arts, des armes, et des loix."[5]

National sentiment, as we know it, was then the product of the break-up of medieval society. It comes with the Renaissance, the modern nation-state. Even that most sceptical, unbelieving intelligence, Machiavelli, was a great patriot in his way, both for Florence and for Italy: you know that his book *The Prince*, that text-book of political realism, not to say cynicism, concludes with a chapter "That Italy may be rid of the Barbarians." It is fairly true to say, as a historical generalisation, that patriotism is at its highest and noblest when a people have been through and surmounted a great danger. That seems to bring forth all the latent capacities of a people, heighten them to the greatest tension of which they are capable. And it is such moments in their history that are apt to be the most creative. Such was the great age of fifth-century Athens after she had triumphantly withstood the Persian Invasion; such the Augustan age at Rome after the long civil wars; such the Elizabethan age in England after the stern test of the struggle with Spain; the golden age of the Dutch seventeenth century, the age of Rembrandt and all the painters and seamen, when Holland had won her independence; the great age in German history, the early nineteenth century, with the repulse of the French Revolution and Napoleon. May it not be that after we have come successfully through our present time of trial, we may be rewarded with an age of creative achievement which will place the twentieth century alongside the Elizabethan age in our history?

For, in the end, patriotism to be good must be constructive and not exclusive. It must take justified pride in the great achievements of one's country, not in everything good or bad just because it is one's own. "My country, right or wrong" is a very questionable principle. It happens that the English people have a wonderful record of creative achievement: in their long record of political success, their poetry — the finest of modern poetries — their achievements in science and industry, upon the sea and now in the air. But other great peoples have similar achievements to be proud of: the French, the Italians, the Germans, the Russians, the Chinese. The ordinary man is perhaps not capable of looking further than his own nation, his own language: his own country is the mental world he inhabits. But he is the really civilised man who is capable of appreciating not only English poetry and English seamanship, but French and Italian and Dutch painting, German music, the Russian novel, Chinese art. For all the great

---

5. France, mother of the arts, of arms, and of law.
Joachim du Bellay

nations have contributed greatly to civilisation, and are ultimately to be judged by that. Is it too much to hope that since men have grown from small tribal loyalties to that greater loyalty to the nation which we call patriotism, one day after these present troubles are over we may achieve some feeling of common pride in the best of each other's achievements and attain something like a European patriotism?

Questions

1. Let us assume that by "scholarship" we mean simply "book-learning." What sorts of scholarship does Rowse use in this essay to establish his definition of patriotism?
2. Rowse suggests that his concept of patriotism is both old in time and relatively new in world history. How does he resolve this paradox?
3. What are Rowse's grounds for identifying England with Athens and Nazi Germany with Sparta? Do you find them convincing?
4. We might immediately assume that an anti-Nazi Englishman of the twentieth century would prefer a republic to an empire. However, Rowse tells us that he finds the Roman Empire more interesting than the Roman Republic. What are his reasons?
5. What connections does the essayist admit between the kind of allegiance which he calls "tribal loyalties" or "regional patriotism," and that he notes as following the break-down of the Roman Empire, and what he calls "true patriotism"?
6. To what extent does Rowse suggest that the "true" or national patriotism which he tries to identify in this essay may be a transient force in history? How does he feel about this possibility?
7. What in the way the essay is put together tells you that Rowse was very aware of the audience he was addressing?

On Patriotism—A Fragment

by William Hazlitt (1778-1803)

Patriotism, in modern times,[1] and in great states, is and must be the creature of reason and reflection, rather than the offspring of physical or local attachment. Our country is a complex, abstract existence, recognized only by the understanding. It is an immense riddle, containing numberless modifications of reason and prejudice, of thought and passion. Patriotism is not, in a strict or exclusive sense, a natural or personal affection, but a law of our rational and moral nature, strengthened and determined by particular circumstances and associations, but not born of them, nor wholly nourished by them. It is not possible that we should have an individual attachment to sixteen millions of men, any more than to sixty millions. We cannot be *habitually* attached to places we never saw, and people we never heard of. Is not the name of Englishman a general term, as well as that of man? How many varieties does it not combine within it? Are the opposite extremities of the globe our native place, because they are a part of that geographical and political denomination, our country? Does natural affection expand in circles of latitude and longitude? What personal or instinctive sympathy has the English peasant with the African slave-driver, or East Indian Nabob? Some of our wretched bunglers in metaphysics would fain persuade us to discard all general humanity, and all sense of abstract justice, as a violation of natural affection, and yet do not see that the love

1. modern times: 1817.

of our country itself is in the list of our general affections. The common notions of patriotism are transmitted down to us from the savage tribes, where the fate and condition of all was the same, or from the states of Greece and Rome, where the country of the citizen was the town in which he was born. Where this is no longer the case, — where our country is no longer contained within the narrow circle of the same walls, — where we can no longer behold its glimmering horizon from the top of our native mountains — beyond these limits, it is not a natural but an artificial idea, and our love of it either a deliberate dictate of reason, or a cant term. It was said by an acute observer, and eloquent writer (Rousseau)) that the love of mankind was nothing but the love of justice: the same might be said, with considerable truth, of love of our country. It is little more than another name for the love of liberty, of independence, of peace, and social happiness. We do not say that other indirect and collateral circumstances do not go to the superstructure of this sentiment (as language,[2] literature, manner, national customs), but this is the broad and firm basis.

Questions

1. What does Hazlitt indicate that patriotism is not and must not be in the "modern times" of 1817? How does he support this?
2. How does the essayist identify "reason and reflection" as it forms the "broad and firm basis" of patriotism?
3. At what point and to what extent does he appear to admit that "local attachment" may have something to do with modern patriotism?
4. To what specific use does Hazlitt put the examples of "savage tribes" and classical Greece and Rome? How is his use different from Rowse's?

Afterword to *The Idea of Patriotism* and *On Patriotism — A Fragment*

Among the famous statements of Dr. Samuel Johnson, one of the most quoted and most misunderstood is, "Patriotism is the last refuge of a scoundrel." The faithful Boswell, who recorded the remark, knew that it was not

2. He who speaks two languages has no country. The French, when they made their language the common language of the Courts of Europe, gained more than by all their subsequent conquests. [Hazlitt's note].

a definition of patriotism, as many have since believed or pretended, but an observation about the behavior of scoundrels. Boswell went on to say, "he did not mean a real and generous love of our country, but that pretended patriotism which so many, in all ages and countries, have made a cloak for self-interest." This "cloak" is what Johnson meant; it is also the "cant term" of which Hazlitt writes — the hypocritical use of the word patriotism, or its slogans, by such a one as a cynical politician in an election campaign. Religion has always been subject to the same abuse.

What Rowse would have us think about is the "real and generous love of our country." At its most natural, this is surely an emotional, spontaneous response rather than the "creature of reason and reflection" that Hazlitt suggests. Reason and reflection may serve to analyze the emotion of patriotism, but we doubt that they are a source of it. Rowse gives us the roots of the word "patriotism" in the Greek *patrios*, "of one's fathers." The gender of the parental metaphor varies from country to country — for some it is the "fatherland," for others, "the mother country." In either case, the image is associated with *home*, and "homeland" is another of the words for one's native place.

Even though he is speaking within the context of England's war for survival against the assault of Nazi Germany, Rowse recognizes that there is even a Nazi patriotism. An inherently good and natural emotion can be invoked for an unworthy object. A man may love his father the thief, or his mother the murderess. Rowse's patriotism leads him to celebrate particular people and virtues of the English as *better*, more deserving of loyalty, than those of Nazi Germany — as he regards the qualities of ancient Athens as more worthy of such devotion than those of its "totalitarian" rival, Sparta. Freedom is his measure, together with the kinds of persons and achievements that may be considered to be, at least in part, freedom's products. But like every other word, "freedom" means different things to different people. We of the West like to call ourselves "the free world," but the reflective man knows that all freedom is limited. Meanwhile, spokesmen for countries behind what we like to call "curtains," whether of iron or bamboo, will make passionate declarations of their own freedom and even, to our amazement, dismiss as frivolous or unworthy many of the expressions of *our* freedom. That was how the Spartans felt about the freedom of the Athenians.

Patriotism at its best can be one of the noble sentiments. The same emotion, at its worst, can be a fatally arrogant pride leading us to regard ourselves as a master race naturally entitled to supersede all others.

Rowse, both as humanist and historian, is aware of these pitfalls of patriotism (so, too, is William Golding, as we will see in "Fable" p. 103). He cites Joan of Arc as an embodiment of the emotion and counsels us to see what Bernard Shaw had to say on the subject in *Saint Joan*. Shaw says a great deal which can only be considered adequately by reading the whole play, but it is interesting to hear just a few lines from one of its characters, a bishop, who fears the change threatening a medieval society whose structural unity is the Church:

> ". . . as a priest I have gained a knowledge of the minds of the common people; and there you will find yet another most dangerous idea. I can express it only by such phrases as France for the French, England for the English, Italy for the Italians, Spain for the Spanish, and so forth. It is sometimes so narrow and bitter in country folk that it surprises me that this country girl can rise above the idea of her village for its villagers. But she can. She does. When she threatens to drive the English from the soil of France, she is undoubtedly thinking of the whole extent of country in which French is spoken. To her the French-speaking people are what the Holy Scriptures describe as a nation. Call this side of her heresy Nationalism if you will: I can find you no better name for it."

The bishop further states the conviction that a world divided into units other than a united Church "will perish in a welter of war."

The same Oxford Dictionary from which Rowse quotes a definition of "patriotism" gives as its first definition of "nationalism": "devotion to one's nation." This sounds close to patriotism, and indeed it is. As close as "nation" is to "country." Yet many people who would defend patriotism choose to use "nationalism" in an unfavorable sense to describe what they regard as the excessive patriotism of another people. So we find once again that with patriotism we are not dealing with a simple, clear-cut, four-square idea but with something subtle, complex, meaning many things to many people, susceptible of virtue, and liable to abuse.

Rowse makes the generalization "that patriotism is at its highest and noblest when a people have been through and surmounted a great danger." One might quibble and suggest the revision, "when a people is experiencing and attempting to surmount a great danger." That seems a surer thing, for while it is true that, if they have emerged safe and successful, the afterglow of triumph may sustain the height of patriotism for a time, history shows it to be often subject to a swift waning, or in different terms, a swift corruption. In the midst of the struggle, it was probably at its purest. Just as it may wane swiftly, it can be aroused swiftly. As Rowse observes, the enemy (and some friends) thought England decadent, believed such old-fashioned virtues as patriotism to be dead there, until her response to attack showed otherwise.

An interesting illumination of this aspect of patriotism may be found in a book called *The Territorial Imperative,* by Robert Ardrey (Atheneum). Speculatively applying to human behavior certain principles which biologists have observed in animal conduct, Ardrey seeks to develop a systematic, scientific principle underlying what has been many times observed, but also often overlooked, that a people will fight far more furiously, far beyond their supposed capacities, in defense of *their place,* than for any other motivation or cause.

In World War II, the people of the United States were generally reluctant to become involved in the war directly, notwithstanding a prevailing sympathy with those who were resisting Hitler in Europe and Japanese expansion in Asia. When Japan devastatingly and without warning attacked Pearl Harbor — *our place* — American determination to fight blazed up fiercely.

The patriotism-inspiring effect of having the homeland, or even a remote outpost that symbolizes it, attacked is in marked contrast to the drastic divisions of opinion we have seen in the United States over the war in Vietnam. Irrespective of the merits of the policy under debate, it is clear that no such uniform patriotism is inspired by such a course of action as when we have been engaged in repelling a direct attack. We come up against one of the most subtle and perplexing of all the many manifestations of patriotism, the claim that the proper love of one's country requires opposition to its policies. This is the ultimate blow to any view of patriotism as a simple emotion.

Hazlitt's short and far more abstractly expressed essay was written at one of those times which Rowse singles out as a high point of patriotism, "when a people have been through and surmounted a great danger." England had held off a threatened invasion by Napoleon and finally, at Waterloo (1815), ended his ascendancy over Europe. Oddly, this is wholly unreflected in the essay, and as a further oddity, Hazlitt had so great a personal admiration for Napoleon as to be a source of friction with some of his friends and a cause of his break with the *Morning Chronicle,* the paper for which he first wrote when he came up to London.

Rowse's essay is the more successful. Examine its organization and development and you will see why. He does, indeed, "pin down" the abstraction, as Hazlitt does not. Rowse seeks to define the term in a formal, linguistic sense, but moves on swiftly to embody and exemplify it in places persons, and events. Also he invokes its *feelings,* especially by his recourse to the poets, and establishes, with evidence, a claim that French poets were the first to celebrate, as Joan of Arc was the first to act upon, the principle of patriotism in the postmedieval world of Europe. He has not forgotten the patriotism of the ancient world, embodied in the tales of Leonidas and the Spartans at Thermopylae or Horatius at the bridge over the Tiber in Rome.

Perhaps some sense of getting off to a wrong start may have led Hazlitt to leave his essay "a fragment." He remarks, "It is not possible that we should have an individual attachment to sixteen millions of men, any more than to sixty millions." By a quirk of historical coincidence, sixty million is not far off the population of the United Kingdom when Rowse wrote *his* essay; as sixteen million was its approximate population in Hazlitt's time. He is writing in the early years of the British Empire. His calling in question the amount of actual attachment we can feel to remote and unseen places recalls one of the superpatriotic slogans of the Empire: "The sun never sets on British soil."

A notable weakness of this fragmentary essay is its excessively sweeping statements. To say that patriotism "is little more than another name for love of liberty, of independence, of peace, and social happiness" carries with it the possibly unintended suggestion that patriotism is little more than the wish to cling to an achieved "good life" and leaves out of account the passionate patriotism possible in those who have yet enjoyed few of those experiences.

His footnote to his closing sentence contains another grossly exaggerated assertion: "He who speaks two languages has no country." The narrowness of this identification of nation with languages goes beyond the fears expressed on the subject by the bishop in *Saint Joan*. It suggests, also, that the man who has mastered languages other than his native one has somehow eroded his loyalties, an assumption far too sweeping for acceptance.

Hazlitt's little piece is a failure by an admittedly great essayist. The likeliest reason for that failure is his neglect to do what Rowse successfully does, to "pin down" the abstraction, and to find exemplification and embodiment for it in people, places, and events.

Foreword to *Wrong Ism*

Like William Hazlitt, John Boynton Priestley is a rural, literary Englishman, and like A. L. Rowse, he is a twentieth century Englishman. Similar backgrounds, geographical and cultural, often accompany similar concerns with particular aspects of a general idea . . . like patriotism. As we shall see, however, Priestley apparently feels about the matter of "regional patriotism" and its alternatives rather differently than do Rowse and Hazlitt.

Perhaps you will find it of significant interest to consider that J. B. Priestley is a somewhat more versatile and popular kind of writer than his two compatriots. He continues to be internationally famous as a practicing novelist, he is a successful essayist and playwright, he is a journalist, and he is even a writer of American secondary-school textbooks.

Wrong Ism

by J. B. Priestley (1894-)

There are three isms that we ought to consider very carefully — regionalism, nationalism, internationalism. Of these three the one there is most fuss about, the one that starts men shouting and marching and shooting, the one that seems to have all the depth and thrust and fire, is of course nationalism. Nine people out of ten, I fancy, would say that of this trio it is the one that really counts, the big boss. Regionalism and internationalism, they would add, are comparatively small, shadowy, rather cranky. And I believe all this to be quite wrong. Like many another big boss, nationalism is largely bogus. It is like a bunch of flowers made of plastics.

The real flowers belong to regionalism. The mass of people everywhere may never have used the term. They are probably regionalists without knowing it. Because they have been brought up in a certain part of the world, they have formed perhaps quite unconsciously a deep attachment to its landscape and speech, its traditional customs, its food and drink, its songs and jokes. (There are of course always the rebels, often intellectuals and writers, but they are not the mass of people.) They are rooted in their region. Indeed, without this attachment a man can have no roots.

So much of people's lives, from earliest childhood onwards, is deeply intertwined with the common life of the region, they cannot help feeling strongly about it. A threat to it is a knife pointing at the heart. How can life ever be the same if bullying strangers come to change everything? The form and colour, the very taste and smell of dear familiar things will be different, alien, life-destroying. It would be better to die fighting. And it is precisely this, the nourishing life of the region, for which common men have so often fought and died.

This attachment to the region exists on a level far deeper than that of any political hocus-pocus. When a man says "my country" with real feeling, he is thinking about his region, all that has made up his life, and not about that political entity, the nation. There can be some confusion here simply because some countries are so small — and ours is one of them — and so old, again like ours, that much of what is national is also regional. Down the centuries, the nation, itself so comparatively small, has been able to attach to itself the feeling really created by the region. (Even so there is something left over, as most people in Yorkshire or Devon, for example, would tell you.) This probably explains the fervent patriotism developed early in small countries. The English were announcing that they were English in the Middle Ages, before nationalism had arrived elsewhere.

If we deduct from nationalism all that it has borrowed or stolen from regionalism, what remains is mostly rubbish. The nation, as distinct from the region, is largely the creation of power-men and political manipulators. Almost all nationalist movements are led by ambitious frustrated men determined to hold office. I am not blaming them. I would do the same if I were in their place and wanted power so badly. But nearly always they make use of the rich warm regional feeling, the emotional dynamo of the movement, while being almost untouched by it themselves. This is because they are not as a rule deeply loyal to any region themselves. Ambition and a love of power can eat like acid into the tissues of regional loyalty. It is hard, if not impossible, to retain a natural piety and yet be forever playing both ends against the middle.

Being itself a power structure, devised by men of power, the nation tends to think and act in terms of power. What would benefit the real life of the region, where men, women and children actually live, is soon sacrificed for the power and prestige of the nation. (And the personal vanity of presidents and ministers themselves, which historians too often disregard.) Among the new nations of our time innumerable peasants and labourers must have found themselves being cut down from five square meals a week to three in order to provide unnecessary airlines, military forces that can only be used against them and nobody else, great conference halls and official yachts and the rest. The last traces of imperialism and colonialism may have to be removed from Asia and Africa, where men can no longer endure being condemned to a permanent inferiority by the colour of their skins; but even so, the modern world, the real world of our time, does not want and would be far better without more and more nations, busy creating for themselves the very paraphernalia that western Europe is now trying to abolish. You are compelled to answer more questions when trying to spend half a day in Cambodia than you are now travelling from the Hook of Holland to Syracuse.

This brings me to internationalism. I dislike this term, which I used only to complete the isms. It suggests financiers and dubious promoters living nowhere but in luxury hotels; a shallow world of entrepreneurs and impresarios. (Was it Sacha Guitry who said that impresarios were men who spoke many languages but all with a foreign accent?) The internationalism I have in mind here is best described as world civilisation. It is life considered on a global scale. Most of our communications and transport already exist on this high wide level. So do many other things from medicine to meteorology. Our astronomers and physicists (except where they have allowed themselves to be hush-hushed) work here. The UN special agencies, about which we hear far too little, have contributed more and more to this world civilisation. All the arts, when they are arts and not chunks of nationalist propaganda, naturally take their place in it. And it grows, widens, deepens, in spite of the fact that for every dollar, ruble, pound or franc spent in explaining and praising it, a thousand are spent by the nations explaining and praising themselves.

This world civilisation and regionalism can get along together, especially if we keep ourselves sharply aware of their quite different but equally important values and rewards. A man can make his contribution to world civilisation and yet remain strongly regional in feeling: I know several men of this sort. There is of course the danger — it is with us now — of the global style flattening out the regional, taking local form, colour, flavour, away for ever, disinheriting future generations, threatening them with sensuous poverty and a huge boredom. But to understand and appreciate regionalism is to be on guard against this danger. And we must therefore make a clear distinction between regionalism and nationalism.

It is nationalism that tries to check the growth of world civilisation. And nationalism, when taken on a global scale, is more aggressive and demanding now than it has ever been before. This in the giant powers is largely disguised by the endless fuss in public about rival ideologies, now a largely unreal quarrel. What is intensely real is the glaring nationalism. Even the desire to police the world is nationalistic in origin. (Only the world can police the world.) Moreover, the nation-states of today are for the most part far narrower in their outlook, far more inclined to allow prejudice against the foreigner to impoverish their own style of living, than the old imperial states were. It should be part of world civilisation that men with particular skills, perhaps the product of the very regionalism they are rebelling against, should be able to move easily from country to country, to exercise those skills, in anything from teaching the violin to running a new type of factory to managing an old hotel. But nationalism, especially of the newer sort, would rather see everything done badly than allow a few non-nationals to get to work. And people face a barrage of passports, visas, immigration controls, labour permits; and in this respect are worse off than they were in 1900. But even so, in spite of all that nationalism can do — so long as it keeps its nuclear bombs to itself — the internationalism I have in mind, slowly creating a world civilisation, cannot be checked.

Nevertheless, we are still backing the wrong ism. Almost all our money goes on the middle one, nationalism, the rotten meat between the two healthy slices of bread. We need regionalism to give us roots and that very depth of feeling which nationalism unjustly and greedily claims for itself. We need internationalism to save the world and to broaden and heighten our civilisation. While regional man enriches the lives that international man is already working to keep secure and healthy, national man, drunk with power, demands our loyalty, money and applause, and poisons the very air with his dangerous nonsense.

Questions

1. How does Priestley characterize the leaders of almost all nationalist movements? What, he writes, is the connection between such leaders and "regionalism"?
2. If Hazlitt connects "true" patriotism to our "rational and moral nature," to what does Priestley attach it? How does he attempt to support his view of the connection?
3. What is the negative idea suggested by the term "internationalism" to Priestley? How does he use the fact of language to illustrate this reaction?
4. In what sense does he present internationalism as a positive, desirable thing? Why does he shift terms as he does so? What endangers the positive good of internationalism and what can nurture and support it in Priestley's view?
5. With what judgment does this essayist conclude his consideration of patriotism (without using the word) as Hazlitt and Rowse each appear to identify it?

Foreword to *The War Prayer*

Mark Twain, an American for a change, is by far the best known of the writers in the "*Pro Patria*" section. Whatever one may associate with him from reading his novels and short stories, here we see him passionately and single-mindedly attempting to present his personal views on the subject of and particularly the fruits of, national patriotism.

We include "The War Prayer" as an essay although its form is narrative (like that of Orwell's "A Hanging" on page 8) and although an ardent literary classifier might insist on calling the piece a *parable* or a *fable*.

Here, for what light or confusion they might bring you as you read "The War Prayer," are a few interesting sentences from Bernard de Voto's Introduction to *The Portable Mark Twain* (Viking Press 1949). They are, of course, about Mark Twain himself.

> His intelligence was intuitive, not analytical. He reasoned fluently, with an avidity which touched most of the surface flow of his time, but superficially and with habitual contradictions. He had little capacity for sustained thought and to get to the heart of a question had to abandon analysis and rely on feeling.

The War Prayer

by Mark Twain (Samuel Clemens) (1835-1910)

It was a time of great and exalting excitement. The country was up in arms, the war was on, in every breast burned the holy fire of patriotism; the drums were beating, the bands playing, the toy pistols popping, the bunched firecrackers hissing and spluttering; on every hand and far down the receding and fading spread of roofs and balconies a fluttering wilderness of flags flashed in the sun; daily the young volunteers marched down the wide avenue gay and fine in their new uniforms, the proud fathers and mothers and sisters and sweethearts cheering them with voices choked with happy emotion as they swung by; nightly the packed mass meetings listened, panting, to patriot oratory which stirred the deepest deeps of their hearts and which they interrupted at briefest intervals with cyclones of applause, the tears running down their cheeks the while; in the churches the pastors preached devotion to flag and country and invoked the God of Battles, beseeching His aid in our good cause in outpourings of fervid eloquence which moved every listener. It was indeed a glad and gracious time, and the half-dozen rash spirits that ventured to disapprove of the war and cast a doubt upon its righteousness straightway got such a stern and angry warning that for their personal safety's sake they quickly shrank out of sight and offended no more in that way.

Sunday morning came — next day the battalions would leave for the front; the church was filled; the volunteers were there, their young faces alight with martial dreams — visions of the stern advance, the gathering momentum, the rushing charge, the flashing sabers, the flight of the foe, the tumult, the enveloping smoke, the fierce pursuit, the surrender! — then home from the war, bronzed heroes, welcomed, adored, submerged in golden seas of glory! With the volunteers sat their dear ones, proud, happy, and envied by the neighbors and friends who had no sons and brothers to send forth to the field of honor, there to win for the flag or, failing, die the noblest of noble deaths. The service proceeded; a war chapter from the Old Testament was read; the first prayer was said; it was followed by an organ burst that shook the building, and with one impulse the house rose, with glowing eyes and beating hearts, and poured out that tremendous invocation —

> "God the all-terrible! Thou who ordainest,
> Thunder thy clarion and lightning thy sword!"

Then came the "long" prayer. None could remember the like of it for passionate pleading and moving and beautiful language. The burden of its supplication was that an ever-merciful and benignant Father of us all would watch over our noble young soldiers and aid, comfort, and encourage them in their patriotic work; bless them, shield them in the day of battle and the hour of peril, bear them in His mighty hand, make them strong and confident, invincible in the bloody onset; help them to crush the foe, grant to them and to their flag and country imperishable honor and glory —

An aged stranger entered and moved with slow and noiseless step up the main aisle, his eyes fixed upon the minister, his long body clothed in a robe that reached to his feet, his head bare, his white hair descending in a frothy cataract to his shoulders, his seamy face unnaturally pale, pale even to ghastliness. With all eyes following him and wondering, he made his silent way; without pausing, he ascended to the preacher's side and stood there, waiting. With shut lids the preacher, unconscious of his presence, continued his moving prayer, and at last finished it with the words, uttered in fervent appeal, "Bless our arms, grant us the victory, O Lord our God, Father and Protector of our land and flag!"

The stranger touched his arm, motioned him to step aside — which the startled minister did — and took his place. During some moments he surveyed the spellbound audience with solemn eyes in which burned an uncanny light; then in a deep voice he said:

"I come from the Throne — bearing a message from Almighty God!" The words smote the house with a shock; if the stranger perceived it he gave no attention. "He has heard the prayer of His servant your shepherd and will grant it if such shall be your desire after I, His messenger, shall have explained to you its import — that is to say, its full import. For it is like unto many of the prayers of men, in that it asks for more than he who utters it is aware of — except he pause and think.

"God's servant and yours has prayed his prayer. Has he paused and taken thought? Is it one prayer? No, it is two — one uttered, the other not. Both have reached the ear of Him Who heareth all supplications, the spoken and the unspoken. Ponder this — keep it in mind. If you would beseech a blessing upon yourself, beware! Lest without intent you invoke a curse upon a neighbor at the same time. If you pray for the blessing of rain upon your crop which needs it, by that act you are possibly praying for a curse upon some neighbor's crop which may not need rain and can be injured by it.

"You have heard your servant's prayer — the uttered part of it. I am commissioned of God to put into words the other part of it — that part which the pastor, and also you in your hearts, fervently prayed silently. And ignorantly and unthinkingly? God grant that it was so! You heard these words: 'Grant us the victory, O Lord our God!' That is sufficient. The *whole* of the uttered prayer is compact into those pregnant words. Elaborations were not necessary. When you have prayed for victory you have prayed for many unmentioned results which follow victory — *must* follow it, cannot help but follow it. Upon the listening spirit of God the Father fell also the unspoken part of the prayer. He commandeth me to put it into words. Listen!

"O Lord our Father, our young patriots, idols of our hearts, go forth to battle — be Thou near them! With them, in spirit, we also go forth from the sweet peace of our beloved firesides to smite the foe. O Lord our God, help us to tear their soldiers to bloody shreds with our shells; help us to cover their smiling fields with pale forms of their patriot dead; help us to drown the thunder of the guns with the shrieks of their wounded writhing in pain; help us to lay waste their humble homes with a hurricane of fire; help us to wring the hearts of their unoffending widows with unavailing grief; help us to turn them out roofless with their little children to wander unfriended the wastes of their desolated land in rags and hunger and thirst, sports of the sun flames of summer and the icy winds of winter, broken in spirit, worn with travail, imploring Thee for the refuge of the grave and denied it — for our sakes who adore Thee, Lord, blast their hopes, blight their lives, protract their bitter pilgrimage, make heavy their steps, water their way with their tears, stain the white snow with the blood of their wounded feet! We ask it, in the spirit of love, of Him Who is the Source of Love, and Who is the ever-faithful refuge and friend of all that are sore beset and seek His aid with humble and contrite hearts. Amen.

(After a pause) "Ye have prayed it; if ye still desire it, speak! The messenger of the Most High waits."

It was believed afterward that the man was a lunatic, because there was no sense in what he said.

Questions

1. To what extent do you think that Mark Twain identifies national patriotism with war in this essay? To what extent does he explain the relationship between war and patriotism?
2. What are the two familiar pictures of war that the writer supplies in "The War Prayer"?
3. The old "lunatic" who says that he comes from the Throne of God has certain qualities of the Old Testament Prophet. What are these qualities? What does this kind of identity add to the force of the essay?
4. What attention, by statement or implication, does Mark Twain pay to the idea of "regionalism" or "local patriotism" which we find in the other essays of this section?
5. In what major respects, particularly in word choice, does Twain's style in "The War Prayer" differ from the styles employed by Hazlitt, Rowse, and Priestley?

General Discussion Questions

1. As mentioned on page 32, James Boswell explains that when Dr. Johnson made his famous remark to the effect that patriotism is the last refuge of the scoundrel, the sage was not attacking patriotism but scoundrels. What possibilities for immoral uses do each of the versions of patriotism considered in this section offer.
2. To what extent do the essayists in this section appear to look upon patriotism not so much as a good thing (or a bad thing) but as an inevitable element in human social existence?
3. Consider your own introduction to the general idea of patriotism. Possibly, as you recall it, this was from your parents, television, or in the primary grades of school. In any case, what exactly are your memories of this earliest encounter? What were your reactions at the time? To what extent have they changed since?

5

Books

"There is no book so bad," said the bachelor,
"but something good may be found in it."

CERVANTES

Foreword to *Fable*

One of the less common, but most rewarding, kinds of essay is that in which an author examines his own work, discussing what he intended in it and the processes by which he wrote it. In "Fable," William Golding, an English novelist, talks of the inception of his first — and though he has since written other excellent books, still his most famous — novel, *Lord of the Flies.*

The book has an unusual history. Upon its first publication in the United States, in 1955, it received some enthusiastic praise from a few critics, but found no responsive public; it sold fewer than 2,500 copies. In 1959 a paperback reprint edition appeared, with no expectation of more than moderate sales. To everyone's surprise, it rapidly became a major bestseller, well in excess of 100,000 copies. It was brought back into print in a hardcover edition, and a motion picture was made of it. More significantly, it became for a time the most liked and most discussed book among students in both colleges and high schools. Teachers, too, shared the enthusiasm and as a result, *Lord of the Flies* became the unusual phenomenon of a book that was simultaneously widely popular and widely studied in classrooms.

The sheer fad aspect of the book has subsided, but *Lord of the Flies* is established as a modern classic and works its fascination upon every one who encounters it.

During the time of its vogue, William Golding made several trips to the United States, lecturing at many colleges and serving for brief times as writer-in-residence at some of them. "Fable" was written, or developed, as one of some lectures for UCLA, in California. He remarks of it: "I elaborated this lecture and took it round a variety of American universities where it answered some of the standard questions which students were asking me. I print it . . . in the hope that it may continue to do so."

Fable

by William Golding (1911-   )

'Nuncle,' says the fool in Lear,[1] 'thou hast pared thy wit o' both sides and left nothing i' the middle. Look — here comes one of the parings.' The paring in question is Goneril and she gives him a dirty look. No one has ever been quite sure what happened to the fool later on. He disappears halfway through the play in mysterious circumstances, but we need not be surprised. He asked time and again for summary measures to be taken against him. Oh, the uncomfortable counsel he gave! 'Thou did'st little good when thou mad'st thy daughters thy mothers.' He tries to comfort Lear; to turn his mind from his sorrows; but ever and again the bitter truth will out. Notice that he never says 'It was a piece of folly to put yourself in the power of your bloody-minded daughters.' Always the truth is metaphorical. So he disappears; and though Shakespeare nowhere says so, it is plain enough to me that Lear's daughters got him in the end. For the fool was a fabulist, and fabulists are never popular. They are those people who haunt the fringes of history and appear in miscellanics of anecdotes as slaves or jesters, rash courtiers, or just plain wise men. They tell the dictator, the absolute monarch what he ought to know but does not want to hear. Generally they are hanged, or beheaded or even bow-stringed, unless they have the wit to get out of that hole with another pretty jest. It is a thankless task, to be a fabulist.

1. Lear: Shakespeare's *King Lear;* the lines are adapted from I, iv, 183-4 and 169-70.

Why this is so is clear enough. The fabulist is a moralist. He cannot make a story without a human lesson tucked away in it. Arranging his signs as he does, he reaches, not profundity on many levels, but what you would expect from signs, that is overt significance. By the nature of his craft then, the fabulist is didactic, desires to inculcate a moral lesson. People do not much like moral lessons. The pill has to be sugared, has to be witty or entertaining, or engaging in some way or another. Also, the moralist has to be out of his victim's reach, when the full impact of the lesson strikes him. For the moralist has made an unforgiveable assumption; namely that he knows better than his reader; nor does a good intention save him. If the pill is not sufficiently sugared it will not be swallowed. If the moral is terrible enough he will be regarded as inhuman; and if the edge of his parable cuts deeply enough, he will be crucified.

Any of Aesop's fables will do as examples to begin with. The fox who loses his tail in a trap and then tries to persuade all the other foxes to cut theirs off, because a fox looks better that way, is a situation that may be paralleled in human experience easily enough. But, you cannot make a scale model. This is why *Animal Farm,* George Orwell's splendid fable, having to choose between falsifying the human situation and falsifying the nature of animals, chooses to do the latter. Often, we forget they are animals. They are people, and Orwell's brilliant mechanics have placed them in a situation where he can underline every moral point he cares to make. We read his funny, poignant book and consent to the lesson as much out of our own experience as out of his. There are fables from other centuries, *Gulliver's Travels, Pilgrim's Progress,* perhaps *Robinson Crusoe.* Children love them, since by a God-given urgency for pleasure, they duck the morals and enjoy the story. But children do not like *Animal Farm.* Why should the poor animals suffer so? Why should even animal life be without point or hope? Perhaps in the twentieth century, the sort of fables we must construct are not for children on any level.

With all its drawbacks and difficulties, it was this method of presenting the truth as I saw it in fable form which I adopted for the first of my novels which ever got published. The overall intention may be stated simply enough. Before the second world war I believed in the perfectibility of social man; that a correct structure of society would produce goodwill; and that therefore you could remove all social ills by a reorganization of society. It is possible that today I believe something of the same again; but after the war I did not because I was unable to. I had discovered what one man could do to another. I am not talking of one man killing another with a gun, or dropping a bomb on him or blowing him up or torpedoing him. I am thinking of the vileness beyond all words that went on, year after year, in the totalitarian states. It is bad enough to say that so many Jews were exterminated in this way and that, so many people liquidated — lovely, elegant word — but there were things done during that period from which I still have to avert my mind lest I should be physically sick. They were not done by the headhunters of New Guinea, or by some primitive tribe in the Amazon. They were done, skilfully, coldly, by educated men, doctors, lawyers, by men with a tradition of civilization behind them, to beings of their own kind. I do not want to elaborate this. I would like to pass on; but I must say that anyone who moved through those years without understanding that man produces evil as a bee produces honey, must have been blind or wrong in the head. Let me take a parallel from a social situation. We are commonly dressed, and commonly behave as if we had no genitalia. Taboos and prohibitions have grown up round that very necessary part of the human anatomy. But in sickness, the whole structure of man must be exhibited to the doctor. When the occasion is important enough, we admit to what we have. It seems to me that in nineteenth-century and early twentieth-century society of the West, similar taboos grew up round the nature of man. He was supposed not to have in him, the sad fact of his own cruelty and lust. When these capacities emerged into action they were thought aberrant. Social systems, political systems were composed, detached from the real nature of man. They were what one might call political symphonies. They would perfect most men, and at the least, reduce aberrance.

Why, then, have they never worked? How did the idealist concepts of primitive socialism turn at last into Stalinism? How could the political and philosophical idealism of Germany produce as its ultimate fruit, the rule of Adolf Hitler? My own conviction grew that what had happened was that men were putting the cart before the horse. They were looking at the system rather than the people. It seemed to me that man's capacity for greed, his innate cruelty and selfishness, was being hidden behind a kind of pair of political pants. I believed then, that man was sick — not exceptional man, but average man. I believed that the condition of man was to be a morally diseased creation and that the best job I could do at the time was to trace the connection between his diseased nature and the international mess he gets himself into.

To many of you, this will seem trite, obvious and familiar in theological terms. Man is a fallen being. He is gripped by original sin. His nature is sinful and his state perilous. I accept the theology and admit the triteness; but what is trite is true; and a truism can become more than a truism when it is a belief passionately held. I looked round me for some convenient form in which this thesis might be worked out, and found it in the play of children. I was well situated for this, since at this time I was teaching them. Moreover, I am a son, brother, and father. I have lived for many years with small boys, and understand and know them with awful precision. I decided to take the literary convention of boys on an island, only make them real boys instead of paper cutouts with no life in them; and try to show how the shape of the society they evolved would be conditioned by their diseased, their fallen nature.

It is worth looking for a moment at the great original of boys on an island. This is *The Coral Island*,[2] published a century ago, at the height of Victorian smugness, ignorance, and prosperity. I can do no better than quote to you Professor Carl Niemeyer's sketch of this book.

Ballantyne shipwrecks his three boys — Jack, eighteen; Ralph, the narrator, aged fifteen; and Peterkin Gay, a comic sort of boy, aged thirteen — somewhere in the South Seas on an uninhabited coral island. Jack is a natural leader, but both Ralph and Peterkin have abilities valuable for survival. Jack has the most common sense and foresight, but Peterkin turns out to be a skilful killer of pigs and Ralph, when later in the book he is separated from his friends and alone on a schooner, coolly navigates back to Coral Island by dead reckoning, a feat sufficiently impressive, if not quite equal to captain Bligh's. The boys' life on the island is idyllic; and they are themselves without malice or wickedness, tho' there are a few curious episodes in which Ballantyne seems to hint at something he himself understands as little as do his characters. . . . Ballantyne's book raises the problem of evil — which comes to the boys not from within themselves but from the outside world. Tropical nature to be sure, is kind, but the men of this non-Christian world are bad. For example the island is visited by savage cannibals, one canoeful pursuing another, who fight a cruel and bloody battle, observed by the horrified boys and then go away. A little later, the island is again visited, this time by pirates (i.e. white men who have renounced or scorned their Christian heritage) who succeed in capturing Ralph. In due time the pirates are deservedly destroyed, and in the final episode of the book the natives undergo an unmotivated conversion to Christianity, which effects a total change in their nature just in time to rescue the boys from their clutches.

'Thus Ballantyne's view of man is seen to be optimistic, like his view of English boys' pluck and resourcefulness, which subdues tropical islands as triumphantly as England imposes empire and religion on lawless breeds of men.'

---

2. *The Coral Island:* novel by Robert Ballantyne (1825-94), Scottish author of "story books for young folks."

Ballantyne's island was a nineteenth-century island inhabited by English boys; mine was to be a twentieth-century island inhabited by English boys. I can say here in America what I should not like to say at home; which is that I condemn and detest my country's faults precisely because I am so proud of her many virtues. One of our faults is to believe that evil is somewhere else and inherent in another nation. My book was to say: you think that now the war is over and an evil thing destroyed, you are safe because you are naturally kind and decent. But I know why the thing rose in Germany. I know it could happen in any country. It could happen here.

So the boys try to construct a civilization on the island; but it breaks down in blood and terror because the boys are suffering from the terrible disease of being human.

The protagonist was Ralph, the average, rather more than average, man of goodwill and commonsense; the man who makes mistakes because he simply does not understand at first the nature of the disease from which they all suffer. The boys find an earthly paradise, a world, in fact like our world, of boundless wealth, beauty and resource. The boys were below the age of overt sex, for I did not want to complicate the issue with that relative triviality. They did not have to fight for survival, for I did not want a Marxist exegesis. If disaster came, it was not to come through the exploitation of one class by another. It was to rise, simply and solely out of the nature of the brute. The overall picture was to be the tragic lesson that the English have had to learn over a period of one hundred years; that one lot of people is inherently like any other lot of people; and that the only enemy of man is inside him. So the picture I had in my mind of the change to be brought about was exemplified by two pictures of the little boy Ralph. The first is when he discovers he is on a real desert island and delights in the discovery.

'He jumped down from the terrace. The sand was thick over his black shoes and the heat hit him. He became conscious of the weight of clothes, kicked his shoes off fiercely and ripped off each stocking with its elastic garter in a single movement. Then he leapt back on the terrace, pulled off his shirt, and stood there among the skull-like coco-nuts with green shadows from the palms and the forest sliding over his skin. He undid the snake-clasp of his belt, lugged off his shorts and pants, and stood there naked, looking at the dazzling beach and the water.

'He was old enough, twelve years and a few months, to have lost the prominent tummy of childhood; and not yet old enough for adolescence to have made him awkward. You could see now that he might make a boxer, as far as width and heaviness of shoulders went, but there was a mildness about his mouth and eyes that proclaimed no devil. He patted the palm trunk softly; and, forced at last to believe in the reality of the island, laughed delightedly again, and stood on his head. He turned neatly on to his feet, jumped down to the beach, knelt and swept a double armful of sand into a pile against his chest. Then he sat back and looked at the water with bright, excited eyes.'

This is innocence and hope; but the picture changes and the book is so designed that our last view of Ralph is very different. By the end, he has come to understand the fallen nature of man, and that what stands between him and happiness comes from inside him; a trite lesson as I have said; but one which I believed needed urgently to be driven home.

Yet if one takes the whole of the human condition as background of a fable it becomes hopelessly complex, tho' I worked the book out in detail.

Let us take, for example, the word 'history.' It seems to me that the word has two common meanings, each of them of awful[3] importance. First there is what might be called academic, or if you like campus history. To my mind this is not only of importance, but of supreme importance. It is that objective yet devoted stare with which humanity observes its own past; and in that stare, that attempt to see how things have become what they are, where they went wrong, and where right, that our only hope lies of having some control over our own future. The exploration of the physical world is an art, with all the attendant aesthetic pleasures; but the knowledge we get from it is not immediately applicable to the problems that we have on hand. But history is a kind of selfknowledge, and it may be with care that selfknowledge will be sufficient to give us the right clue to our behaviour in the future. I say clue; for we stand today in the same general condition as we have always stood, under sentence of death.

But there is another kind of force which we call history; and how uncontrollable that force is even in the most detached of men was amusingly demonstrated to me only the other day. I was being driven over the last battleground of the War Between the States, a historical episode which I am able to observe with some objectivity. My driver was a southerner and scholar. His exposition to me of the situation was a model of historical balance. He explained to me how the south had embarked on a war which they could not hope to win, in support of a pattern of society which could not hope to survive. He was perhaps a little harder on the south than a northerner would have been; but judicially so. As the day wore on, his voice began to return to its origins. Emotion crept in — not very far, because of course he was a scholar, and scholars are detached and unemotional are they not? — At a discreet forty miles an hour we followed the

3. awful: very great.

wavering fortunes of battle down into Virginia. Here, he told me, Lee had performed that last incredible tactical feat in the defence of Richmond; here, Grant had sidestepped — but what was this? His voice had lost all pretence of scholarship. Insensibly the speed of the car had increased. When we came to Appomattox, this educated and indeed rather cynical man grunted — 'Aw, shucks!' and drove past the place where Lee surrendered to Grant at seventy-five miles an hour.

This is a different force from campus history. It is history felt in the blood and bones. Sometimes it is dignified by a pretty name, but I am not sure in my own mind that it is ever anything but pernicious. However this is a political and historical question which we need not settle here and now. My point is that however pathetic or amusing we find these lesser manifestations of prejudice, when they go beyond a certain point no one in the world can doubt that they are wholly evil. Jew and Arab in the name of religion, Jew and Nordic in the name of race, Negro and white in the name of God knows what.

And it is not only these larger more spectacular examples of frozen history which do the damage. I am a European and an optimist. But I do not believe that history is only a nominal thing. There have been many years when as I contemplate our national frontiers, I have fallen into something like despair. Frontiers in Europe may be likened to wrinkles in an aged face, and all that will remove them is the death of the body. Now I know you will point out to me that Europe is already moving towards some confederation; and I would agree and add that that confederation has the full support of every man of goodwill and commonsense. But the wrinkles are so deep. And I cannot think of a confederation in history where the members voluntarily bowed to supranational authority without at least one of the members fighting a war to contest it. In Europe there is and has been a terrible fund of national illwill, handed down from generation to generation. There are habits of feeling which have acquired the force of instinct. These habits of feeling may be encouraged in school or college, but they are rarely taught there. They are an unconscious legacy wished on children by their parents. A woman, like one old French lady I knew, who had gone through the business of being conquered three times, in 1870, 1914 and 1940, had acquired an attitude to the Germans which was a hate so deep that she shook when she thought of them. Indeed, as I make these words, I am aware in myself of resents, indignations and perhaps fears which have nothing to do with today, with the England and Germany of today, in a word, with reality, but are there, nevertheless. I got them from off-campus history; and unless I make a conscious effort I shall hand them on. These impulses, prejudices, even perhaps these *just* hates which are nevertheless backward-looking are what parents luxuriating in a cheap emotion can wish on their children without being properly conscious of it and so perpetuate division through the generations. A less painful example of this is the way in which where one Englishman and one American are gathered together, that sad old story of the eighteenth century will raise its head, so that the American whose ancestors have perhaps been in the States since 1911 will be arrogating[4] to himself all the splendours of that struggle, while the Englishman who may have spent his life in the pursuit and furtherance of liberal principles may find himself forced into the ridiculous position of defending his fellow Englishman George III. My own technique on these occasions is to start talking about the vicious occupation of my country by the Romans[5] and the splendid resistance to them by our own heroes, Queen Boadicea[6] and King Arthur.[7] Some of these examples are silly, meant to be silly, and are understood as silly by the contestants. They are less severe than the partisanship roused by games of one sort or another; nevertheless they are symptomatic. We ought not to underestimate the power or the destructiveness of these emotions. The one country to leave the British Commonwealth of Nations in recent centuries is the Union of South Africa, forced out by a universal, if sometimes smug condemnation of her policy towards her own black population. But a quarter of a century ago England and Australia were shaken to the very roots of their common interests by a game of cricket. Those of you who find this incredible either do not understand the tenuousness of the bond that holds Australia and England together, or else do not understand the fierce passions that can be roused by cricket. But the point is that many Englishmen and Australians did in fact begin to think of each other as objectionable, irrational, ill-disposed, vindictive. For a moment each nation, or at least the sillier members of each — and there are always enough silly people in any country to form a sizeable mass-movement — each nation stood squarely behind their culture heroes, the one a very fast and accurate bowler, the other a batsman who objected to being struck repeatedly on the head. If the random agglomeration of nations which is the commonwealth seems to you to have any power for good, you may consider it lucky that England and Australia are twelve thousand miles apart. Had they

---

4. arrogating: taking on with no justification.
5. occupation . . . Romans: the Romans were in control of large parts of which is now England from 43 A.D. until the middle of the fifth century.
6. Queen Boadicea: queen who poisoned herself in 62 A.D. when defeated by the Romans.
7. King Arthur: legendary sixth century king of the Briton who resisted Saxon invasions, not Roman.

been separated, not by half a world, but by a relatively small ocean, Australia might have taken her bat and gone off fiercely to play cricket by herself. It was George Orwell who commented on the destructive force of international contests. Anyone who has watched a television programme of a game between two European nations must agree with him. There's savagery for you. There's bloodlust. There's ugly nationalism raising its gorgon[8] head.

What I am trying to do is to add together those elements, some horrible, some merely funny, but all significant, which I suppose to be the forces of off-campus history. They are a failure of human sympathy, ignorance of facts, the objectivizing of our own inadequacies so as to make a scapegoat. At moments of optimism I have felt that education and perhaps a miracle or two would be sufficient to remove their more dangerous elements. When I feel pessimistic, then they seem to constitute a trap into which humanity has got itself with a dreary inevitability much as the dinosaur trapped itself in its own useless armour. For if humanity has a future on this planet of a hundred million years, it is unthinkable that it should spend those aeons in a ferment of national self-satisfaction and chauvinistic idiocies. I was feeling pessimistic when I tried to include a sign for this thing in a fable.

The point about off-campus history is that it is always dead. It is a cloak of national prestige which the uneducated pull round their shoulders to keep off the wind of personal self-knowledge. It is a dead thing handed on, but dead though it is, it will not lie down. It is a monstrous creature descending to us from our ancestors, producing nothing but disunity, chaos. War and disorder prolong in it the ghastly and ironic semblance of life. All the marching and countermarching, the flags, the heroism and cruelty are galvanic twitches induced in its slaves and subjects by that hideous, parody thing. When I constructed a sign for it, therefore, it had to be something that was dead but had a kind of life. It had to be presented to my island of children by the world of grownups. There was only one way in which I could do this. First I must take the children at a moment when mature council and authority might have saved them as on so many occasions we might have saved our own children, might have been saved ourselves. Since a novelist ought not preach overtly in a fable, the situation had to be highlighted by the children having some dim knowledge that wisdom, that commonsense even, is to be found in the world of grownups. They must yearn for it, now they have begun to find the inadequacy of

8. gorgon: snaky-haired female in Greek mythology so frightful that anyone who looked at her face was turned to stone.

their own powers. I took a moment therefore, when they had tried to hold a council meeting to discuss ways and means but had found that other questions came up — questions which they would sooner have ignored. Finally the meeting breaks down. The children who are retrogressing more rapidly have gone off into the war dance with which they fortify their own sense of power and togetherness. It is dark. The few remainder, puzzled, anxious, surrounded by half perceived threats and mysteries; faced with a problem which once looked so simple of solution, the maintenance of a fire on the mountain, but which proved to be too much for them — these few, men of goodwill, are searching for some hope, some power for good, some commonsense.

'If . . . only they could get a message to us,' cried Ralph desperately. 'If only they could send us something grown up . . . a sign or something.'

What the grown-ups send them is indeed a sign, a sign to fit into the fable; but in the fable sense, that arbitrary sign stands for off-campus history, the thing which threatens every child everywhere, the history of blood and intolerance, of ignorance and prejudice, the thing which is dead but won't lie down.

'There was no light left save that of the stars. The three bigger boys went together to the next shelter. They lay restlessly and noisily among the dry leaves, watching the patch of stars that was the opening towards the lagoon. Sometimes a little 'un cried out from the other shelters and once a big 'un spoke in the dark. Then they too fell asleep.

'A sliver of moon rose over the horizon, hardly large enough to make a path of light even when it sat right down on the water; but there were other lights in the sky, that moved fast, winked, or went out, though not even a faint popping came down from the battle fought at ten miles' height. But a sign came down from the world of grown-ups, though at that time there was no child awake to read it. There was a sudden bright explosion and a corkscrew trail across the sky; then darkness again and stars. There was a speck above the island, a figure dropping swiftly beneath a parachute, a figure that hung with dangling limbs. The changing winds of various altitudes took the figure where they would. Then, three miles up, the wind steadied and bore it in a descending curve round the sky and swept it in a great slant across the reef and the lagoon towards the mountain. The figure fell and crumpled among the blue flowers of the mountain-side, but now there was a gentle breeze at their height too and the parachute flopped and banged and pulled. So the figure, with feet that dragged behind it, slid up the mountain. Yard by yard, puff by puff, the breeze hauled the figure through the blue flowers, over the boulders and red stones, till it lay huddled among the shattered rocks of the mountain-top. Here the breeze was fitful and allowed the strings of the parachute to tangle and festoon; and the figure sat, its helmeted head between its knees, held by a complication of lines. When the breeze blew the lines would strain taut and some accident of this pull lifted the head and chest upright so that the figure seemed to peer across the brow of the mountain. Then, each time the wind dropped, the lines would slacken and the figure bow forward again, sinking its head between its knees. So as the stars moved across the sky, the figure sat on the mountain-top and bowed and sank and bowed again.'

I have no time to prolong this quotation, nor is it necessary since I am glad to say the book itself remains in print. But it is perhaps worth noticing that this figure which is dead but won't lie down, falls on the very place where the children are making their one constructive attempt to get themselves helped. It dominates the mountaintop and so prevents them keeping a fire alight there as a signal. To take an actual historical example, the fire is perhaps like the long defunct but once much hoped-over League of Nations.[9] That great effort at international sanity fell before the pressures of nationalism which were founded in ignorance, jealousy, greed — before the pressures of off-campus history which was dead but would not lie down.

Having got thus far, I must admit to a number of qualifications, not in the theory itself but in the result. Fable, as a method, depends on two things neither of which can be relied on. First the writer has to have a coherent picture of the subject; but if he takes the whole human condition as his subject, his picture is likely to get a little dim at the edges. Next a fable can only be taken as far as the parable, the parallel is exact; and these literary parallels between the fable and the underlying life do not extend to infinity. It is not just that a small scale model cannot be exact in every detail. It is because every sort of life, once referred to, brings up associations of its own within its own limits which may have no significant relationships with the matter under consideration. Thus, the fable is most successful *qua* fable when it works within strict limits. George Orwell's *Animal Farm* confines itself to consideration and satire of a given political situation. In other words, the fable must be under strict control. Yet it is at this very point that the imagination can get out of hand.

I had better explain that I am not referring now to normal exercises of imagination, which we are told is the selection and rearrangement of pictures already latent in the mind. There is another possible experience, which some may think admirable and others pathological. I remember,

---

9. League of Nations: an ineffective world organization of nations set up after the first world war and dissolved in 1946.

many years ago, trying to bore a hole with a drilling machine through armour plate. Armour plate is constructed to resist just such an operation — a point which had escaped me for the time being. In my extreme ignorance, I put the drill in the chuck, held by half an inch of its extreme end. I seized the handle and brought the revolving drill down on the armour. It wobbled for a second; then there was a sharp explosion, the drill departed in every direction, breaking two windows and taking a piece of my uniform with it. Wiser now, I held the next drill deep in the chuck so that only the point protruded, held it mercilessly in those steel jaws and brought it down on the armour with the power behind it of many hundred horses. This operation was successful. I made a small red-hot hole in the armour, though of course I ruined the drill. If this small anecdote seems fatuous,[10] I assure you that it is the best image I know for one sort of imaginative process. There is the same merciless concentration, the same will, the same apparently impenetrable target, the same pressure applied steadily to one small point. It is not a normal mode of life; or we should find ourselves posting mail in mailboxes which were not there. But it happens sometimes and it works. The point of the fable under imaginative consideration does not become more real than the real world, it shoves the real world on one side. The author becomes a spectator, appalled or delighted, but a spectator. At this moment, how can he be sure that he is keeping a relationship between the fable and the moralized world, when he is only conscious of one of them? I believe he cannot be sure. This experience, excellent for the novel which does not claim to be a parable, must surely lead to a distortion of the fable. Yet is it not the experience which we expect and hope the novelist to have?

It might be appropriate now to give an example of a situation in which something like this happened. For reasons it is not necessary to specify, I included a Christ-figure in my fable. This is the little boy Simon, solitary, stammering, a lover of mankind, a visionary, who reaches commonsense attitudes not by reason but by intuition. Of all the boys, he is the only one who feels the need to be alone and goes every now and then into the bushes. Since this book is one that is highly and diversely explicable, you would not believe the various interpretations that have been given of Simon's going into the bushes. But go he does, and prays, as the child Jean Vianney[11] would go, and some other saints — though not many. He is really turning a part of the jungle into a church, not a physical one, perhaps, but a spiritual one. Here there is a scene, when civilization has already begun

---

10. fatuous: silly.
11. Jean Vianney: French Catholic saint (1786-1859).

to break down under the combined pressures of boy-nature and the thing still ducking and bowing on the mountaintop, when the hunters bring before him, without knowing he is there, their false god, the pig's head on a stick. It was at this point of imaginative concentration that I found that the pig's head knew Simon was there. In fact the Pig's head delivered something very like a sermon to the boy; the pig's head spoke. I know because I heard it.

'You are a silly little boy,' said the Lord of the Flies, 'just an ignorant, silly little boy.'

Simon moved his swollen tongue but said nothing.

'Don't you agree?' said the Lord of the Flies. 'Aren't you just a silly little boy?' Simon answered him in the same silent voice.

'Well then,' said the Lord of the Flies, 'you'd better run off and play with the others. They think you're batty. You don't want Ralph to think you're batty, do you? You like Ralph a lot, don't you? And Piggy, and Jack?'

Simon's head was tilted slightly up. His eyes could not break away and the Lord of the Flies hung in space before him.

'What are you doing out here all alone? Aren't you afraid of me?'

Simon shook.

'There isn't anyone to help you. Only me. And I'm the Beast.'

Simon's mouth laboured, brought forth audible words.

'Pig's head on a stick.'

'Fancy thinking the Beast was something you could hunt and kill!' said the head. For a moment or two the forest and all the other dimly appreciated places echoed with the parody of laughter. 'You knew, didn't you? I'm part of you? Close, close, close! I'm the reason why it's no go? Why things are what they are?'

The laughter shivered again.

'Come now,' said the Lord of the Flies. 'Get back to the others and we'll forget the whole thing.'

Simon's head wobbled. His eyes were half-closed as though he were imitating the obscene thing on the stick. He knew that one of his times was coming on. The Lord of the Flies was expanding like a balloon.

'This is ridiculous. You know perfectly well you'll only meet me down there — so don't try to escape!'

Simon's body was arched and stiff. The Lord of the Flies spoke in the voice of a schoolmaster.

'This has gone quite far enough. My poor, misguided child, do you think you know better than I do?

There was a pause.

'I'm warning you. I'm going to get waxy. D'you see? You're not wanted. Understand? We are going to have fun on this island. Understand? We are going to have fun on this island! So don't try it on, my poor misguided boy, or else —'

Simon found he was looking into a vast mouth. There was blackness within, a blackness that spread.

'— Or else,' said the Lord of the Flies, 'we shall do you. See? Jack and Roger and Maurice and Robert and Bill and Piggy and Ralph. Do you. See?

Simon was inside the mouth. He fell down and lost consciousness.

That then is an example of how a fable when it is extended to novel length can bid fair to get out of hand. Fortunately the Lord of the Flies' theology and mine were sufficiently alike to conceal the fact that I was writing at his dictation. I don't think the fable ever got right out of hand; but there are many places I am sure where the fable splits at the seams and I would like to think that if this is so, the splits do not rise from inepitude or deficiency but from a plentitude of imagination. Faults of excess seem to me more forgivable than faults of coldness, at least in the exercise of craftsmanship.

And then I remind myself that after all, the last lecture on sign, symbol, fable and myth, and this one more particularly on fable, are exercises not in craftsmanship but in analysis. I suspect that art, like experience, is a continuum and if we try to take elements out of that continuum, they cease to be what they were, because they are no longer together. Take these words, then, as efforts to indicate trends and possibilities rather than discrete things. May it not be that at the very moments when I felt the fable to come to its own life before me it may in fact have become something more valuable, so that where I thought it was failing, it was really succeeding? I leave that consideration to the many learned and devoted persons who, in speech and the printed word, have explained to me what the story means. For I have shifted somewhat from the position I held when I wrote the book. I no longer believe that the author has a sort of *patria potestas*[12] over his brainchildren. Once they are printed they have reached their majority and the author has no more authority over them, knows no more about them, perhaps knows less about them than the critic who comes fresh to them, and sees them not as the author hoped they would be, but as what they are.

At least the fable has caught attention, and gone out into the world. The effect on me has been diverse and not wholly satisfactory. On the good side it has brought me here, seven thousand miles from home, jet-propelled tho' somewhat jaundiced. It has subjected me to a steady stream of letters. I get letters from schoolmasters who want permission to turn the book into a play so that their classes can act it. I get letters from schoolmasters telling

12. *patria potestas:* the power of a father (Latin).

me that they *have* turned the book into a play so that their classes can act it. Now and again I get letters from mothers of boys whose schoolmasters have turned the book into a play so that their classes can act it. I get letters from psychiatrists, psychologists, clergymen — complimentary, I am glad to say; but sometimes tinged with a faint air of indignation that I should seem to know something about human nature without being officially qualified.

And at the last — students. How am I to put this gently and politely? In the first place, I am moved and fulfilled by the fact that anyone of your generation should think a book I have written is significant for you. But this is the standard form of the letters I get from most English speaking parts of the world.

Dear Mr. Golding, I and my friend so and so have read your book *Lord of the Flies* and we think so forth and so forth. However there are some things in it which we are not able to understand. We shall be glad therefore if you will kindly answer the following forty-one questions. A prompt reply would oblige as exams start next week.

Well there it is. I cannot do your homework for you; and it is in some ways a melancholy thought that I have become a school textbook before I am properly dead and buried. To go on being a schoolmaster so that I should have time to write novels was a tactic I employed in the struggle of life. But life, clever life, has got back at me. My first novel ensured that I should be treated for the rest of my days as a schoolmaster only given a longer tether — one that has stretched seven thousand miles.

Questions

1. Golding tells us early in "Fable" that fabulists are never popular, that it is a thankless task to be a fabulist. How does he support this assertion? To what extent does he appear to contradict or at least qualify it as he goes on?
2. What exactly is the moral lesson which Golding says he felt impelled to teach when he wrote *Lord of the Flies*? Why does he call it trite and obvious? What grounds does he offer for teaching it anyway?
3. What distinction does Golding make between "campus history" and "off-campus history"? What has his consideration of the two kinds of history to do with the "truism" he says he wants to represent in *Lord of the Flies*?
4. What basic difference between *Lord of the Flies* and Ballantyne's *The Coral Island* does Golding emphasize? Why?
5. To what end does Golding direct his anecdotes about sightseeing in Virginia and about the drill press? What kind of tone do these as well as his analogy between modern clothing and the nature of man supply in this "literary" essay?

Afterword to *Fable*

The movement of this essay has a wavelike pattern — sweeping in, drawing back, in and back, several times over. It goes from the general ("fabulists," what they are, how people respond to them) to the particular (his own book); from this, back again to the general (history, the nature of the fable) and back once more to the writing of *Lord of the Flies*. Golding has a gift many authors do not share, of being articulate about his intentions and his means of achieving them — one might call it the stamp of the schoolmaster until one remembers some inarticulate schoolmasters.

Golding intimates, without specifically saying, that he borrowed from Ballantyne's simplified and optimistic *The Coral Island*, the core situation of his own story, and possibly even the names "Ralph" and "Jack" for its major figures. The differences between the two books are so great, in spite of their few common elements, as to show how something may be borrowed and given a wholly new dimension by another point of view.

Though the subject matter of "Fable" is literary, and weighty historical, philosophical, or theological ideas are introduced, it has the most winning quality of an essay — the one of a human voice. Golding is a good enough writer to gain this effect in other essays written directly for print, but the structure of so complex a piece as "Fable" certainly is kept loose, flexible, by the fact that it was prepared to be spoken and takes its final form from the modifications it underwent in the course of being delivered many times. Revision, for sharpening and focusing, is one of the principal technical tasks of the professional writer. The experienced speaker, if he happens to be a writer also, finds live audiences to be a useful anvil on which the work can be pounded and shaped while hot.

There are interesting overlappings of thought between some points in A. L. Rowse's "The Idea of Patriotism" (p. 79), and "Fable." Golding's statement about detesting and condemning his country's faults reminds us of an important distinction Rowse makes between patriotism and nationalism. The differentiation made here between "campus history" (which he flatters by a sweeping assumption of its objectivity) and "off-campus history" by which he means emotional attitudes, prejudices, conditions, derived from experience or passed on to us through some direct association such as parents, also finds association with ideas in Rowse's essay.

At the heart of "Fable," and also of *Lord of the Flies*, is the concept of the nature of man as the essential determining force in what happens to man, or what man does. He tells us that the shock of the historical events precipitated by Nazi Germany purged him of an optimistic notion that man was moving through progressive stages of improvement toward self-perfection.

Yet he is tempted at least twice, in the essay itself, to lapse from his own central insight (he is quite aware of it, of course). Speaking of the possibility of society completely curing its own ills, he says, "It is possible that today I believe something of the same again. . . ." Also he remarks (qualifying it by the words "you will point out to me") that, "Europe is already moving towards some confederation." In the few years since the essay was written (1962) the prospects of such a confederation are not much brighter. He cites with melancholy the failure and disappearance of the League of Nations, but since his writing, another question which he does not raise, has grown acute: will the United Nations go the same way sooner or later, due to nationalism and "off-campus history"?

In purely literary terms, one of this essay's more valuable passages is the discussion of the problems and limits of fable as a medium. Golding isolates "control" as the principal problem, and suggests the paradox that in theory the fable works best when carefully limited in scope, together with the possibility that (like many productive scientific experiments) the fable may achieve the most when it slips slightly out of control and overleaps its intended limits.

Foreword to *The Lord of the Hobbits: J. R. R. Tolkien*

Another sort of literary essay (among many kinds) is descriptive and appreciative. Edmund Fuller describes J. R. R. Tolkien's *The Lord of the Rings* series in considerable detail. Perhaps you have read Tolkien; if not, you will learn a good deal about his books as you read "The Lord of the Hobbits: J. R. R. Tolkien." If you *have* read him, your profit from the essay will be somewhat different and more complicated. You will be able to measure and assess your own responses to the work by comparison with those of the essayist.

If a critic has high regard for a work (possibly even enthusiasm, though some critics by temperament regard such an emotion as beneath them), one of his aims is to lead other people to read it. Consider whether this essay succeeds in doing that.

If the reader has already read the work under discussion, another of the critic's aims is to reveal aspects of it, or meanings in it, that perhaps the reader has not seen before.

This essay was first published in 1962, well before the recent dramatic increase in public interest in Tolkien's work, which has made these books bestsellers, especially in colleges and schools. To that degree, the essay was prophetic.

The Lord of the Hobbits: J. R. R. Tolkien

by Edmund Fuller (1914-)

J. R. R. Tolkien has defined fantasy as "the making or glimpsing of Other-worlds." As such a maker, his own accomplishment is extraordinary. It is embodied in a four-part work introduced by *The Hobbit* and developed through the trilogy called *The Lord of the Rings.*

The other world which he has invented carries us back into untold depths of pre-history to what he calls the Third Age of Middle-earth. It is a time when men have already long existed, have experienced heights and depths of being, and still share the world with other rational creatures of several different orders, with some of whom, in fact, they have interbred.

For this world he has created a self-contained geography, with maps, a mythology and balladry, a history in great depth and completeness of organization, stretching back far behind the time-span of his story. He has created several languages and runic[1] alphabets, and within them traced elaborate linguistic interrelationships and pursued many etymologies. The historical frame of his world is filled out with genealogies and what might be called ethnic treatises on his other-than-human species. There are extensive flora and fauna in addition to those already known to us. All these elements are woven through the tale, but so deep is Tolkien's immersion in this world that at the end of the trilogy there are six appendices, totaling 103 pages, elaborately footnoted, dealing with the subjects remarked

1. runic: mysterious, riddling.

above. Though the appendices contribute to the persuasive verisimilitude of the tale, they are not necessary for such a purpose. They reflect Tolkien's own intensity of inner experience and total absorption in his act of sub-creation. It is this that makes his spell so great and in turn draws readers with him into these further compilations of data about an imaginary world they are loath to leave.

The four-part structure of the work is analogous to Wagner's[2] Ring cycle of operas. A shorter, relatively childlike wonder tale *(Das Rheingold* and *The Hobbit* respectively) in each case introduces a massive trilogy. It is odd and interesting that a ring of power is central to both stories and lends its name to their titles, and that dragons and a broken sword to be mended by a warrior hero occur in each. But noting these coincidences between the *Ring of the Nibelungs* and *The Lord of the Rings* is as far as comparison should be carried in a discussion which is not concerned with tracing the incidence of familiar mythic motifs. Tolkien's great work is astonishingly underivative in terms of any specific sources or borrowings. To whatever he has drawn, as all must do, from the common cultural heritage of the human race, he has brought something uniquely his own.

Hobbits are Tolkien's authentic contribution to the lore of imaginary species. They are a small folk, manlike in shape and manner, somewhat furred, seldom attaining more than three feet in stature, but well formed. He tells us they are

> an unobtrusive but very ancient people, more numerous formerly than they are today, for they love peace and quiet and good tilled earth . . . They do not and did not understand or like machines much more complicated than a forge-bellows, a water mill, or a hand-loom, though they were skilled with tools. Even in ancient days they were, as a rule, shy of "the Big Folk," as they call us, and now they avoid us with dismay and are becoming hard to find.

Although hobbits belong to the large and mysterious genre of little people, they are a distinct and fresh invention, richly elaborated in all their histories, habits, and generic idiosyncrasies. Sometimes they are called "halflings" by the men of the story, and are already legendary within its frame so that many are astonished to learn that they really exist. They inhabit a gentle region of Tolkien's geography called The Shire, which has much the character of the Cotswold country.

The sheer creative feat of bringing a new creature into the realm of fairy story is almost too much for some to accept. Sir Stanley Unwin, Tolkien's publisher, told me that the first negotiations for German publication

2. Wagner: Richard Wagner, German composer (1813-83).

of *The Hobbit* were broken off abruptly when the publishers wrote that they had searched through all the encyclopedias and found that there was no such thing as a hobbit.

Yet it is part of the meaning of these books that this simple, obscure people should play a central role in a great contest involving the welfare of all earth. And it is not that people as a group, but a few individuals from among them, who play the determining role, thrust irresistibly from their wonted quiet into the heart of a vast struggle.

In *The Hobbit,* Bilbo Baggins is inveigled into an expedition by some dwarfs who seek stratagems to destroy a dragon who has long usurped their halls and treasures. The small size and ability for unobtrusive movement of the hobbit is deemed valuable for reconnaissance. In a memorable episode of the journey, Bilbo acquires a ring which he keeps secret for a long time. It has the power of conferring invisibility, which is all that Bilbo knows about it.

The Hobbit is a story which young children love. It can be read to, or by, them from seven years up. To this extent it may be called a children's book. But like any fine story that may lie within a child's range, it is not limited to children and, indeed, can scarcely be relished with ultimate appreciation by them. The more mature the reader, the more added qualities he can discern in it. Stories written not for their own sake, but "for children," seldom are of enduring merit for children or anyone else.

On the other hand, *The Lord of the Rings* cannot be approached by children as young as those who can cope with *The Hobbit.* It is more difficult in language and concept, and prospective child readers must wait a few years. Yet I know from experience that it can be read aloud to an intelligent nine-year-old with immense involvement and response. But the trilogy is an adult book, on any terms.

Its three parts are: *The Fellowship of the Ring, The Two Towers,* and *The Return of the King.* In the trilogy, the nature and significance of Bilbo's ring has been discovered by one of the major figures, Gandalf the Gray, a benevolent wizard. The aged Bilbo has turned over the ring to his nephew, Frodo. It proves to be a long-lost and portentous artifact.

A runic rhyme tells of:

Three Rings for the Elven-kings under the sky,
    Seven for the Dwarf-lords in their halls of stone,
Nine for Mortal Men doomed to die,
    One for the Dark Lord on his dark throne
In the Land of Mordor where the Shadows lie.
    One Ring to rule them all, One Ring to find them,

One Ring to bring them all and in the darkness bind them
In the Land of Mordor where the Shadows lie.

Bilbo's Ring proves to be the "One Ring to rule them all." It had been wrought in an earlier age, in the land of Mordor, by Sauron the Great, a malevolent being of immense powers, now devoted to absolute evil. In the past history of the world, he has had times of ascendancy and decline. His earlier loss of the Ring forced him into a long withdrawal, during which he has planned a new campaign. He knows that the Ring has been found. Already he has launched his dark, terrible and corrupt forces to recover it. If he succeeds, all earth and its creatures will be brought under his total sway.

It devolves upon Frodo to attempt to dispose of the powerful Ring in the only way by which it can be destroyed. This is to fling it into the Cracks of Doom, into the heart of the volcanic fire of Orodruin, Mount Doom, in the land of Mordor itself, near the tower which is the seat of Sauron's rule. This heroic attempt and its terrible hazards comprise the story of the trilogy.

The tale is spun out in a masterly way. It is plotted with an astonishing prodigality of invention that never fails in the approximate 600,000 words of the whole. Tolkien can evoke hideousness, terror, horror and dreadful suspense, as well as beauty, laughter, nobility and joy. The style is always graceful, often highly eloquent, occasionally lyrical with descriptive passages of much loveliness and color. Tolkien is an adept painter of scenes and evoker of images, who can orchestrate his narrative and descriptive effects with flexibility and variety, from pianissimo to forte, while keeping his themes or motifs tightly interwoven and steadily developing. Also he is a poet of much skill in the special veins appropriate to the work. He creates runic rhymes and bardic songs in a wide range of moods and meters, from comic to heroic to elegiac, in the modes of those that characterize Anglo-Saxon and Scandinavian literature.

The Lord of the Rings is a fairy tale in the highest aspect of its kind — which requires some discussion. *Fairy* is prominent in the long lexicon of words ruined by the nasty vulgarism of our time — at least in the American culture. It is probably irrecoverable for several generations because it has been made a sniggering, derisive synonym for homosexual. This unhappy association with effeminacy clearly came out of a saccharine sentimentality that previously had vulgarized an ancient and noble conception into a sickly-sweet, flutter-winged miniature image that flourished in Victorian times. To be fair, this corruption had earlier roots, and it has since reached its peak of nauseousness in the excruciating cuteness of Walt Disney. (God forbid that he should lay his sticky hands upon hobbits!) What, then, was a fairy before this despoiling, and how is he to be restored to his lost stature and quality?

Here Tolkien has done a great rehabilitation, not only in the hobbit books, but in a long essay, "On Fairy-Stories," originally delivered as a lecture at St. Andrews University, in Scotland, and printed in the memorial volume, *Essays Presented to Charles Williams* (Oxford, 1947), and since then, in this century, in a volume called *Tree and Leaf* (Houghton Mifflin, 1965). Professor Tolkien deprecates his expertness, but it is the most profound and illuminating discussion of the subject I have ever seen.

"Faërie," in its essence, means "enchantment." As a *place name*, perhaps its best usage, Faërie is the realm or world of enchantment, whether viewed as remote and separate in time and place or superimposed upon our own, for Faërie is wherever and whenever the enchantment is operable, when men have entered or fallen under it. A "fairy" is one of the denizens of that realm, the people of Faërie, the agents of its natural spells, the masters of its enchantments. A better name than fairy for such a being is Elf, and it is so used by Tolkien as it was by Spenser.

In Tolkien's story the Elven peoples are of major importance. It is before the separation of the ways of men and Elves, before the withdrawal (not the end) of the latter. The Elves are of an antiquity greater than man; are uncorrupted, of tall stature and handsome visage, bear themselves with dignity and joy, preserve their ancient tongue and songs, have rich arts and crafts, which men call enchantments. It is the character of their workmanship to "put the thoughts of all that we love into all that we make." They use their powers benevolently; are immortal but not unconquerable. In a few instances they have wedded with men, producing a race of the Half-elven, still a noble kind though their powers are less and in them immortality is diminished to long living. All this is in Tolkien's canon. Fairy-tale at large has a tradition of bad fairies along with good, but I suspect that in primal origin the relationship is not unlike that of the fallen angels to the good.

It is important to remember that this realm of Faërie encompasses all the natural phenomena and creatures known to us, augmented by much else in plants, animals, and intelligent beings. In Tolkien's world there are not only Elves and men, but hobbits, dwarfs, and some unique creatures, such as Ents, his oldest living species, a kind of walking, talking tree. There are beornings — a sort of were-bear. We also meet an individual figure, unclassifiable other than as some primal nature spirit, Tom Bombadil. The passage about him is one of the most joyously lyrical and contains, too, one of the finest of the work's many poems.

There are wizards, also. The greatest of these, Gandalf, has profound aspects for further discussion. A wizard, as here drawn, is partly an enigma but seems to be in essence a man, but possessed of long life and magical powers. Following the lead of Tolkien, I have avoided the word "magic" in relation to Elves. Not that it may not be used, but that it may confuse a fine distinction. Enchantment is not a technique that Elves use, rather it is the total natural mode of their being and action. The wizard commands magic as an acquired technique and lore, consciously employed for specific effects, good or bad. From ancient times the lore of magic has known both the black magician and the white magician. Merlin was one of the latter, and even the poet Virgil was sometimes considered so.

Tolkien's world also has a variety of malevolent creatures. At the center are demonic powers, greatest of whom is Sauron, who is unmistakably a satanic figure, who might be nothing less than one of the fallen angelic host, and whose very name suggests the serpent. Orcs form the largest category of his mortal servants — goblin creatures of a debased order — but other mysterious powers, demonic or wraith-like, also are deployed under his command.

Here, then, is summarized the basic frame and cast. It seems wise not to attempt anything in the line of detailed synopsis. On this much we can attempt some examination of the story's meaning. In the first place, it is itself, at its face value, rich with inherent meaning, inescapably bonded with the events and characters. This is meaning of a sort that the reader translates into appropriate analogies for his own life, if he is so minded: as in the fact that courage and integrity, seen in any context, are enhancements and encouragements of those qualities wherever we have need of them. Beyond the inherent meaning lies the possibility of allegorical elements, in which there are many implications, subject to argument and disagreement among interpreters.

As to the inherent meaning, we are confronted basically by a raw struggle between good and evil. This contest offers challenge and demands decisions of several kinds. The power of evil is formidable and ruthless. The initial decision, in which many of the characters participate, is whether or not to attempt to resist it at all. So great and discouraging are the odds involved in resistance that the possibility of surrender, terrible as it may be, seems only in degrees more terrible than the fight — unless the deciding element is the moral choice of rejecting evil regardless of consequences.

Before some of the great ones is dangled the old temptation, "If you can't lick 'em, jine 'em." A corrupted wizard seeks to persuade Gandalf:

> A new Power is rising. Against it the old allies and policies will not avail us at all . . . This then is one choice before you, before us. We may join with that Power . . . Its victory is at hand; and there will be rich reward for those that aided it . . . the Wise, such as you and I, may with patience

> come at last to direct its courses, to control it. We can bide our time . . . deploring maybe evils done by the way, but approving the high and ultimate purpose: Knowledge, Rule, Order . . . There need not be . . . any real change in our designs, only in our means.

Tolkien pursues still further that most ancient and insidious moral dilemma, the problem of ends and means. If Sauron recovers his Ring, his power will be irresistible. The only means of assuring that he can never recover it is the awful one of carrying it right to the heart of his own realm and casting it into the volcanic fire in which it was first forged and that alone can destroy it. Yet an alternative constantly confronts the Fellowship in its resistance to Sauron. The Ring could be used to overthrow him by any one of several persons with advanced mastery of great powers. It is the nature of the Ring to give power according to the stature of its user — petty powers to the unknowing or inconsequential, vast ones to the strong and adept.

But the Ring and its potencies are evil, conditioned by its maker and his motives. It participates in the essence of its maker. At several crucial times the appeal arises: "Let the Ring be your weapon . . . Take it and go forth to victory!" Each time that counsel is rejected, as here in the words of Elrond Half-Elven:

> We cannot use the Ruling Ring . . . Its strength . . . is too great for anyone to wield at will, save only those who have already a great power of their own. But for them it holds an even deadlier peril. The very desire of it corrupts the heart . . . If any of the Wise should with this Ring overthrow the Lord of Mordor, using his own arts, he would then set himself on Sauron's throne, and yet another Dark Lord would appear. And that is another reason why the Ring should be destroyed: as long as it is in the world it will be a danger to the Wise. For nothing is evil in the beginning. Even Sauron was not so. I fear to take the Ring to hide it. I will not take the Ring to wield it.

Here we are brought to the classic corrupting quality of power in direct proportion to its approach to the absolute. Yet, of course, it is not simply the power, in itself, that corrupts, but the pride which power may engender, which in turn produces the swift corruption of the power. The primal nature of the sin of Pride, bringing the fall of angels before the seduction and fall of Man, is the wish to usurp the Primal and One source of Power, incorruptible in His nature because He *is* Power and Source and has nothing to usurp, in being All.

The Ring had found its way into the hands of the hobbit Bilbo, who, in his old age, at the advice of the wizard Gandalf, reluctantly entrusts it to Frodo. Upon the back of the younger hobbit descends this monstrous burden. None of the great dare lift it from him. Frodo's first response is that of anyone caught abruptly in a responsibility too great to contemplate. "I wish it need not have happened in my time."

> "So do I," said Gandalf, "and so do all who live to see such times. But that is not for them to decide. All we have to decide is what to do with the time that is given us."

Then, further, Frodo protests:

> ". . . I wish I had never seen the Ring! Why did it come to me? Why was I chosen?"
> "Such questions cannot be answered," said Gandalf. "You may be sure that it was not for any merit that others do not possess: not for power or wisdom, at any rate. But you have been chosen and you must therefore use such strength and heart and wits as you have."

The merit of Frodo, then, is not any built-in endowment, but the painfully, gradually ripening fruit of his response to the challenge set before him.

How Frodo fails or succeeds is the burden of the story — and it is not simple. Comparable tests are placed before other characters and are passed or failed in varying degrees, so that, in all, there are few aspects of challenge and response in the area of inexorable moral responsibility that Tolkien does not exemplify for us in this tale.

The next significant aspect involves the ability of the hobbits to cope with the actively malevolent Ring, so dreaded by greater and wiser than they. It is not to be assumed that the Ring does not work upon them, yet some circumstances help to shield them from its powers, at least at the outset. In the episode in *The Hobbit* when Bilbo acquired the Ring, he began his ownership with an act of pity which had an insulating effect. At the beginning of the trilogy he voluntarily gives it up — something which he alone has ever done — though not without a wrench. In turn, Frodo, though subject to corruption like any creature, begins his guardianship of the Ring unwillingly and without ambition, accepting it as an obligation thrust upon him.

With so heavy odds, against so formidable an adversary, a significant factor provides one hopeful element in the grim web of Sauron's network of agents, tracking down the Ring. In Sauron's very nature, he is incapable of anticipating the policy adopted by his enemies. He cannot conceive that they would voluntarily relinquish the Ring and destroy it, for it would be incompatible with his nature to do so. Thus, the one move that he does not expect is that they would themselves convey it to his threshold in an ultimate renunciation and destruction of its power.

Yet counterbalancing this small advantage is a demonstration of the fact that creaturely life does not always offer us clear choices of good or evil. Often we must choose between degrees of evil, and we are fortunate when we know that is what we are doing. Frodo, at times, is compelled to use the Ring for its power of invisibility as the immediate alternative to losing all. Yet every time he does so, two bad results are involved: the always baleful influence of the Ring gains perceptibly over Frodo, and Sauron is instantly aware of its use and his mind is able to grope, in a general way, toward its location, like a radio direction-fix. The expedient of employing it thus is doubly harmful each time momentary necessity forces it. In addition, the nearer Frodo gets to his destination, the heavier becomes the physical burden and the greater the influence of the Ring — consequences of its approach to its source. The question of endurance therefore is progressively acute.

At the outset, the Fellowship of the Ring comprises the wizard Gandalf; an Elf, Legolas; a Dwarf, Gimli; two men, Aragorn and Boromir, and four hobbits: Frodo, his servant Sam, and two others called Merry and Pippin. All the non-malevolent rational species thus have a hand, as well as a stake, in the enterprise. The Fellowship is dispersed early. Frodo must make his grim attempt with the aid only of his loyal servant, Sam. In shuttling narrative patterns of the most prolific story-spinning, the others play a variety of necessary roles in the widely dispersed secondary campaign against Sauron's far-ranging forces.

Now we shall shift to another level of meaning. In this story there is no overt theology or religion. There is no mention of God. No one is worshipped. There are no prayers (though there are invocations of great names of virtue). Yet implicit in the conflict between good and evil is a limited eschatology for the Third Age of Middle-earth. A theology contains the narrative rather than being contained by it. Grace is at work abundantly in the story.

In the Judeo-Christian scriptures, God is seen at work in history, taking an initiative, intervening in the affairs of His creatures. Even in the pagan Homeric literature (and in all other primitive literatures) the heroes are seen operating, as in the *Iliad* and the *Odyssey*, with the constant intervention and support of the gods, without which their enterprises and achievements would be impossible.

In Tolkien's Third Age an Ultimate Power is implicit. There is the possibility of Sauron gaining total sway over Middle-earth, but it is clear that there are other realms where his machinations are inoperable. The "Blessed Realm" lies in the mystery of the West, beyond the Sea, and certain characters sail toward it in an image akin to the passing of Arthur to Avalon.

It is a premise of Christian theology that man must cope with certain of his problems with all his own resources. There are things in which it is up to him to succeed or fail. Yet the Will of God, if not completed through one option, will complete itself through another, and in all contingencies there are helps of which a man may avail himself. The Christian rejects utterly the notion that God is dead, or will be mocked, or even that He has withdrawn Himself from human affairs.

In Tolkien's Third Age, the powers that Gandalf and the High Elves can bring to bear against Sauron clearly are derived from the Prime Source, Who is in some way identified with the Blessed Realm. The great ancient names of men and Elves often invoked, are on His side. Running through the story is a thread of prophecy being fulfilled, and Frodo is regarded as "chosen" for his heavy task.

Bilbo's acquiring of the Ring was not just a combination of chance and the power of the Ring itself to work its way back toward its master. Gandalf says to Frodo:

> Behind that there was something else at work, beyond any design of the Ring-maker. I can put it no plainer than by saying that Bilbo was *meant* to find the Ring, and *not* by its maker. In which case you also were meant to have it.

A mysterious, over-arching purpose is manifested, too, in the enigmas of the odd, repulsive, but fascinating creature called Gollum, who had treasured the Ring for a long time before Bilbo came upon him. He haunts the Ring through the whole chronicle. There are moments when he is spared only in remembrance of Gandalf's early words:

> . . . he is bound up with the fate of the Ring. My heart tells me that he has some part to play yet, for good or ill, before the end; and when that comes, the pity of Bilbo may rule the fate of many – yours not least.

The intricacy of Tolkien's web of cause and effect, of the interactions of motives and wills, natural and supernatural, is extraordinary and — notwithstanding the frame of fantasy — profoundly realistic.

As for the choosing of Frodo, it is said:

> This quest may be attempted by the weak with as much hope as the strong. Yet such is oft the course of deeds that move the wheels of the

world: small hands do them because they must while the eyes of the great are elsewhere.

There is no evading the problem of the Ring:

. . . they who dwell beyond the Sea would not receive it: for good or ill it belongs to Middle-earth; it is for us who still dwell here to deal with it.

And so it is that the hobbit, Frodo, quietly, reluctantly, in a sustained action surely as brave as any recorded in imaginative literature, assents:

"I will take the Ring," he said, "though I do not know the way."

Thus, at its core, still leaving unreckoned all the wealth of its detailed unfolding, this wonder tale is rich with teaching for life as *we* lead it. This places it among the true elite of books that can claim to offer such rewards.

Yet so far we have dealt only with inescapable inherent meanings. Possible allegorical elements can be discerned in it, whether or not they were a part of Tolkien's conscious purpose. It is true that things can be got out of a work of art that its creator did not knowingly put in. Yet rather than say it *is* an allegory, which is too rigid for so large, free and flexible a story, I will say that it has allegorical possibilities and suggestions underlying the face value of the narrative. It is some of these which suggest themselves to me that I put forward, rather than any complete and systematic scheme. Tolkien vigorously rejects any formal allegorical or other elaborately schematized "interpretations" of his stories. These tend to proliferate even more in the wake of the immense surge in the popularity of the books since this essay was first published in 1962. Reluctantly he concedes the right of readers to find certain "correspondences" to the modern world if they insist. The intent of this essay is no more than that. He really wishes we would read his work at its face value and keep quiet about it. One cannot blame him, or help feeling slightly guilty about such a discussion as this.

It has for me an allegorical relation to the struggle of Western Christendom against the forces embodied, successively but overlappingly, in Nazism and Communism. The work was conceived and carried forward when the darkest shadow of modern history was cast over the West and, for a crucial part of that time, over England in particular.

Although the notion of the Blessed Realm in the true West is an ancient motif, it is no simple association that also makes the Westernese of Middle-earth — Numenor as he calls it (which suggests land of spirit) —

and its men, the hope for justice, peace and order. In the story, men are the inheritors of earth and theirs is the new age coming. The other creatures are withdrawing, having completed their destinies, but a man is king again in the West and the future lies with his kind.

For those to whom Christianity — not any political or economic or military system — is the one possible counterpoise to the Communist doctrine of man, Tolkien's image of the West is a meaningful parable. He shows us a challenge that must be met, or to which surrender is the only other alternative. All the seductions and rationalizations are there, including that of accepting a "wave of the future," or of using power in such ways as to supplant the enemy with nothing better than ourselves corrupted into his own image. Though Tolkien could not have foreseen it, a natural analogy arises between the hydrogen bomb and the Ring of power which by its nature could not be used to achieve anything that could be called good.

In both the Third Age and our world, evil is never defeated once for all. Even men who fight evil devotedly are not themselves free of its taint:

> Always after a defeat and a respite, the Shadow takes another shape and grows again . . . The evil of Sauron cannot be wholly cured, nor made as if it had not been . . . Other evils there are that may come; for Sauron is himself but a servant or emissary. Yet it is not our part to master all the tides of the world, but to do what is in us for the succor of those years wherein we are set, uprooting the evil in the fields that we know, so that those who live after may have clean earth to till.

If we survive the hydrogen crisis, we will find new technologically pressing moral dilemmas, from genetics to space-colonization. There is never a hiding place, or a time when the perennial but Protean[3] moral dilemma has been solved forever. Though we feel with Frodo, "I wish it need not have happened in my time," we must accept the fact that "The wide world is all about you: you can fence yourselves in, but you cannot forever fence it out." We are faced with what Aragorn, foremost of the men in the story, sternly calls "The doom of choice . . . There are some things that it is better to begin than to refuse, even though the end may be dark."

> "How shall a man judge what to do in such times?"
> "As he ever has judged," said Aragorn. "Good and ill have not changed since yesteryear; nor are they one thing among Elves and Dwarves and another among Men."

3. Protean: Proteus was a Greek mythological sea god who could change shape at will; protean means unfixed or perversely changeable.

So, likewise, one faces with Frodo the necessity that he expresses: "It must often be so, Sam, when things are in danger: some one has to give them up, lose them, so that others may keep them."

The parallels for our world continue:

> . . . in nothing is the power of the Dark Lord more clearly shown than in the estrangement that divides all those who still oppose him.

Part of this divisive power is the force with which everyone sometimes nurses the thought

> that he was offered a choice between a shadow full of fear that lay ahead, and something that he greatly desired: clear before his mind it lay, and to get it he had only to turn aside from the road and leave the Quest and the war against Sauron to others.

We have seen enough to show that it is impossible not to be haunted by parallels between Tolkien's Middle-earth and our here and now. Greater than the samples that are offered is the cumulative effect of the whole tale. It is a moral fable on a scale commensurate with its narrative scope.

Other things remain unremarked. The blight of Mordor, and the damage sustained as far away as The Shire, are images of the blight which the first half-century of the industrial revolution laid upon fair lands, especially England. The sins of the Christian West in that era are directly visited upon the heads of the generations since, in the warped and fragmentary version of the neglected Christian ethic which, since Marx, has been the ideological appeal of the adversary.

We have noted already the general harmony of the elements in this story with Christian theology. It is clear from the nature and powers of Sauron — not always evil, but become so, and not himself the greatest of his kind — that he is a type of the fallen Angels. In the era of the making of the twenty Rings of the runic rhyme, even certain of the sub-angelic High Elves were for a time deceived by him and, with biblical and Faustian parallels,[4] ensnared by "their eagerness for knowledge." We learn that "It is perilous to study too deeply the arts of the Enemy, for good or for ill."

I shun a too-eager search for supposed Christ figures in literature, and excessively elaborate constructions in pursuit of them. But it is possible to say that both Gandalf and Frodo, each in his way, appear not as Christ

4. biblical and Faustian parallels: Adam and Eve disobeyed God by eating the fruit "of the tree of the knowledge of good and evil"; Faust sold his soul to the devil in exchange for worldly power and knowledge.

equivalents, but as partial anticipations of the Christ. With Frodo, quite simply and movingly, it lies in his vain wish that the cup might be taken from him, and since it may not, he goes his long, dolorous way as Ring-bearer — a type of the Cross-bearer to come. More mystically with Gandalf, indicative of the operation of an unexpressed Power behind the events, the wizard undergoes a harrowing prefiguring of the death, descent into Hell, and rising again from the dead. Also he experiences something of the temptation in the wilderness in his refusal of the Ring which he has power enough to wield.

In a conversation in June of 1962, too late for inclusion in the original printing of this essay, Professor Tolkien was explicit about the nature of Gandalf. In response to my question he said, unhesitatingly, "Gandalf is an angel." He went on to explain that Gandalf had voluntarily accepted incarnation to wage the battle against Sauron. Gandalf the Gray does indeed die in the mortal flesh in the encounter with the Balrog in the Mines of Moria. Gandalf the White, who returns, is the angel in the incorruptible body of resurrection.

Professor Tolkien worked on the whole enterprise for more than fourteen years. He brought to it, apart from his great inventive gifts as what he nicely insists on calling a Sub-creator, a background as an authority on Anglo-Saxon language and literature. He is richly steeped in an enormous lore — but it is not that he has pillaged it for his story. Rather he has so profoundly penetrated the spirit of a genre that he has created a modern work in its mode.

Internal evidence indicates that *The Hobbit* was begun as a complete and self-sufficient tale. Somewhere in the stages of its growth, I believe the vision of the larger projection in the trilogy came upon him, and that the gathering darkness and gloom over the remnants of the West in the Third Age of Middle-earth grew from the darkness and threats looming over Western Christendom in the 1930's when *The Hobbit* was written. The trilogy was produced during and after the years of World War II, a circumstance which seems to support much of what I read into it.

The volumes of the trilogy appeared in 1954 and 1955, and were received with a critical acclaim so great as to carry in it the danger of faddism and an inevitable counter-reaction — a natural hazard of any work unique in its time that kindles a joy by its very freshness. The names of Spenser, Malory, and Ariosto[5] were immediately invoked in the search for comparisons.

---

5. Spenser, Malory, and Ariosto: all involved in "the making or glimpsing of Other-worlds," in Tolkien's words: Edmund Spenser, 16th century English poet; Sir Thomas Malory, 15th century English translator of French Arthurian romances; Lodovico Ariosto, early 16th century Italian poet; all wrote epic romances.

Tolkien is not admired by all. Naturally some eight or nine years later, in our succession of glutted publishing seasons, the books are no longer on everyone's tongue. This, together with an apparent total temperamental antipathy, led Philip Toynbee, in an article in the London *Observer* in the late summer of 1961, to make a rashly sweeping assumption.

> There was a time when the Hobbit fantasies of Professor Tolkien were being taken very seriously indeed by a great many distinguished literary figures. Mr. Auden is even reported to have claimed that these books were as good as "War and Peace"; Edwin Muir and many others were almost equally enthusiastic. I had a sense that one side or other must be mad, for it seemed to me that these books were dull, ill-written, whimsical and childish. And for me this had a reassuring outcome, for most of his more ardent supporters were soon beginning to sell out their shares in Professor Tolkien, and today those books have passed into a merciful oblivion.

As a small shareholder, I challenge Mr. Toynbee. His case against the books rests on four adjectives. It is clear that the hobbits are not his cup of tea, and he may rest on the unassailable privilege of personal taste. Still — "dull?" This is a judgment only possible for someone allergic to the basic genre. If you cannot or will not enter its realm then you could not truly encounter its proliferating invention and narrative pace. "Ill-written" is a more strange indictment. I am puzzled as to how he can look upon the writing of our time and say this, unless his basic resistance to the story's content has made him impervious to its expression. "Whimsical" is a more difficult and complex idea. Philip Toynbee gives the word a pejorative tone. But whimsical means so many things, and is in some respects so fitting to this tale that a more concrete bill of particulars needs to be offered. What kind of whimsy? How much of it in the proportions of the work? And what is bad about it? There are occasional touches of whimsicality that might not reach one reader, or might irritate another, but they are swallowed up in the scale and scope of the story. Mr. Toynbee seems to have equated "whimsical" with his final accusing word, "childish." Here he has elected the unfavorable suffix, where I would say "child*like*." The kingdom of wonder, like that of Heaven, is one scarcely to be entered except ye be as a little child. I am afraid that the critic here is too anxious to preserve his adult standing because the work lies within the reach of children and contains elements altogether mistakenly thought by some to be reserved exclusively for them.

Philip Toynbee blinds himself totally to the substance and weight of the profound elements in the story which I have demonstrated here. He might wish to challenge their worth, rejecting the conceptual structure of the work, but he either does not know it is there, or simply chooses to disregard it. Challenge would be a legitimate critical posture — lack of perception is not. His conclusion is, "today those books have passed into a merciful oblivion."

What Toynbee mistakes for oblivion is, instead, a constantly growing following. To continue his own metaphor, those of us who have held on to our shares feel them to be gilt-edged securities. The audience is certain to go on expanding, for it consists of enthusiasts, upon whom the work has made a lasting impression, who reread it, lend it, present it, and always publicize it by word of mouth — that greatest of all media for the dissemination of a book. Because this is not happening in Toynbee's own circle, he is unaware of it.

The English edition of Tolkien has been reprinting steadily from 1954 to 1959. The sale of *The Hobbit* is extremely large. *The Lord of the Rings* has sold over 35,000 sets in England alone. It is an expensive set of books, which means that an unusually high percentage of its readership is through libraries. The double advantage it has of being the kind of book that its enthusiasts want their children to know, and that children in general love, gives it a prospect enviable for any book. If it were to go out of print forthwith it would be certain of a long-continuing audience. Sir Stanley Unwin[6] expressed to me the opinion that the hobbit books were more likely to outlast his own time and his son's than anything else he had ever published, in a career that would include many of the foremost literary figures of our day. Tolkien, retired from Oxford, is at work on another saga creation of comparable scale, to be called *The Silmarillion.* Actually begun before *The Lord of the Rings,* it is a vast myth of the Creation and the Fall. It portrays the earlier ages and some of the history out of which *The Lord of the Rings* arises. There are many of us awaiting it eagerly.

I think it safe to say that whatever anyone might hold to be the flaws, idiosyncrasies, or excesses of the hobbit story, this extraordinary imaginative feat in the making of an Other-world, meaningfully related to our own, is likely to be one of the most tenacious works of fiction in this present age of Middle-earth. It gives joy, excitement, a lift of spirits, and it contains the kind of wisdom and insight which, if applied to the world we inhabit, might help our sore-beset race to hang on through the present shadows of modern Mordor into yet another age.

6. Sir Stanley Unwin: British publisher.

Questions

1. What distinction does Fuller make between *The Hobbit* and *The Lord of the Rings?* To what extent does the essayist appear to evaluate them comparatively?
2. What, as Fuller describes them, are the qualities and properties of the ring given to Frodo by Bilbo Baggins?
3. What relationships or correspondences does Fuller find between the modern world and the world created by Tolkien in *The Hobbit* and *The Lord of the Rings* trilogy?
4. What are Philip Toynbee's objections to the Tolkien books? How does Fuller deal with these objections?

Foreword to *Faulkner, Extra-Special, Double-Distilled*

Like the other essays in this section, "Faulkner, Extra-Special, Double-Distilled" is a work of personal reflection on a particular book or series. But while Golding explains how he has successfully undertaken a particular kind of story-telling in *Lord of the Flies,* and while Fuller explains to the reader why he appreciated the "Ring" books, Clifton Fadiman describes his own negative reaction to William Faulkner's famous *Absalom, Absalom.*

In one way, Fadiman appears to be taking on more of a task than do the other two literary essayists. There are far more impassioned defenders of Faulkner (and almost anything he has written) than there are of either Golding or Tolkien. To many astute readers and critics, *Absalom, Absalom* is in fact one of William Faulkner's masterpieces. In another way, of course, this essayist enjoys something of an advantage, since the reading audience is often titillated by the spectacle of attack on an established giant.

Mr. Fadiman published this essay in *The New Yorker* when *Absalom, Absalom* first appeared in 1940 and perhaps he no longer endorses all he writes in it . . . though, of course, it is likely enough that he does. This is not immediately relevant to the reader of essays, just as it is not immediately relevant whether you agree with his judgment, or for that matter, with the judgments of Golding and Fuller. We repeat, essays are personal statements; if they are clear, knowledgeable, and interesting, we may owe them our attention (to our profit). We never necessarily owe them our agreement.

Faulkner, Extra-Special, Double-Distilled

by Clifton Fadiman (1904-   )

At one point in "Absalom, Absalom!" William Faulkner makes Quentin Compson, who is telling the story, say to his auditor, "You can't understand it. You would have to be born there." This seems to me not merely one (or two) of the few comprehensible sentences in the entire novel, but also beyond a doubt the truest. At any rate, it is my particular Out. Not hailing from Mississippi (which Mr. Faulkner, in his best Greek-tragedy mood, calls "a land primed for fatality"), I figure I'm not required to understand Mr. Faulkner's novels. I should like to state, therefore, in all humility, that I do not comprehend why "Absalom, Absalom!" was written, what the non-Mississippian is supposed to get out of it, or, indeed, what it is all about. Nor do I understand why Mr. Faulkner writes the way he does. And, having gone so far, I may as well break down and state my conviction that Mr. Faulkner's latest work is the most consistently boring novel by a reputable writer to come my way during the last decade. Duty also bids me report the opinion of the publishers, who see it as his major work, "his most important and ambitious contribution to American literature."

One may sum up both substance and style by saying that every person in "Absalom, Absalom!" comes to no good end, and they all take a hell of a long time coming even that far. The story runs from 1807 to 1910, with the major action concentrated between 1833, when Thomas Sutpen appears in Jefferson, Mississippi, and 1869, when he is rather regretfully murdered by an old family retainer. Thomas Sutpen is a monomaniac, known familiarly to the other characters as The Demon. It is never quite clear what makes him so villainous, except that he has a habit of engaging in gouge-as-gouge-can fights with Negroes, and has the odd power of scaring ladies first into marrying him and then into conniption fits. However, he's the fellow you're supposed to shudder at, and if you understand Mr. Faulkner, you'll shudder. If you don't, I guess you just won't. The Demon's second wife, Ellen Coldfield, gives birth to two children, Henry and Judith, goes dotty, and dies after a while. Her younger sister, Rosa, is insulted by The Demon and also goes dotty, though it takes her much longer to die. The father of Rosa and Ellen goes nuts when the Civil War arrives, nails himself up in a garret, and perseveringly starves himself to death. Now, young Henry, upon finding out that his best friend, Charles Bon, engaged to be married to his sister Judith, is (a) his half-brother and (b) part Negro, also goes dotty in a complicated way, and finally shoots Charles dead. By the end of the story Henry has been reduced to straight, simple idiocy and is kept shut up in the attic. Judith, after some years passed in a vacant-eyed trance, passes out as a result of smallpox, a death so natural as to strike a rather jarring note. There is also Clytemnestra Sutpen, daughter of Thomas Sutpen (that's dat Ole Demon Sutpen) and a Negro slave. Clytie sets fire to herself and the idiot Henry, and so finishes her career in a fine blaze of pyromaniacal lunacy.

Then there are the Joneses. Wash Jones is a daft hanger-on of Ole Demon Sutpen. He has a granddaughter, Milly. Milly gives birth to a child (it's the Ole Demon's handiwork), Ole Demon insults her, Wash gets sore, shoots Milly, shoots the child, cuts Ole Demon in two with a scythe, and then commits suicide. The Joneses furnish the nearest thing to comic relief in the book. Now, if you'll think back a few lunatics or so, you will remember Charles Bon, preserved from incest and miscegenation by Henry Sutpen's fraternal bullet. Charles had an octoroon mistress, name and mental condition unrecorded, by whom he engendered the boy Charles Etienne. Charles Etienne, realizing that he is a few thirty-seconds Negro, promptly runs amuck. He dies rather dully, of smallpox, but not before he has begotten, with the assistance of a full-blooded Negress, a son Jim. Jim is the real McCoy, a legitimate idiot. (I mean one specifically so called by Mr. Faulkner.) At the end of the book, he is the only living descendant of the accursed Sutpens, which shows you what can happen to a family once they have committed themselves to Mr. Faulkner's tender care.

I think I've got them all in. There's a stray lunatic aunt here and there, but I'm no stickler for details. Come to think of it, there's the young man named Quentin Compson, whose grandfather had befriended Ole Demon Sutpen, and who tells the Sutpen saga to his college chum many years after all these murders, near-incests, fires, suicides, etc., occurred down on the

Sutpen farm in Old Mississipp'. Neither Quentin nor his roommate carries on what you would call normal conversations, but as there is no evidence of either of them having married his grandmother, or roasted his grandfather over a slow fire (under the impression that the latter was merely a mulatto first cousin with a trace of chimpanzee blood), I think they should be accepted as Mr. Faulkner's concession to the gray, tawdry, nonMississippian universe in which the rest of us poor folks live, if Mr. Faulkner can bring himself to call it living.

This cheerful little fable is filtered through the medium of a style peculiar to Mr. Faulkner. It seems peculiar to me, too. First, we have the Non-Stop or Life Sentence. The first two and a half pages of "Absalom, Absalom!" consist of seven sentences, composed of 123, 155, 9 (something wrong here), 146, 66, 93, and 135 words respectively. Average: 104. To penetrate Mr. Faulkner's sentences is like hacking your way through a jungle. The path closes up at once behind you, and in no time at all you find yourself entangled in a luxuriant mass of modifiers, qualifications, relative clauses, parenthetical phrases, interjected matter, recapitulations, and other indications of a Great Style. All of Mr. Faulkner's shuddery inventions pale in horrendousness before the mere notion of parsing him.

After the Life Sentence comes the Far Fetch, or Hypertrope.[1] Very few things in the book remain themselves. Each one reminds Mr. Faulkner of something else. "Her legs hung . . . clear of the floor with that air of impotent and static rage like children's feet." See it? No? Join me at the foot of the class, where you belong.

Then we have what may be called Anti-Narrative, a set of complex devices used to keep the story from being told. Mr. Faulkner is very clever at this. He gets quite an interesting effect, for example, by tearing the Sutpen chronicle into pieces, as if a mad child were to go to work on it with a pair of shears, and then having each of the jagged divisions narrated by a different personage: the author, Rosa, Quentin, Quentin's father, Quentin's grandfather. All these people do a neat job of mixing up the time sequences, delaying climaxes, confusing the reader, and otherwise enabling Mr. Faulkner to demonstrate that as a technician he has Joyce and Proust[2] punch-drunk. I should add that everybody talks the same language, a kind of Dixie Gongorism,[3] very formal, allusive, cryptic. Appar-

---

1. Hypertrope: Mr. Fadiman's coinage; "trope" means "figure of speech"; "hypertrophy" means "abnormal growth in complexity."
2. Joyce and Proust: James Joyce, Irish writer (1882-1941) and Marcel Proust, French writer (1871-1922), both master technicians and innovators in their respective languages and literatures.
3. Gongorism: from Luis de Góngoray Argote, 17th century Spanish poet, whose style was ornate and obscure.

ently the entire population of Jefferson, Mississippi, consists of rhetoricians who would blench at the sight of a simple declarative sentence. On the other hand, it is only fair to say that there are a score of pages (Rosa Coldfield's section of the narrative) full of remarkable prose poetry, beautiful in itself, if magnificently irrelevant.

Seriously, I do not know what to say of this book except that it seems to point to the final blowup of what was once a remarkable, if minor, talent. I imagine that many of my respected colleagues will see in it a tragic masterpiece, a great lament for the old dead South, a Sophoclean study of a doomed family. Perhaps they are right. For me, this is a penny dreadful[4] tricked up in fancy language and given a specious depth by the expert manipulation of a series of eccentric technical tricks. The characters have no magnitude and no meaning because they have no more reality than a mince-pie nightmare. If we are to have tales of violence and sadism, let the violence and sadism be drawn from the behavior of grownups, let them be more than the melodramatic gestures of childish maniacs. A study of defeat can have great tragic weight, but only if the defeated are akin to us, which these mumbling, muttering, frozen-faced Sutpens surely are not. I fail to see why we must go into a spasm of ecstatic shivering just because Mr. Faulkner is a clever hand at fitting up a literary asylum for the feebleminded. It takes more than these fake sepulchral voices, these synthetic incests, these Monk Lewis[5] allusions, to scare ordinary sober citizens. Ole Demon Sutpen is a mechanical bogeyman, and the rest of his gang are no better. The whole affair reminds one more of "The Tavern" than of Greek tragedy, and I have the horrid suspicion that if enough people were to say boo the entire structure of "Absalom, Absalom!" would disappear in smoke. Does anyone care to say boo?

---

4. penny dreadful: any cheap novel of violence and crime for its own sake.
5. Monk Lewis: Matthew Gregory Lewis, nicknamed Monk, English writer (1775-1818) who wrote a number of novels and stories filled with horrible happenings.

Questions

1. One of the techniques employed by Fadiman in writing this literary essay is to emphasize a particular "stance," a personality and position of himself as essayist on his subject. What is this "stance"? By what means does he present it? Have you any reason to believe that it is artificial . . . that the real Mr. Fadiman is not the Mr. Fadiman presented here? Discuss.
2. Early in the essay Fadiman undertakes to tell us in simple terms what happens in the plot of *Absalom, Absalom*. To what extent is that venture successful? How much do you know from reading the essay of what happens in the novel? To what extent is his summary for some other purpose than such enlightment?
3. What particular criticisms has Fadiman to make about Faulkner's *style* in *Absalom, Absalom?* What specifically does he have to say about the *form* or structure of the novel?
4. What inferences can you draw as to what Fadiman's reactions might be to the principles on which the essays of Golding and Fuller each rests?

General Discussion Questions

1. Grant that the three essays in this section might be classified in order of appearance under the labels: *explanation, appreciation,* and *attack*. What elements do the three still have in common? Yet how do the personal '"stances" suggested by the labels affect these common elements?
2. Of course you might follow the model of any one of these essays and write on a book with which you are familiar. Instead of this easy venture, try writing a single essay in which you describe how you would write about one book if you *were* going to treat it in each of the manners of Golding, Fuller, and Fadiman.

6

Education

> If a little knowledge is dangerous, where is the man who has so much as to be out of danger?
>
> THOMAS HENRY HUXLEY

Foreword to *New Eyes For Old*

Richard McKenna was born in American desert country, grew up something of a loner, and became what nowadays is called a high school "drop-out." He joined the Navy and served for twenty-two years in the Pacific. After World War II, in his forties, he left the Navy, with the rank of machinist's mate, entered the University of North Carolina and completed the four-year course for a B. A. degree. He married one of the University librarians, settled in Chapel Hill, and became a writer.

His first novel, *The Sand Pebbles,* hit the jackpot. It was the Harper Prize Novel, was serialized in the *Saturday Evening Post,* was a Book-of-the-Month Club selection, was sold for paperback publication, and for a motion picture. In 1964, when he had scarcely begun to develop his abilities in this new career, McKenna died abruptly of a heart attack. In 1967, a posthumous book appeared, *The Sons of Martha and Other Stories* (Harper & Row), containing the first third of his unfinished novel-in-progress, and also another valuable essay, "Journey with a Little Man," describing his development as a writer.

The essay "New Eyes for Old" was written in 1962 and delivered as a talk at the Faculty Club of the University of North Carolina. Here the essayist attempts to put before his audience a fascinating experience: that of a man whose excited hunger for learning drives him to find it when his time for formal education would appear to be long past. This essay will be discussed in a joint afterword with Louis B. Salomon's "How Impractical Are the Humanities?"

New Eyes For Old

by Richard McKenna (1913-1964)

For most of my life the word education has, to me, meant book learning. I understand well enough now the notion of character-formation contained in the word. But I must understand also that not one of the billions of people whom I am conveniently leaving out of this discussion has reached or will reach maturity without gaining that kind of education, no matter how deficient he may be in book learning. His whole society is his teacher and no one can play hooky from that school.

In my own formative years I never encountered the equivalent of Mark Hopkins;[1] I know him best even now as a tall, glassheaded structure in San Francisco within which almost anything might happen. Yet the other end of my log was by no means untenanted. Lumberjacks and miners, old cowboys and Indian fighters, Basque sheepherders and Mexican section hands all sat there. As a boy I was drawn to old men and to men of exotic origins. Later there were old sailors and beachcombers of a dozen nationalities and many Japanese and Chinese in Far Eastern seaports. I have forgotten most of their names. No single one of them stays in my

1. Mark Hopkins (1802-1887) was an American educator long associated with Williams College. The allusion to the "log" that follows the mention of his name derives from a remark by President James A. Garfield that his ideal of a college would be "a log in the woods with a student at one end and Mark Hopkins at the other." The "tall, glassheaded structure" is the well-known Mark Hopkins Hotel in San Francisco.

memory as a tremendously impressive individual. Yet I am convinced that in their aggregate they would outweigh Mark Hopkins. I think men's characters are more formed by their casual daily encounters with other ordinary people, as ball bearings are brought to perfect sphericity by randomly tumbling against each other in a barrel, than by any skilled institutional machine work.

No man has to go questing after a moral education. Some kind of moral education, and commonly the most useful kind, is going to be unavoidably thrust upon him. In a course in Anthropology here I was pleased and amused to learn the distinction anthropologists make between the overt and the covert value-systems of a culture. Their methodology is much older than the science which uses it. First, they ask a representative sample of the people what they would do in various hypothetical situations involving choice, and they make notes of the answers. Then, saying nothing, they observe what the people actually do when they are confronted with similar real situations, and they make a different set of notes. I think in our own culture that kind of anthropological fieldwork is perforce begun by every child at about the age of five. When he reaches a point, if ever, where he can be once more unconscious of the discrepancy, his moral education may be said to be complete. Insofar as our society has institutionalized means of anaesthetizing the pain caused by the split in our moral personality, perhaps one might after all speak of a quest for moral education. Since I never undertook that quest, I must disqualify myself from further remarks upon it. I will talk only about book learning.

My early book learning came to me as naturally as the seasons in the public school of the little town in which I grew up. I did well, but I think I studied primarily only to please my teachers. I seemed able to appease my curiosity about the nature of things simply by looking at the world around me without much discrimination. Quite early I began to find a special charm in an unpeopled world, the waste of lava rock and sagebrush desert surrounding my home. I was much alone in that desert and I never felt lonely. I was often more purely happy at such times than I think I have ever been since.

For many years I felt obliged to think ill of myself and hold those memories a guilty pleasure. Then I met Thoreau[2] and later, here at the University, I met William Wordsworth[3] and I have been relieved of that small pain.

When I was a very young man I went to China as a United States

---

2. Thoreau: Henry David Thoreau, American writer, amateur naturalist (1817-62).
3. William Wordsworth: English poet, great lover of nature (1770-1850).

sailor. I had no very keen regrets that my education, in the sense of supervised book learning had ended. My modest store was still greater than that of most of the men among whom I lived. I was busy learning military life and steam engineering without the mediation of books. I learned how to be alone on a ship at sea simply by leaning on the rail and looking out to the horizon. The sea yielded me the same curious pleasure that the desert had. I found that I could wander the streets and temple courtyards of Oriental cities much as I had once lingered in the desert. A screen of strangeness stood between me and the busy human living I observed. I could be tolerated as observer without being demanded to participate. So then it seemed to me that I could and often did participate in their lives with the same strange sympathy I knew how to feel toward forms in the desert. They would feel it too. Without a word of language in common, possibly by virtue of that, we could often exchange smiles or join in laughter or make a little game with children. No human interaction has ever seemed more real to me.

That was education, but it was not book learning. In connection with book learning, I want to recount just one memory of that other sort. It is a memory that often forced itself to my attention in the years when I was learning that I would have to attend a university.

There was a little bar, run by a Japanese man and his wife, in the Wanchai district of Hong Kong. It had only two tables and six or eight chairs and it was clean and neat and orderly beyond the average of such places. I never saw anything really rowdy go on there. The unique feature of the place was a large wire cage on a shelf at one side of the room. In the cage were four white rats.

The rats were the entertainers. They were lean and hollow of flank and their eyes were a fierce red. They would prowl the straw litter in the bottom of their cage and from eyes red with hatred they would watch the sailors drinking beer at the tables. When a customer passed near their cage they would press against the bars, squeaking faintly and hoping to get a nip at him.

The sailors relished the helpless hatred of the rats. Often a man would tease them with a finger through the bars. The rats would fly around inside their cage almost like birds, in a great squeaking rage, trying to catch the teasing finger. If the man kept it up long enough, one of the rats would usually catch his finger. Then we would all laugh while the mamasan came to unclamp the rat's jaw. The rats would not bite the mamasan.

When closing time was near, around midnight, the mamasan would put an egg into the cage. I think the rats were deliberately kept starved, because I never saw any water or any other food go into the cage. The egg made the best show of all. Instantly the rats would be at it. They knew there was food inside. But they were not able to break the egg. They would bite at it, but they could not open their jaws wide enough to get a purchase with their teeth. Their teeth would just slide off. They would all be frantic to get at it at once. The egg would disappear inside what looked like a white ball of interwoven rats. The ball of rats would roll slowly around the floor of the cage, with a constant muffled squeaking and a constant writhing pulsation of its surface.

After a while they would break the egg, and no one ever saw just how they did it. Almost always it took them half an hour or longer. On the rare occasions, when they broke it in a few minutes, the sailors felt cheated.

When the egg was broken, the rats would eat it. Afterward they would not fly at a man's finger with anything like their former enthusiasm. For that reason the mamasan seldom gave them their egg until about an hour before closing time.

I did not spend as much time in bars as this particular reminiscence might seem to indicate. If for no better reason, I simply could not afford it. I found time to read many books, but seldom with the sense of consciously seeking enlightenment. I felt that I was reading for entertainment. Books were hard to come by and I found entertainment in more than one unlikely volume. Ships had no libraries. Others had only a few western stories. I could not often afford to buy a new book. But in the thieves' market of Hong Kong I would sometimes find a few books for sale among the other junk. There was quite a good second-hand bookstore in Shanghai. And I soon learned that in the scores of cheap bookstores in Japanese cities there would usually be far back in the rear, a few secondhand books in English.

Thus I did not lack for books, although I had to read a weirdly varied lot of them. Finding them in my trips ashore, was one of my chief enjoyments. The only gripe I had was my trouble in keeping them once I had read them. Lockers for personal gear were designed to hold just the prescribed outfit of uniforms, provided that they were rolled or folded very compactly. There was no room for books. I would hide books away in crannies all over the engineering spaces the way a squirrel hides acorns. When I transferred to a new ship, I would just have to leave most of them. Now that I live ashore I will not relinquish any book and I have already had to move once to a larger house.

Very little of all that I read excited any sharply focused intellectual curiosity in me. An exception was the frequent references one encounters to Nietzsche's statement that God is dead. That seemed to me a pretty enormous thought. I knew a beachcomber in Guam, a towering old Englishman who was said to have once been a scholar at Oxford, and I asked him about it. He confirmed the statement, but he could not explain it. He gave me a worn copy of "Thus Spake Zarathustra,"[4] to which I clung through three transfers, but I never did succeed in understanding it. I did not really try very hard to understand it. I was content to read it as I did poetry, simply to enjoy the excitement and wonder it could arouse.

The turning point came for me with World War II, when I was twenty-eight years old. I had long intended to serve out my twenty years and retire in the Orient as many men did in those days. When I had to return to the States, with the uneasy conviction that those old days were gone forever, it was not pleasant. My future was suddenly all uncertain. I had let myself become too deeply aware of the common humanity I shared with Chinese and Japanese to force myself easily into the mental and emotional state proper to wartime. My ship came into San Francisco in March 1942 at the time when Americans of Japanese ancestry were being dispossessed and imprisoned. The mood of the people, as I sampled it in the places where I went ashore, seemed to me almost that of a lynch mob. A few unpleasant experiences quickly taught me that it was dangerous to speak my thoughts and possibly a sin even to think them. I had to relieve my feelings with drunken mutterings to which no one listened. I ached with self-contempt and a shattering sense of opposed loyalties which I could not reconcile. I was undergoing a genuine crisis of faith and I began to understand at last what Nietzsche was talking about.

I went all through the war in that state. Thinking back to it now, I am reminded of a verse from Kipling:

It is not learning, grace nor gear,
Nor easy meat and drink,
But bitter pinch of pain and fear
Which makes creation think.

For it was then for the first time in my life that I began to think, deliberately to think, as clearly and as coldly as I could. For the first time I began to read books in clear, conscious pursuit of the thought in them. I was no longer seeking entertainment only, but information and the hope of a way out of pain. I would no longer skip over a difficult passage after a brief puzzlement. I would worry at it for an hour and only leave it undigested, if I had to, with a sense of baffled defeat. I was gaining an entirely new conception of the nature of books and the way a man must read them.

The time was propitious for that change in my bent. The men around me were a cross-section of civilian America temporarily in uniform and

4. "Thus Spake Zarathustra" — long treatise on the doctrine of the superman by the German philosopher, Friedrich Wilhelm Nietzsche (1844-1900).

there was always someone with whom I could discuss ideas. With my modest share of wartime prosperity I could buy any book that I wanted. The paperbound armed forces editions began coming aboard ship. Few of them were froth and many were very solid books indeed. I had never before read so many books of worth and substance, one after another. And one of those armed forces paperbacks, I thought privately at the time, almost literally saved my life. Now I think a more accurate word would be salvaged.

That book was Thoreau's "Walden." I know it has long meant much to many people. But I doubt whether it has often happened that "Walden," or any other book, has come so providentially into the hands of a man so desperately in need of it. It showed me a middle way between trying to be a Nietzschean herd-man and trying to be a Nietzschean superman and failing at both. It not only gave me back my sense of personal worth and significance, but it established that sense more firmly in me than I had ever had since I had become a man. For the first time since childhood I knew again certainly that I had a right to exist, that I really did exist. I could read "Walden" with the emotional response proper to poetry and at the same time understand it rationally. The book seemed to me so radically subversive that I wondered how it could be permitted aboard any ship in wartime.

Well, I will not go on about "Walden." No doubt I have read many a better book when I was not so peculiarly ready to make a total response to it. Perhaps it is only possible to have a book-experience such as mine with "Walden" once in a lifetime and a great many other books can trigger and serve it. But for me it was "Walden," and from it I shaped a new future for myself. I planned to retire from the navy to a cabin in the Nevada desert, stock it with books, and live there as simply and richly as Thoreau had lived by Walden Pond. I began accumulating books for that purpose. I went on reading books with an even stronger will to know and to understand.

And now at last I come to something I hope may be of a genuine professional interest. My design was to gain a formal education, to acquaint myself with all areas of thought, simply by reading books. I kept at it year after year, I was very resolute about it, and in the end I had to acknowledge failure. I was forced to conclude that, for me at least, there was no substitute for a college education.

I met books that I could not read. I spent months on some of them. I suspected that the treasure they withheld from me was proportional in richness to the difficulty of getting at it. I would start over again and again, trying to pinpoint the precise page and then paragraph and finally the single word at which my comprehension began to fail. I would squint and scratch my head and chew my pencil. I would writhe my feet and ankles in among the rungs of my chair and sometimes I would grip a book hard enough to tear it. When the unconscious physical expression of my frustration reached that pitch I would become conscious of it and relax and laugh.

At those times I would be irresistibly reminded of the Hong Kong rats so frantic to break their egg. Once I had laughed at them and now by some trans-human justice I was in their predicament. No rats were present to laugh at me, so I laughed for them.

To begin with, I had thought a dictionary would be all the help I would need. I did not give up that notion easily. I don't know how many times I looked up the word ontology and grasped at it as futilely as the Hong Kong rats would bite at their egg. I used to go into bookstores and look up that word in every dictionary they had, vowing to buy the first one in which I could understand the definition. I never found such a dictionary.

What I did discover was the existence of a kind of vocabulary of a higher order, a fundamental outfit of ideas which the writers of the books I could not read assumed their readers to possess. The ideas would appear on the printed page only as a casual reference or a literary allusion, yet a full knowledge of them was necessary in order to follow the author's argument. I began to understand it as a kind of shorthand of thought which permitted the author to convey to the initiated clearly on one page what might require fifty pages to be made clear to my more limited comprehension. It was not enough to be literate in letters; one had also to be literate in ideas. When I had learned the hard way, I decided that I must attend a university before retiring to my desert Walden.

I knew that it would require several years but I expected it to save me a great deal of time in the long run. I meant to come out of it equipped to read and understand in a week books that might otherwise tantalize me for a month and evade me at the end of it. I meant to develop a metaphorical set of teeth and gape of jaw that could crack any egg in print.

Let me say that I found the University of North Carolina abundantly able to supply what I lacked. I can now read almost any book in English that I wish to read. In addition I can tell quite soon whether any particular book is to me worth reading. I no longer assume that anything difficult is good for me in direct proportion to its turgid impenetrability. I remember ruefully now certain almost worthless books into which I poured Herculean efforts in the old days. Those eggs were shell all the way to the center. Nothing like that can fool me now.

Thus I found the University of North Carolina able to supply what I knew I lacked. But I found here also other gains for which I had not bargained. I discovered other lacks of mine which I had not realized until I knew them being supplied me. And I now think those were the most important.

Each new thing I learned seemed to fit as a bridge between two things that I already knew. I had brought to the University a great, chaotic rat-hoard of miscellaneous information. As my studies progressed, I could appreciate how it was all being subtly rearranged into some kind of form and order. It was being made more useful and available to me and charged with renewed interest. It took me more than a year to understand clearly what was happening and then I learned the principle of the organizing scheme. I put to myself the problem of how to state in one sentence what I hoped to gain from the University. The answer was no longer that I wanted to learn how to read books. The new answer was itself a question: What is a man? The answer to that question was what I sought both from the University and from all the books I meant to read afterward.

From the moment I began my studies the appearance of the world began to alter for me. I mean that quite literally. I started the summer of 1953 with a course in physical geology. I was fascinated to learn the origin and history of land forms. The many slow processes that were shaping the face of the earth all around me, hitherto unknown and unnoticed, caught my eye everywhere I walked. There was a granite boulder in front of Battle Dorm that was a perfect example of spheroidal weathering. I passed it every morning and nodded to it. Sometimes, walking home up Franklin Street in a heavy rain, I would loiter for half an hour to watch part of the life history of a river valley in a rivulet cutting across the gravel sidewalk. In my mind I might be assisting at the creation of the Grand Canyon of the Colorado. Thus the simplest, most unregarded things took on a new and vital interest for me. It pleased me to see change everywhere in seeming permanence. Nothing is fixed. Nothing lasts forever. That was what those poetic symbols of permanence, the very rocks themselves, were saying in stony dumb-show. There is nothing like physical geology to stretch a man's time-sense out to the breaking point.

Almost every course I took added its own kind of increment to the process I am describing. I only have time here to mention a few of them. For instance, that same beginning summer I took English 21 and discovered "Paradise Lost." We were required to read only parts of it but I read it all and some parts repeatedly. Later, in a full semester course on Milton, "Paradise Lost" became and remains for me one of the finest approaches to the secret of What is a man? that I am ever likely to find in English. But at first encounter, even with the aid of the University, I could not crack that shell.

With my first fall semester I continued geology and started botany. Botany opened for me new windows on living things. Insensibly through the years my vision had been dulled by familiarity. I looked through a microscope into the fine structure of leaves and flowers and stems. I discovered the whole world of meaningful form and color, of beauty and wonder, that lies beyond the reach of natural human vision. The cumulative experience of it sharpened my natural vision to a finer discrimination than it had ever had. What had before been a mass of unregarded green all around me as I walked became a crowding of individual forms all beautifully interrelated and full of meaning. With natural vision we see only surfaces and infer solidity. In the strangest kind of way I felt that I was learning to see in three and even in four dimensions. In the same way that I could see solidity by inference, I began almost seeing down into the piled strata of the earth, into the busy micro-structure of leaves and flowers, back through time to the seed of a plant or the form of a hill a million years ago. That vision of the mind's eye fused unbidden with the natural vision and infused the whole with wonder. I thought how William Blake could see the world in a grain of sand and heaven in a wild flower and I suspected that I might have broken into that realm of poetic experience through a door not open to men until the last few generations.

By the time I knew surely that I was seeking the answer to What is a man? I was almost through with the physical sciences and well launched into the social sciences. Anthropology was another great breakthrough for me, this time through the screen of stereotyped familiarity hiding from me man and his works. It taught me new ways to look at familiar experiences. That was true of all that I learned in the University. In some measure, great or small, each course contributed to making all things new. It even made the past new. All of my memories cried out for reworking under a different light, one I had not known how to cast on them before. As I had begun by pestering Dr. White with questions about land forms remembered from my travels, so I ended by pestering Dr. Honigmann with my reminiscences of military life in China. For one term paper we were asked to write a brief anthropological description of our home towns. I had been so long gone from my home town that I wrote up a ship instead. I am now expanding that term paper into my second novel.

I never did expect to learn any final or complete answer to What is a man? I would almost instinctively have rejected any that was offered me. The nearest thing I have to an absolute conviction is the sense that man himself is neither final nor complete and never will be in all of linear time. I always knew that I would have to put together the most satisfactory master-answer that I could from my own insights and the partial answers

I could learn from other men and their books. I sought as many partial answers as I could get from science, because science is not shackled to absolutes. When some seemingly fundamental principle of science requires revision the scientists are free to revise it or scrap it without the necessity of burning large numbers of helpless people. Science leaves man room to grow and to go on discovering himself.

Such wisdom as I have gained tells me that it would be wise if I stopped talking at this point. But I feel obliged to comment, however briefly, on the current controversy over American education. I will not be as bold as Admiral Rickover.[5] I have already said as much as I know of my own knowledge: that there is no easy and perhaps no possible substitute for a university education to forward a man along the way I wanted to go in the world. I have affirmed that for me the University of North Carolina was all that I had expected and far more. But I could not help knowing that many of the youngsters in the classes I attended were not finding it anything like the enthralling experience it was to me. I observed only those few who chanced to sit near me in class and to whom I sometimes talked. I have not thought at all deeply about what I observed and what I have to convey is no more than an impression.

Overwhelmingly, my impression was of passiveness. Some of the boys seemed dutifully to sit there expecting the professors to give them an education much as they would expect a barber to give them a haircut. Others sat braced as grimly as they might in a dentist's chair. They were finding it unpleasant but they were going to sweat it out. Whatever the emotional tone, however, the attitude seemed predominantly passive. They were undergoing an education, not undertaking it.

What I am calling passiveness is a more subtle and deeply-founded quality than I can readily convey. Probably no adjuration from without nor anything less than the most desperate act of will from within can much relieve or change it. It seems to be a kind of fundamental life-attitude which colors all effort, no matter how great. I sometimes think it springs from a self-identity founded on thingness, on a sense of the self as object plastic to events which happen to it. There is possible another sense of the self as process, as continuous event, over which the man has a measure of control and for which he has a full measure of responsibility. Probably they are complementary aspects of something unstatable in words and too much one-sidedness either way might be regrettable. I just do not know enough to talk about it.

---

5. Admiral Hyman Rickover (b. 1900), physicist, frequently called "the father of the nuclear submarine," has been an outspoken critic of standards in American education.

Even the best and most eager of the students I observed, however, seemed not to be free of what I am calling passiveness. In some measure they were all doing what was expected of them and as a reward for it they expected to receive their education gift-wrapped in a piece of parchment at graduation. They seemed to lack the full pleasure of discovering their education as they went, of living it day by day, of being lured on by the continuous, exhilarating wonder of it, knowing no greater lure than that.

In my own thinking I link that passiveness with underdeveloped imagination. I am more pessimistic than Admiral Rickover. I fear it will not be enough no matter how expertly Johnny learns to read unless he also learns to read creatively. By reading creatively, or by listening creatively to a lecture, I mean getting up the same order of spiritual sweat as the writer or lecturer. I mean trying desperately to match him stride for stride instead of assuming that it is possible to get there by riding on his back. Those who can do it already will know what I mean; no amount of verbal amplification can make it clear to those trapped too much in passiveness.

I fear also that, increasingly these days, Johnny takes his bent toward passiveness and away from imagination long before he encounters the alphabet. His toys grow more elaborate and differentiated each year, restricting the freedom of his imagination. They tend to pre-program his play. His dolls and teddy bears and monsters are becoming animated and vocal with batteries and transistors. They no longer give him even the small pleasure and reassurance of winding up a spring. The toys are threatening to become more real than the children.

Yet if he did not have such toys, any normal child could make do with a stick and a tin pot and a bundle of rags transfigured to order for any play-occasion by the unhampered power of his developing imagination. In healthy measure his toys would be his own creations. His play-worlds would be his own creations with himself in command of them instead of subject to them. Soon enough anyway the adult thing-world would close in on him. But if he had been able to play creatively, he might find it easier later in life to read and to listen and to look at the world creatively.

What I have just said springs from too insufficient base of observation to be taken at all seriously. It is the most tentative of suggestions. I have already talked myself into a position where I may be accused of wanting to shoot Santa Claus and bring American children up like starving rats. So I had better pipe down and batten my hatches.

Questions

1. For the individual, what are the practical distinctions McKenna makes between "book learning" and "moral education"?
2. What have the Hong Kong rats to do with (1) the establishment of the essayist's person in the reader's consciousness; (2) depicting his motives for education; and (3) illustrating what the act of book learning was like for him?
3. The late Richard McKenna was a promising novelist and by temperament very much a literary man. Note, however, his interest in the various scientific subjects he pursued at the University of North Carolina. What does he indicate in this essay that he expects from science?
4. What particular changes in McKenna's views on education and in his life style does he record in "New Eyes for Old"?
5. All essays are personal; some are much more intensely so than others. What are the elements in this one which bring the general subject of education into focus on the unique Richard McKenna? Consider both matter and style.

Foreword to *How Impractical Are the Humanities?*

Professor Louis B. Salomon is a member of the Department of English, Brooklyn College. He is a novelist, as well as a scholar in American and 19th-century English literature. This essay deals with probably the most-debated question in modern education: whether the foremost emphasis should be placed upon the scientific, or the humanistic, studies. In part, it examines the question of how valid are the assumed distinctions between them. In the Afterword, it is compared to Richard McKenna's essay, "New Eyes for Old," in which some of the same questions are latent, yet which is a piece of writing of quite a different kind.

How Impractical Are The Humanities?

by Louis B. Salomon (1908-   )

I

While the average American undergraduate may not realize that his time and attention during his four college years have long been the disputed territory in a cold war between the three major educational powers, his teachers know it; even those who may not have taken an active part have been close enough to hear the blasts and counterblasts from spokesmen of the humanities, the natural sciences, and the social sciences.

The humanities, of course, have seen their once-mighty empire eaten away by nibbling attacks until they currently find themselves entrenched in a sort of Formosa-bastion[1] from which they now and then issue manifestoes full of faith and determination, and from which even their supposed enemy — the awesome combine of the natural and social sciences — has so far made no serious effort to dislodge them. Why have they been left so relatively unharried? Is the enemy craftily planning new Koreas and Indo Chinas? Is he massing his forces for a final engulfment? Or does he merely find the present position of the humanities so innocuous as to be worth no more than occasional harassment? If the defenders' heaviest artillery can fire nothing more telling than star-shells like "cultural her-

1. Formosa-bastion: Formosa (now called Taiwan) is an island off the southeast coast of China controlled by the Nationalist Republic of China, which established itself there when it was ousted from mainland China by the Communists in 1949; a bastion is a stronghold or fortress.

itage," "esthetic values," "appreciation of beauty," which sparkle against the night sky like Fourth of July rockets without setting anyone's shingles on fire, perhaps even the enemy can afford to watch and enjoy the fireworks. But when the scientists zero in on you with a salvo of "practicals," you know you've been hit.

While I, as a teacher of literature, stand committed to the Formosa-garrison of the humanities, I do not share the suspicion of some of my comrades-in-arms that the science-mainland harbors a sinister, grasping breed. If the mainland-dwellers regard us patronizingly instead of respecting us as equals, it may well be because we answer their blockbusters with skyrockets while our own heavy weapons rust unused in our arsenals. As for the outsider, who takes no interest in doctrinaire squabbling and demands to see "results," if all we have to show him is time-hallowed phrases, he can hardly fail to think of us as merely clinging to the shreds of our gentility instead of coming to slug it out in the forum with those who cry, "Look, folks, this culture stuff is all very well if you can afford it, but let me tell you some *facts* . . . some *useful* facts . . . some *practical* facts."

Now, aside from the fact that words like *practical, useful, factual,* lend themselves just as easily to incantatory mumbo-jumbo as do words like *cultural, esthetic,* and *beautiful* — just how impractical is this culture stuff, which in academic circles goes by the more genteel name of the humanities? First of all, what *are* the humanities?

II

When I use the term *humanities,* I do not automatically include all the subjects taught by departments of language, literature, philosophy, and fine arts. Insofar as a student takes a course purely for his financial or social advancement (e.g., Spanish, to qualify as a commercial attaché in Bolivia; philosophy, to get a job as a philosophy teacher; classical Greek drama, for "alertness credit" or so he may flabbergast his pseudo-intellectual friends at cocktail parties), such a student is engaged in vocational training no less than if he were boning up on metallurgy or soil chemistry. Some of the departments conventionally classed among the humanities distribute booklets ("Careers for English Majors," "Jobs for Fine Arts Majors," etc.) listing business and professional openings which their students are equipped to fill. These ventures serve an undeniably useful purpose, since a bachelor of arts graduates with the same appetite for porterhouse and penthouse as a bachelor of science or of laws — but they simply do not deal with the approach to experience which I regard as the distinguishing characteristic of the humanities.

It is a question not of subject-matter alone but of an attitude toward subject-matter. Any subject-matter, however frivolous or nonutilitarian it may seem (e.g., antique-collecting), may conceivably be put to use as the basis for a thriving business, if only through snob-appeal; and the most obviously practical skills of one time or place (say, papyrus-manufacture or falcon-breeding) may become the mere leisure hobby or museum curiosity of another society. I know at least one teacher of mathematics who insists that math should be classed as one of the humanities — surely not because it helps an engineer to figure how much concrete he needs for a bridge pier or an actuary to calculate an insurance premium. And one of the most eminent chemists of our time, Dr. James B. Conant, writes of science in terms that might well embarrass the defenders of the "practical":

> To my mind, the significance of the fabric of scientific theories that have been produced in the last three hundred and fifty years is the same as the significance of the art of the great periods in history, or the significance of the works of the musical composers. For most scientists, I think the justification of their work is to be found in the pure joy of its creativeness; the spirit which moves them is closely akin to the imaginative vision which inspires an artist.

III

By what sign, then, do you distinguish the humanities, if not from the kind of science Dr. Conant describes, at least from the kind most people have in mind when they say that we must train more scientists if we want to keep up with the Russians?

Basically, it is the difference between a parable and a case-history. In preparing a case-history, you look for every single fact you can discover about Mr. A——: when and where he was born, what he ate when he was a child, what he refused to eat, what his father did to him for refusing to eat it, etc. — just as a chemist notes every phenomenon that occurs in the course of a laboratory experiment, because any scrap of information, no matter how irrelevant it may seem at the moment, may, in conjunction with other data, not yet observed or not previously considered important, close a circuit which will throw a brilliant light on the whole subject under investigation. The more facts the psychiatrist or chemist observes about his topic, the better he is qualified to build a reliable hypothesis explaining what goes on in patient or test tube. This is science. Its business is to reduce experience as far as possible to finite quantities, which can be assessed by finite understandings, so that men and women may make plans — whether for a picnic or for a space-ship, for wangling a marriage proposal or a presidential nomination with the greatest probability of success. For this business it is the best method yet contrived or likely ever to be contrived.

The case-history, however, can never be complete; no matter how many facts you have recorded, there will always be some, minute or otherwise, which have escaped detection. Hence, any hypothesis about what makes Mr. A—— want to kill his grandmother is perpetually subject to revision or discard on the basis of new evidence or new tools for evaluating the old evidence. The Piltdown Man, the unsplittable atom, phlogiston, the "possession" theory of lunacy — the discredit that has befallen these and countless other once-proved truths testifies to the readiness of science to divest itself of intellectual garments as soon as they begin to look shabby. It was only with the development of that readiness that modern science began.

The humanities, on the other hand, speak characteristically in parables. The artist, unless he subscribes to the pursuit of an illusory "naturalism" (in other words, misguidedly tries to make himself a scientist), approaches his subject qualitatively rather than quantitatively. What he perceives to be the truth of his subject may seem mid-summer madness to many others, but one's impression of its truth or falseness bears no relation to the size of the subject or to the amount of time the artist has spent gathering data. It is unlikely that Rembrandt compiled an exhaustive dossier on a grizzled old man before painting his portrait, inconceivable that the painting would have seemed truer if he had. Imagine Shakespeare doing "research" on Hamlet, or any reader of *Hamlet* feeling the reality of the play suddenly shot to pieces if he should discover, say, that the Danish prince really had spent his freshman and sophomore years at Jena rather than at Wittenberg!

This has nothing to do with the "sublimity" of Shakespeare or Rembrandt *versus* the earthbound achievements of Edison or Pasteur, nor with daring anyone to think *Hamlet* a crashing bore and *The Night Watch* an unfortunate waste of good tent-material. I merely want to indicate a difference in kind, not in value, between the two methods. Mark Antony used the humanistic approach when he remarked of Brutus that the elements were "So mixed in him that Nature might stand up/And say to all the world, 'This was a man' "; the aim of the scientific approach would be to so disentangle those elements that they might be listed as: patriotism 32%, self-sacrifice 19%, antagonism to authority 28%, etc.

Now, a popular syllogism seems to run like this: since the two methods are very different, and the scientific method is unmistakably practical, the humanities must be impractical. Which is as much as to say: hammers and saws are very different; hammers are practical; therefore saws are impractical. Science and the humanities are also tools, devices to help mankind come to grips with the "facts" of life. But there is more than one order of facts (the facts of modern relativistic science, indeed, appear to the layman more topsy-turvy than those of *The Arabian Nights);* and just as there are more ways to kill a cat than stuffing it with cream, and more ways to roast a pig than burning down a house, so there are more ways for a man or woman to be a useful, happy citizen than operating a lathe or a public opinion poll, than running a bank or a gin-mill, than splitting atoms or common stocks. The humanities offer their way, just as the sciences offer theirs.

IV

Let us take a look as some of those ways.

First, the humanities and their discipline are vital to the defense of science itself: *i.e.*, to the liberty of scientists to continue their pursuit of truth. From what quarters have the efforts to muzzle scientists always come? Not from the humanists — secure in their conviction that no matter how carefully you measure the finite parts of reality the sum will never add up to 100%, they never fear that science will undermine the foundations of order and belief. Rather it has been from the supporters of a logical, codified set of doctrines that assigned everything, including God, its place in a system as definitive as the periodic table of elements. The quarrel of the church with Galileo, like the antagonism of totalitarian governments to free scientific speculation, was really a jurisdictional dispute: a union which had staked out its claim to sole possession of *the* answers to all questions saw its franchise threatened by anyone who suggested that even one of those answers might be wrong. Those who have followed the discipline of the humanities feel no such threat to their security; they know that whether the earth moves around the sun or the sun moves around the earth or both scramble about like a pair of mad jitterbugs in a crowded ballroom, there will always be questions which the mere observation of bodies in motion will never resolve. In so far as Galileo's view of terrestrial motion enables anyone to make life more comfortable, they will applaud it, just as they will applaud his law of the pendulum — yes, and take up a collection to buy him better lenses for his telescope and a more reliable chronometer than his pulse-beat. They are too keenly aware of the fallibility of all rational judgments to feel alarmed because one more time-honored doctrine goes out of fashion.

Less dangerous to science than the threat of interference from its enemies, but, I should think, equally embarrassing, must be the sort of adulation it receives from a public that has not only placed it on a pedestal but firmly chained it there. Clad, however unwillingly, in the Nessus-shirt[2] of omniscience, the "expert" cannot step down if he wants to; the public will impute his disclaimers not to modesty but to mere churlishness. It is the average layman, not the scientist, who ascribes witch-doctor powers to the man with the microscope or the electronic control-panel or even just the blackboard covered with eerie equations. It is the layman who has made the words "Science says . . ." the most potent ritual incantation of our time. Though he has watched theory after theory thrown into the discard, he never loses his childlike faith that *this* time science has settled the question once and for all.

As time goes by, in fact, your science-fan behaves more and more like a yokel eagerly shelling out his money for nostrums at a country fair. He takes his ulcer or his broken shin to the physician as trustingly as he takes his auto to the mechanic or his TV set to the repairman, his melancholy to the psychiatrist, his theological qualms to the pastor, his domestic squabbles to the marriage counselor, his employment difficulties to the personnel man, his educational frustrations to the education expert, or his quest for total security to the chairman of the appropriate Congressional committee. Saying: find the loose connection; devise the perfect curriculum; prescribe the miracle drug; rearrange our sex-life; set up the fool-proof security test — just don't ask us to do any thinking, and be sure the answer is RIGHT.

He is indeed like Tennyson's infant crying for the light, and with no language but a cry. But how many scientists take the trouble to tell the infant bluntly: "If you're after a sure thing, you may cry your little eyes out; the light is as far away as ever"? Meanwhile, you can learn the same bitter but necessary lesson simply by reading the stories of people who consulted the oracles of the gods — people who also wanted the sure thing, the error-free answer, to help them achieve their desire; but whether the answer came in such cryptic terms that human intelligence could not rightly interpret it, or whether it foretold a clear and explicit doom, it afforded mortals no vantage-grip on their own destiny, no way to beat the game.

If conscientious scientists sometimes find it embarrassing to be regarded as oracles even in their specialties, how much more annoying must

2. Nessus-shirt: poisoned garment which caused the death of Hercules in Greek mythology.

they find an attitude that so often runs perversely concomitant with this: namely, the view that the specialist, though infallible in his own field, has no competence whatever in any other. I, for one, were I a brilliant theoretical physicist, for instance, would find it quite humiliating to be told that I had no right to expect my views on politics, ethics, or religion even to be taken seriously in grown-up company. But I don't know where I'd go for comfort or support if not to literature. I can't think of a single "great book" that pictures a man of dazzling brilliance in one field as being a dolt in every other respect. Yet from earliest times myth-makers have recognized that the populace would so regard the expert: even as the strong-armed Trojans hauled the wooden horse through their streets, their companions were telling Cassandra to go back to her knitting.

Study of myth and literature, indeed, has often furnished scientists with useful instruments for tackling their own problems. Freud could presumably have isolated psychic complexes without the help of Ovid and Homer, but his choice of labels suggests his acknowledgment that the stories of Oedipus, Electra, and Narcissus carry the same significance as *The Interpretation of Dreams* and are a good deal more readable. Dr. Frederic Wertham based one of his most fascinating case-studies on the *Hamlet* story. Anthropologists find in a people's fables a far more quintessential clue to its values, taboos, and ideas than can be sifted out of its kitchen-middens or codes of law.

V

You don't have to be a scientist, however, to profit from the aid afforded by the materials of the humanities. In the long run, practical success or failure reflects the extent of your understanding of your fellow-man; hence, your ability to face his whims and vagaries without surprise, and perhaps even to anticipate them more often than not. The contributions of science to this end need no advertising — but it would be a sad waste of available materials if we overlook the wealth of insights furnished by literature and the arts to whoever examines them as closely as he would have to examine, say, Newton's *Principia*. Thus, if you want to study man as a political animal, you can learn as much from *Coriolanus* or *Civil Disobedience* as from a political science textbook; if you want to become a successful diplomat you can learn as much about a country's mores (and hence, how to avoid giving or taking unintended offense) by studying its truly popular literature than by memorizing its import-export balance sheets for the past half-century; if you want to see the disturbed personality in action you can learn as much from *King Lear* or *Crime and Punishment* as from a volume of case-histories; if you want to discover whether men have courage you can find the answer in the stories of Beowulf or Protesilaus as well as from a statistical summary of casualties and decorations in World War II. If you want a quick glimpse of the problems brought on by old age you can find it in the myth of Tithonus or of the Cumaean Sibyl, or in Swift's picture of the Struldbrugs, as well as in the almost brand-new science of geriatrics. If you want to scare yourself into fits over the prospects of a totalitarian society you can get as good results from a reading of *1984* as of the latest correspondent's book about Russia; and if you want to comfort yourself with a reminder of man's indomitable urge to assert himself as an individual you will find more encouragement in *Walden* than in the C.I.A. estimate of the strength of the underground behind the Iron Curtain.

Actually, most people use and respect the humanistic approach in practical affairs a good deal more than they realize. What for instance, do we mean when we call a man "a good judge of character"? Not, obviously, one who declines to form any judgment about a stranger until he has amassed and digested a "file" on him, and then limits his estimate to what the facts in that file prove beyond a reasonable doubt. This is the method of caution, of distrust — in a word, the method of science — but, while it has its advantages, it will hardly avail a juror confronted with two or more witnesses telling conflicting stories. Rather, we think of a person who may base his judgment of another on a single interview, perhaps a single act, a single gesture — and yet turn out to be right at least as consistently as any scientific character-evaluation would be.

Scientists show a sorry inconsistency when they reproach the Federal security system for using methods which it has learned (however clumsily) from them. Scientific character-analysis measures and dissects what I did yesterday, and the day before, and all my yesterdays, then tickets me, say, as one who can be trusted with "secret" secrets but not with "top-secret" secrets; thus it acts to bar me from making whatever contribution I might possibly make if I had access to all information, and still does not cushion the general dismay when I am discovered to have sold an enemy the information — still pretty valuable — that I do have. The "good judge of character" forms a total judgment of me as a trustworthy person or an untrustworthy one; he may be mistaken, but if right he stands to win bigger rewards, and if wrong will he be any wronger than the screening-system which gave clearance to Klaus Fuchs?

I don't mean that such character-divination occurs only in people who have read a lot of great books or heard a lot of great symphonies. It would be a denial of the very spirit of the humanities to assume that compulsory exposure to great works of art and philosophy will automatically produce a humane spirit in the people so exposed. You can no more guarantee to make people humane by giving humanities courses than you can guarantee to make them reverent by building churches. A student might quite possibly come away from *Don Quixote* with nothing but a feeling of pity that the old man lived too early to be straightened out by a psychiatric clinic; his reaction to the Bovary household might be that they demonstrate the need for competent marriage-counseling; he might shake his head over the tragedy of Sohrab and Rustum and point out that if they had carried identity cards the unfortunate duel might have been averted; or he may find in *Moby Dick* only a reason to congratulate himself that he lives in the day of radar navigation and electric harpoons. In such a case, to debate whether he should take three, six, or sixteen hours of humanities courses is about as meaningful as to debate whether to shoot him with a Colt or a Smith and Wesson.

I do mean that the spirit (not the mere letter) of the great books and symphonies constitutes a decidedly usable approach to experience: a compound of humility and boldness, an acceptance of the fact that absolute certainty can never be reached, together with a confidence that the sort of certainty which the human mind can attain through non-logical processes has a pragmatic value of its own. This, it seems to me, is the spirit that imbues all classical tragedy, and leads to that catharsis, that "calm of mind, all passion spent," which Americans pay their psychiatrists so many millions of dollars a year to induce. If this should mean that you can make as deep a dent in your Oedipus complex by an attentive, sympathetic study of *Oedipus Rex* as by spending the same amount of time on an analyst's couch (I suggest it only as a possibility), then surely no one would question the practicality of a good dose of Sophocles.

If furthermore it is true, as alleged, that aggression by individuals or by nations results largely from human beings' inner tensions and inhibitions, then perhaps the very survival of the species depends on an ever-widening submission to the discipline of the humanities. In these days when every newspaper blazons tidings of a heavier doom than ever Cassandra dreamed of, I do not recall having seen a single allegation that our present danger may be due to a poet, a painter, a philosopher, or a musician. If, on the other hand, we hear very few voices calling on the poets, painters, philosophers, and musicians to avert catastrophe, this does not necessarily mean that they are incapable of doing so. I believe they have an antitoxin which at best can save the human race from self-destruction, and at worst can help it meets its end not with a whimper but a bang; but their remedy, like any other, can function only if the patient uses it. Smallpox vaccination itself was once regarded as impractical, even by some scientists. Cotton Mather (not a scientist), for advocating it, had a bomb thrown through his window.

VI

Whether science is more practical than humanities or vice versa depends pretty much on what you're after — and on what you mean by science. In its brash youth, a century or more ago (though the great myths of *hybris* and its downfall — Lucifer, Adam and Eve, Prometheus, Faustus, the tower of Babel, etc. — were available then to scientists and humanist alike), ultimate comprehension through observation and logic seemed possible. Today, when scientists look beyond their test tubes, their microscopes, even their cyclotrons, and attempt to construct an epistemology, a philosophical tool for grasping not the atom or the avalanche but the whole nature of reality, they are apt to be found in attitudes of humility which stem directly *from* the startling advances in scientific thought of the past few decades. Modern scientific philosophy, as in these words of physicist P. W. Bridgman, winner of a Nobel Prize, sounds remarkably like mysticism:

> The structure of nature may eventually be such that our processes of thought do not correspond to it sufficiently to permit us to think about it all. . . . We are now approaching a bound beyond which we are forever estopped from pushing our inquiries not by the construction of the world, but by the construction of ourselves.

In other words, science, a Johnny-come-lately, has finally arrived where the humanities have been all along.

This unanimity of viewpoint, however, is to be found only at the top level of scientific theorizing, where, except for differences in vocabulary, it makes little difference whether a student reads Emerson or Einstein. As you go down from there, the road forks, and the farther you get from the top the more vital it becomes to choose your guide according to where you want to go. If you want to make synthetic diamonds or pulverize a city, look for the man in the technician's apron, not the one in the artist's smock. If you want to find out where to go from there, don't stir without at least hearing what the other fellow has to say.

Very recently I read a jocular but startling boast by the scientist in charge of General Electric's successful experiment in making synthetic diamonds (based in large measure, incidentally, on Professor Bridgman's studies). Explaining that his laboratory helpers are now able to reproduce the conditions of heat and pressure that would be found at greater and greater depths within the earth's torrid core, he proudly announced their goal: "To hell by 1956."

I, for one, have confidence in these fellows, and I would be the last one in the world to bet that they will not make it. But, if Dante doesn't happen to be around when they arrive, who will show them the way back?

Questions

1. This is obviously an argumentative essay. As such, it requires an identified position to oppose. What is this position? Is it "science"? Is it a certain attitude towards life? How does the essayist define and describe this opposition?
2. Granting that Dr. Salomon is an English professor, what else can you suppose about his point of view, his "stance", simply from your reading of the essay? What implications, for example, do you find in his figures of speech, his choice of references, his topical allusions, the title he chose?
3. What exactly does the essayist mean by "the humanities"? How does his meaning of the term tell us what he means by "practical" and "impractical"?
4. At what point and in what way does the author indicate what he believes to be the importance, and the extent of the importance, of the "humanities"?
5. In what ways, if any, do you feel the author has used, in his defense of the "humanities," heavier artillery (to use his metaphor) than "star-shells like 'cultural heritage,' 'esthetic values,' 'appreciation of beauty' "? In other words, how convincing do you find his argument?

Afterword to *New Eyes For Old* and *How Impractical Are the Humanities?*

"New Eyes For Old" and "How Impractical Are the Humanities?" make an interesting contrast. Having the common subject of education, and a shared attitude of measuring educational values in terms of *man*, they are nevertheless wholly unlike each other in method.

McKenna, essentially the novelist, the storyteller, approaches the subject through narrated personal experience. Though he reflects upon the meaning of his experiences, still the principal force of the essay comes from the concrete account of what he did and why he did it. His search for education is a powerful example of what is called in the jargon of educationists, "incentive," or in older and better terms, a hunger and thirst for knowledge and understanding. The irony of the age of universal public education is that many students come into school resentfully because it is required, forced upon them. Thus it is rare in our time to hear a man who had dropped out describe his craving for the education from which he had turned away and to see him take strikingly original steps to get that education years later.

Early in his essay, McKenna tells us the unusual story of the rats and the egg in the Hong Kong bar. It holds our attention simply as a happening, but later we see why McKenna has introduced it here. It is a vivid metaphor of his own hard struggle to break the shell enclosing some kinds of knowledge.

Turning to the Salomon essay we go from concrete narrative to an abstract intellectual exercise. Professor Salomon is *debating* a series of points. As a professional educator he is *arguing* about aspects of education. McKenna began by looking at institutionalized education from the outside; Salomon sees it from inside. His essay is a skirmish in a war with the educational establishment. This dispute, or at the least this uneasy and suspicious coexistence between the sciences and the humanities, has spread down from the university level under discussion here to the schools. You, reading these essays in this book, are involved in that debate.

Professor Salomon defends the humanities vigorously. Yet there is an irony about his argument. His title shows a defensive posture. He takes the classical view of education as something good in itself rather than as a means to some other end. Yet he goes on to argue that the humanizing, worthwhile-in-themselves fruits of education are *also* useful, or practical, in a variety of ways. You *can* earn a living from art. The pen sometimes *is* mightier than the sword. And "In the beginning was the word."

There is a story about Michael Faraday, the 19th-century English scientific genius, showing a small, unspectacular experiment to a visitor to his laboratory. The visitor, unimpressed, asked, "Of what use is it, Mr. Faraday?" The scientist asked in turn, "Of what use is a new-born child?" The Faraday story, McKenna's experience, Salomon's argument, if viewed perceptively, all point to the inextricable intermingling in knowledge, education, art, science, and the processes of living, of what is useful and what has value beyond immediate usefulness.

It would be profitable to compare by close reading Salomon's sections V and VI with the last eight paragraphs of McKenna's essay. You will see how these two pieces, so unlike in method, draw together in implicit value assumptions, and both suggest that the individual finally determines what he wants and gets in the way of education.

Foreword to *On the Classics*

Gilbert Keith Chesterton brought to every subject a fresh, personal view, giving such new insights into the familiar, and upsetting so many common assumptions, that he has been called the master of paradox. He was a novelist, biographer, critic, and poet, as well as one of the most engaging and prolific essayists.

On the Classics

by G. K. Chesterton (1874-1936)

In a moment of fine frenzy a young man has stood up and declared that "the study of Latin and Greek is not of much use in the battle of life," and gone on to demand that the young should be instructed chiefly in the science of Health — that is, in the facts and the functions of the body. The young man in question will be gratified to know that I, for one, consistently neglected to do any work at the school in which I was supposed to be learning Latin and Greek, though I am not sure that the mere fact of idleness and ignorance can be said to have armed and drilled me for the battle of life. But, when I consider such armour or armament, some faint memories come to me from the learning that I neglected. There flits across my mind the phrase *aes triplex*, and I remember how Stevenson used it for a title to his essay defending a cheerful contempt for medical fussing; and how he cited the example of Dr. Johnson, who dreaded death and yet disdained any vigilance against disease; and whose "heart, bound with triple brass, did not recoil before the prospect of twenty-seven individual cups of tea." It is, doubtless, terrible to think that Stevenson took his Stoical image of triple brass from a Latin poet; and still more terrible to think that Johnson would have approved of Stevenson for quoting the Latin poets. But though Stevenson and Johnson were superficially about as different as any two men could be in everything except in this weakness for traditional scholarship, I do not think that either of them can be said to have come off so badly in fighting the battle of life.

The trouble about always trying to preserve the health of the body is that it is so difficult to do it without destroying the health of the mind. Health is the most unhealthy of topics. Those who support such hygienic culture always profess to be very practical, and compare their own healthy materialism with the visionary futilities of everybody connected with the classics from Julius Caesar to Johnson. But, in fact, it is in practice that their practical ideal breaks down. There is no difficulty about talking and writing in general terms of the facts of nature, or what are commonly called the God-given functions of man. It is when people really begin to teach these things, as if they were algebra or geography, that they discover a surprising number of difficulties — not to say diseases. Upon this point of practical application I will only mention one example out of the statement referred to above. The young man in question frankly admits that he would dislike having to read a list of hideous malformations or foul diseases to an infant school or a row of staring babies. He says that this might, doubtless, be inadvisable, and lead to morbid fears and fancies. Anyhow, he disapproves of such physiology in the nursery; every man has a sane spot somewhere. But he goes on to say that big boys, presumably towards the end of their school career, should have learnt to balance and appreciate such knowledge; and it is such knowledge which they ought above all things to know.

Now it seems to me that the argument is very much the other way. The period when many boys, we might almost say most boys, are capable of morbidly misusing a medical knowledge is exactly the period at which he proposes to give it to them. I imagine it would do, in comparison, precious little harm to a child of five. If you talk to a child about an aortic aneurism, he will not be frightened; he will only be bored. If you talk to a boy of fifteen or sixteen about it, and give only a few fragmentary hints of what it is like, he will very probably come to the rapid conclusion that he has got one. All that is necessary is to have odd sensations round the heart; and digestion, or indigestion, will do that at any time of life, but rather specially at the time when digestion is tried by unripe apples or cob-nuts before lunch. Youth is a period when the wildest external carelessness often runs parallel to the most gloomy and concentrated internal cares. An enormous number of normal youths are quite abnormal for a time. Their imagination is working inwards, and on nothing more commonly than on imaginary maladies. To throw a medical encyclopaedia at the head of a young man in this condition is simply to provide him with a handbook of One Thousand Ways of Going Mad. A doctor once told me that even among medical students there is a perceptible proportion of this medical mania; and they have all the correcting elements of a special vocation, of a scientific atmosphere, and of more complete and therefore more balanced knowledge. Ordinary people receiving an ordinary smattering of such knowledge are very likely indeed to find that little knowledge a dangerous thing.

But the essential truth is that those who talk to us about facts have not faced the chief fact of all — and, indeed, the fact is also a paradox. Facts as facts do not always create a spirit of reality, because reality is a spirit. Facts by themselves can often feed the flame of madness, because sanity is a spirit. Consider the huge accumulations of detail piled up by men who have some crazy hobby of believing that Herodotus wrote Homer or that the Great Pyramid was a prophecy of the Great War. Consider the concrete circumstances and connected narratives that can often be given at vast lengths and in laborious detail by men who suffer from a delusion of being persecuted, or being disinherited, or being the rightful King of England. These men are maddened by material facts; they are lunatics not by their fancies but by having learned too many facts. What they lack is proportion: a thing as invisible as beauty, as inscrutable as God. And when we thus realize the real problem of morbidity and medicine we may begin to catch a far-off glimpse of something distant, but not quite so dispensable as we had supposed; and find ourselves once more faintly conscious of the presence of the case for Classical Education, so useless in the battle of life.

What culture does, or ought to do, is to give a health of the mind that is parallel to the health of the body. It is ultimately a matter of intellectual instincts that are almost like bodily instincts. A sane man knows when something would drive him mad, just as a man standing up knows at what angle he would fall down. He does not have to calculate the angle with a mathematical instrument, or fall flat on his nose forty times in a series of scientific experiments. The body, like the mind, knows its own equilibrium. But it knows it better than the mind; because the problem is simpler, and the physical instincts are less paralysed by false teaching. Now the true teaching, which strengthens and steadies the mind so that it knows and rejects madness at sight, has, in fact, come down to us very largely from the culture of those great languages in which were written the works of the last Stoics and the first Saints, the Greek Testament and the Roman Law.

To be of the company of such men, to have the mind filled with such words, to remember the tone of their orators or the gesture of their statues, is to feel a steadying power upon the spirit and a love of large spaces and large ideas, rather than of little lunacies and secrecies. It is something that understands at once modesty and dignity; something that is never servility and never pride. It is the power in the mind that can keep order among the virtues, often almost as dangerous as the vices. No catalogue of facts will give it; yet we can hear it instantly in the sound of some random Roman verse. That is why the great men I have named, so different in their natures, felt that the classics did count somehow in the battle of life. When

Johnson says, "The shepherd in Virgil became acquainted with love, and found him a native of the rocks," we know that his rage against Chesterfield will never go beyond a grand restraint; when Stevenson says, "We have heard perhaps too much of lesser matters. Here is the door, here is the open air. *Itur in antiquam silvam*,"[1] we know that for such a mind lunacies will always be lesser matters and sanity be like the open air.

---

1. *Itur . . . silvam:* "It leads into an ancient forest" (from Virgil's *Eclogues*).

Questions

1. What particular "science" does Chesterton choose to oppose with what particular department of the "humanities" in this essay? What grounds for his doing so – or for his choosing otherwise – can you imagine?
2. Chesterton starts his essay by quoting a young man who, "in a fine frenzy," used the term "the battle of life." How, and with what effect does the essayist continue to employ "the battle of life" cliché (explicitly or implicitly) as he proceeds with his argument?
3. How does Chesterton apparently intend his observation about the particular concern of young men with their supposed bodily ailments to reflect on the credibility of his opposition? On what does the success of his intention depend? To what extent is it successful in your case?
4. Why do you suppose that Chesterton chose Johnson and Stevenson as examples in this essay?
5. How, and with what effect, does Chesterton introduce the idea of insanity into the pattern of his argument?

General Discussion Questions

1. The essays in this section are obviously in favor of formal education – or systematic "book-learning." What common assumptions do they make about it? Any significant differences in their approaches?
2. These days, abounding books and articles call for various sorts of *reform* in education. Some contend that the materials of conventional education are too distant from the realities of current life. Others complain that education today is excessively directed at social order and discipline, rather than at learning. To what extent do you find the essays in this section concerned with educational reform? To what extent do you find them opposed to much change?

7

Childhood Remembered

Backward, turn backward, O Time, in your flight,
Make me a child again just for tonight!

ELIZABETH AKERS ALLEN

Foreword to *A Memory of Father, Brownsville,* and *Once More to the Lake*

The three essays in this section are in part recollections from childhood. We say "in part" because each goes beyond remembrance to implicit reflections on things as they are in the present perspectives of its author. Each is intensely personal, but each also is a statement about the conditions of life in twentieth-century America.

The black scholar and author, J. Saunders Redding, recalls in his essay (taken from his book, *No Day of Triumph*) something of what his life as an American, middle-class black child was like. Notice as you read him that the author and especially his father are unique individuals who live lives that are not completely definable by the stereotypes that blind us these days. They are not of the "ghetto," they do not react predictably within such worn labels as "militant" or "Uncle Tom." But the world Redding discloses through his black childhood is in some sense the world we all face (whatever our age or color) and his essay must inform us as well as move and interest us.

The idea of the "ghetto" is important in Alfred Kazin's "Brownsville." This eminent critic and editor shows us the shabby corner of New York City where he grew up, a section inhabited by poor, immigrant Jews who live there because, for economic, social, and even psychological reasons, they must live there until they are no longer poor or immigrant. At that point they leave eagerly, as Kazin himself did, but, like him, they cannot escape the continuing reality of Brownsville. This, too, is a condition of American life in general — a circumstance drawn from the past with its continuing implications for the present.

Finally, the American essayist E. B. White depicts in "Once More to the Lake" the effect of childhood experience from what might seem to be the most comfortable and conventional of perspectives, that of the white Anglo-Saxon, and relatively prosperous, Protestant. Here too, however, we see the particular and sensitive consciousness reacting at once uniquely and familiarly to a certain fraction of universal experience – nostalgia, nature, and the passage of time.

A Memory of Father

by J. Saunders Redding (1906-   )

As far back as I can remember, it was necessary for my father to eke out his small government salary by doing all sorts of odd jobs after his regular hours and on his vacations. He belonged to a waiters' association, and frequently he served at dinners, banquets, and parties from early evening until dawn. On these occasions he wore the swallow-tailed coat in which he had been married and the black broadcloth trousers which he had picked up at a secondhand shop. This outfit always amused us, for the trousers did not cover his ankles and his big feet spread beneath them in a truly monumental fashion. The coat had a greenish tinge and fitted across his thick shoulders like a harness. My mother had to sew up the shoulder seams after every use. My father cared little about the appearance of his clothes. "So long as they're clean, children," he used to say, when for reasons of pride we used to fidget with his tie, fold down his collars, and see to it that he was wearing a proper belt in his trousers. Our attentions amused him, and he would wink at our mother and say, "Girl, they've all got your side's pride."

Sometimes he would bring from these parties a satchel bulging with steaks, chicken, butter, rolls, and ice cream; and then we feasted — not because we ever went hungry, but because all this was extra and had to be eaten before it spoiled.

My father always took his annual vacation in the late summer or early fall, for then he could find employment among the farmers a few miles outside the city. He would contract to cut corn or harvest potatoes. Sometimes he stayed in the country, but when he did not, he was always back long after we were in bed and gone again before dawn. Often my brother and I, in the room next the bathroom, would wake up in the night and hear my father thrashing about in the tub and murmuring wearily to my mother, who always waited for him late in the night.

As I look back upon it now, I know that my father was driven by more than the necessity to provide a living for his family. Surrounded by whites both at home and at work, he was driven by an intangible something, a merciless, argus-eyed spiritual enemy that stalked his every movement and lurked in every corner. It goaded him every waking hour, but he could not get at it, though he felt it to be embodied in almost every white man he met. Because of this, he moved with defensive caution, calculating the effect of every action and every utterance upon his unseen enemy. Every day he won defensive victories, but every day the final victory seemed more impossible. He was up at dawn, painting the trim, repairing the roof, putting out ashes, shoveling snow from the sidewalk. In fifteen years he was never late for his work, and only once did he allow an illness to keep him home. His endurance was a thing of spirit.

But the other necessity was there too, the physical need to provide for a family that soon increased to seven. We were a problem. We helled through our clothes, and especially our shoes. My father mended our shoes with thick leather patches that balled clumsily on the soles. He trimmed our hair. When it seemed safe, he avoided doctors' bills by purging us with castor oil, plastering us with goose grease, and swathing us in flannel. I myself was often sick with ruinous colds that threatened a serious illness. I was almost constantly under the care of Dr. Elbert, who spent his time thumping my chest and giving me nauseating medicines. But no saving was too trifling, no economy too stringent for my father to make. Sometimes it was a joking matter. Our garbage pail seldom contained anything but vegetable parings and bones, for my mother, too, knew the value of a penny. Indeed, her thrift was generally more effective and yet less severe than my father's. She had a reasonableness in the matter which he lacked. Sometimes she raised objections — futilely, for instance, to my father's spending his vacation harvesting potatoes or cutting corn. She argued the point of his health, but my father's answer was always the same: "Work wouldn't hurt a man."

When I was fourteen or fifteen, I spent a Saturday on one of these corn-cutting expeditions with him. It was the last weekend of his two-weeks vacation, and he had been working on a farm eight miles out of the city. We left home before daylight and reached the farm just at dawn. It was a large farm, and only a part of it was under cultivation. Before we set to work, the farmer joined us. He was a buck-toothed post of a man, with a skin raw and peeled-looking by the sun. The corn field lay some distance from the house and the land sloped away gently to a flat, rocky strip beyond which the corn field rose abruptly. The brown corn stood in marching rows on the side of the hill. The field had not been cared for. High weeds tangled the rows.

"Well, you overstretched yourself, looks like," the farmer said, looking at the uncut corn on the hill.

My father took off his coat and drew his corn knife from the ground, where he had left it the evening before. I saw his jaw tighten like a fist.

"I'll need a knife for my boy here," he said. "We'll get it done. The weeds will hamper us some, but we'll get it done."

"Maybe you will at that," the farmer said, kicking in a mat of weeds. "Didn' have no time to do nothin' with this crop out here myself. Had another colored feller workin' for me, but he ups an' quits 'bout the time I needed him most. Wasn' much of a loss to me, I don't reckon. He sure was a lazy one. This your boy, hunh?"

"Yes," my father said. He looked past the man. "We'll get it done all right."

"I'm from Missouri," the farmer said.

When he came back with the long-bladed corn knife, he stood for a while and watched us work. I had never cut corn before but it was simply a matter of bending one's back and swinging one's blade as close to the roots as one could. When an armful of stalks was cut, we bound them together and stood them up to finish drying for fodder. The weeds were already giving us trouble. They were wet and tough with dew and they tied themselves around our ankles. But for a while the work did not seem hard to me. My father worked easily, making of bending, swinging, grasping one flowing, rhythmic action.

"The other colored feller sure was a lazy one," the farmer said after a while.

My father did not look up, but I watched the farmer spraddle down the hill and across the rocky gully.

"Damn him," my father said. "Damn him!" It was the only time I ever heard him curse. "Sure. That other colored fellow was lazy. Come on, son. Do you want him to think we're lazy too?"

It began to be hard work cutting uphill, and pretty soon the sun was at us. The weeds grabbed at our blades and we had to hack through them to get at the corn. My father cut very fast and determinedly, paying no attention to me. By nine o'clock my legs were rubbery with fatigue. I could hear my father working the dry, screeching corn somewhere ahead and to the left of me. He made an aspirant sound every time he swung his blade, and this came to me quite distinctly. "Hac. Hac. Hac." I seemed to be floating. My head felt enormously swollen. Bending to the corn, I could feel myself falling, but I had no strength to prevent it. I fell face down in the weeds, struggled up. Then suddenly the earth exploded in my face with blackening, sickening force.

When I came around again, my father was kneeling beside me. His face was gray and hard and his eyes and mouth were like Grandma Redding's. My nose was still bleeding a little and blood was on my shirt and smeared on the damp rag with which my father was stroking my face. He had stuck a twig under my upper lip.

"What's the matter, son?" my father asked. "Feel all right now?"

I spit out the twig. "I can't keep up."

"That's all right. I shouldn't have brought you." He was still stroking my face with the wet, blood-smeared rag. It was unpleasant. I smelled and tasted blood. He looked across the gully toward the house that stood naked and ugly in the broad stroke of the sun. "I'll give that farmer a piece of my mind yet," he said.

"When he said, 'I'm from Missouri,' that's slang," I said. "People say I'm from Missouri when they don't believe you can do something. They say, 'Show me'."

"I'll show him," my father said.

After lunch I felt strong enough to work again, but my father made me lie under the lip of the hill out of the sun, and all afternoon I listened to the sound of his working moving farther and farther away from me. He finished the field just before dark.

Questions

1. What are the reactions of the children, the mother, and the father himself towards the outfit which the father wears when he moonlights as a waiter? Why does Redding begin with this particular memory?
2. How do the details of Redding's memory of what the farmer said and the appearance of his farm depict the man himself?
3. To what characteristics of his father does Redding direct our attention in this essay? How does the essayist use himself, as a boy, and the farmer to develop his depiction of this admirable and tormented man?
4. Redding knows in retrospect that his father "was driven by more than the necessity to provide a living for his family, was driven by . . . a merciless

argus-eyed spiritual enemy." Is this enemy simply the white man, perhaps as represented by the farmer? Why does Redding also call it "an intangible something"?

5. While the father is the central figure of the essay, and what he does is the central event, neither is the end of the writing itself. What does Redding really want to tell us?

Brownsville

by Alfred Kazin (1915-   )

Every time I go back to Brownsville[1] it is as if I had never been away. From the moment I step off the train at Rockaway Avenue and smell the leak out of the men's room, then the pickles from the stand just below the subway steps, an instant rage comes over me, mixed with dread and some unexpected tenderness. It is over ten years since I left to live in "the city" — everything just out of Brownsville was always "the city." Actually I did not go very far; it was enough that I could leave Brownsville. Yet as I walk those familiarly choked streets at dusk and see the old women sitting in front of the tenements, past and present become each other's faces; I am back where I began.

It is always the old women in their shapeless flowered housedresses and ritual wigs I see first; they give Brownsville back to me. In their soft dumpy bodies and the unbudging way they occupy the tenement stoops, their hands blankly folded in each other as if they had been sitting on these stoops from the beginning of time, I sense again the old foreboding that all my life would be like this. *Urime Yidn.*[2] *Alfred, what do you want of us poor Jews?*

The early hopelessness burns at my face like fog the minute I get off the subway. I can smell it in the air as soon as I walk down Rockaway

1. Brownsville: section of Brooklyn, N. Y.
2. *Urime Yidn:* poor, unfortunate Jews (Yiddish).

Avenue. It hangs over the Negro tenements in the shadows of the El-darkened[3] street, the torn and flapping canvas sign still listing the boys who went to war, the stagnant wells of candy stores and pool parlors, the torches flaring at dusk over the vegetable stands and pushcarts, the neon-blazing fronts of liquor stores, the piles of *Halvah*[4] and chocolate kisses in the windows of the candy stores next to the *News* and *Mirror,* the dusty old drugstores where urns of rose and pink and blue colored water still swing from chains, and where next door Mr. A.'s sign still tells anyone walking down Rockaway Avenue that he has pants to fit any color suit. It is in the faces of the kids, who before they are ten have learned that Brownsville is a nursery of tough guys, and walk with a springy caution, like boxers approaching the center of the ring. Even the Negroes who have moved into the earliest slums deserted by the Jews along Rockaway Avenue have been infected with the damp sadness of the place, and slouch along the railings of their wormy wooden houses like animals in a cage. The Jewish district drains out here, but eddies back again on the next street; *they* have no connection with it. A Gypsy who lives in one of the empty stores is being reproached by a tipsy Negro in a sweater and new pearl-gray fedora who has paid her to tell his fortune. *You promis' me, didnja? Didnja promis', you lousy f . . .?* His voice fills the street with the empty rattle of a wooden wheel turning over and over.

The smell of damp out of the rotten hallways accompanies me all the way to Blake Avenue. Everything seems so small here now, old, mashed-in, more rundown even than I remember it, but with a heartbreaking familiarity at each door that makes me wonder if I can take in anything new, so strongly do I feel in Brownsville that I am walking in my sleep. I keep bumping awake at harsh intervals, then fall back into my trance again. In the last crazy afternoon light the neons over the delicatessens bathe all their wares in a cosmetic smile, but strip the street of every personal shadow and concealment. The torches over the pushcarts hold in a single breath of yellow flame the acid smell of half-sour pickles and herrings floating in their briny barrels. There is a dry rattle of loose newspaper sheets around the cracked stretched skins of the "chiney" oranges. Through the kitchen windows along every ground floor I can already see the containers of milk, the fresh round poppy-seed evening rolls. Time for supper, time to go home. The sudden uprooting I always feel at dusk cries out in a crash of heavy wooden boxes; a dozen crates of old seltzer bottles come

3. El-darkened: "El" refers to the huge structure of the elevated train tracks running down the middle of, in this case, Rockaway Avenue.
4. Halvah: candy; sesame seeds in honey.

rattling up from the cellar on an iron roller. Seltzer is still the poor Jew's dinner wine, a mild luxury infinitely prized above the water out of the faucets; there can be few families in Brownsville that still do not take a case of it every week. It sparkles, it can be mixed with sweet jellies and syrups; besides, the water in Europe was often unclean.

In a laundry window off Dumont Avenue a printed poster with a Star of David at the head proclaims solidarity with *"our magnificent brothers in Palestine."* A fiery breath of victory has come to Brownsville at last! Another poster calls for a demonstration against evictions. It is signed by one of those many subsidiaries of the Communist Party that I could detect if it were wrapped in twenty layers of disguise. "WORKERS AND PEOPLE OF BROWNSVILLE . . . !" Looking at that long-endured word *Landlord,* I feel myself quickening to the old battle cries.

And now I go over the whole route. Brownsville is that road which every other road in my life has had to cross.

When I was a child I thought we lived at the end of the world. It was the eternity of the subway ride into the city that first gave me this idea. It took a long time getting to "New York"; it seemed longer getting back. Even the I.R.T.[5] got tired by the time it came to us, and ran up into the open for a breath of air before it got locked into its terminus at New Lots. As the train left the tunnel to rattle along the elevated tracks, I felt I was being jostled on a camel past the last way stations in the desert. Oh that ride from New York! Light came only at Sutter Avenue. First across the many stations of the Gentiles to the East River. Then clear across Brooklyn, almost to the brink of the ocean all our fathers crossed. All those first stations in Brooklyn — Clark, Borough Hall, Hoyt, Nevins, the junction of the East and West Side express lines — told me only that I was on the last leg home, though there was always a stirring of my heart at Hoyt, where the grimy subway platform was suddenly enlivened by Abraham and Straus's windows of ladies' wear. Atlantic Avenue was vaguely exciting, a crossroads, the Long Island railroad; I never saw a soul get in or out at Bergen Street; the Grand Army Plaza, with its great empty caverns smoky with dust and chewing-gum wrappers, meant Prospect Park and that stone path beside a meadow where as a child I ran off from my father one summer twilight just in time to see the lamplighter go up the path lighting from the end of his pole each gas mantle suddenly flaring within its corolla of pleated paper — then, that summer I first strayed off the block for myself, the steps leading up from the boathouse, the long stalks of grass wound between the steps thick with the dust and smell of summer — then, that

5. I.R.T.: Independent Rapid Transit, one of the subway lines of New York City.

great summer at sixteen, my discovery in the Brooklyn Museum of Albert Pinkham Ryder's cracked oily fishing boats drifting under the moon. Franklin Avenue was where the Jews began — but all middle-class Jews, *alrightniks,* making out "all right" in the New World, they were still Gentiles to me as they went out into the wide and tree-lined Eastern Parkway. For us the journey went on and on — past Nostrand, past Kingston, past Utica, and only then out into the open at Sutter, overlooking Lincoln Terrace Park, "Tickle-Her" Park, the zoo of our adolescence, through which no girl could pass on a summer evening without its being understood forever after that she was "in"; past the rickety "two-family" private houses built in the fever of Brownsville's last real-estate boom; and then into Brownsville itself — Saratoga, Rockaway, and home. For those who lived still beyond, in East New York, there was Junius, there was Pennsylvania, there was Van Siclen, and so at last into New Lots, where the city goes back to the marsh, and even the subway ends.

Yet it was not just the long pent-up subway ride that led me to think of Brownsville as the margin of the city, the last place, the car barns where they locked up the subway and the trolley cars at night. There were always raw patches of unused city land all around us filled with "monument works" where they cut and stored tombstones, as there were still on our street farmhouses and the remains of old cobbled driveways down which chickens came squealing into our punchball games — but most of it dead land, neither country nor city, with that look of prairie waste I have so often seen on my walks along the fringes of American cities near the freight yards. We were nearer the ocean than the city, but our front on the ocean was Canarsie — in those days the great refuse dump through which I made my first and grimmest walks into the city — a place so celebrated in New York vaudeville houses for its squalor that the very sound of the word was always good for a laugh. CAN-NARR-SIE! They fell into the aisles. But that was the way to the ocean we always took summer evenings — through silent streets of old broken houses whose smoky red Victorian fronts looked as if the paint had clotted like blood and had then been mixed with soot — past infinite weedy lots, the smell of freshly cut boards in the lumber yards, the junk yards, the marshland eating the pavement, the truck farms, the bungalows that had lost a window or a door as they tottered on their poles against the damp and the ocean winds. The place as I have it in my mind still reeks of the fires burning in the refuse dumps. Farms that had once been the outposts of settlers in Revolutionary days had crumbled and sunk like wet sand. Canarsie was where they open the sluice gates to let the city's muck out into the ocean. But at the end was the roar of the Atlantic and the summer house where we stood outside watching through lattices the sports being served with great pitchers of beer foaming onto the red-checked tablecloths. Summer, my summer! Summer!

We were of the city, but somehow not in it. Whenever I went off on my favorite walk to Highland Park in the "American" district to the north, on the border of Queens, and climbed the hill to the old reservoir from which I could look straight across to the skyscrapers of Manhattan, I saw New York as a foreign city. There, brilliant and unreal, the city had its life, as Brownsville was ours. That the two were joined in me I never knew then — not even on those glorious summer nights of my last weeks in high school when, with what an ache, I would come back into Brownsville along Liberty Avenue, and, as soon as I could see blocks ahead of me the Labor Lyceum, the malted milk and Fatima signs over the candy stores, the old women in their housedresses sitting in front of the tenements like priestesses of an ancient cult, knew I was home.

We were the end of the line. We were the children of the immigrants who had camped at the city's back door, in New York's rawest, remotest, cheapest ghetto, enclosed on one side by the Canarsie flats and on the other by the hallowed middle-class districts that showed the way to New York. "New York" was what we put last on our address, but first in thinking of the others around us. *They* were New York, the Gentiles, America; we were Brownsville — *Brunzvil,* as the old folks said — the dust of the earth to all Jews with money, and notoriously a place that measured all success by our skill in getting away from it. So that when poor Jews left, *even* Negroes, as we said, found it easy to settle on the margins of Brownsville, and with the coming of spring, bands of Gypsies, who would rent empty stores, hang their rugs around them like a desert tent, and bring a dusty and faintly sinister air of carnival into our neighborhood.

Questions

1. "Rage, dread, and some unexpected tenderness" are what Kazin writes are his reactions to going back to Brownsville. What does he suggest are specific sources for these triggered emotions as he describes what he sees, smells, and hears?
2. Time, perhaps *the* inexorable fact of mortal life, is also one of the ungraspable mysteries of our existence. To what extent is it evident in the essay that both the essayist and Brownsville *have* changed in ten years? In what sense is it none the less true that when he returns, Kazin is back where he began?
3. What distinctions among Kazin's brief pictures of ethnic minorities, Jews, Negroes, and Gypsies, do you find in this essay?
4. Besides his own origins and childhood, what does Brownsville apparently represent to Kazin as a general circumstance in modern American life?

Once More to the Lake

by E. B. White (1899-   )

One summer, along about 1904, my father rented a camp on a lake in Maine and took us all there for the month of August. We all got ringworm from some kittens and had to rub Pond's Extract on our arms and legs night and morning, and my father rolled over in a canoe with all his clothes on; but outside of that the vacation was a success and from then on none of us ever thought there was any place in the world like that lake in Maine. We returned summer after summer — always on August 1st for one month. I have since become a salt-water man, but sometimes in summer there are days when the restlessness of the tides and the fearful cold of the sea water and the incessant wind which blows across the afternoon and into the evening make me wish for the placidity of a lake in the woods. A few weeks ago this feeling got so strong I bought myself a couple of bass hooks and a spinner and returned to the lake where we used to go, for a week's fishing and to revisit old haunts.

I took along my son, who had never had any fresh water up his nose and who had seen lily pads only from train windows. On the journey over to the lake I began to wonder what it would be like. I wondered how time would have marred this unique, this holy spot — the coves and streams, the hills that the sun set behind, the camps and the paths behind the camps. I was sure that the tarred road would have found it out and I wondered in what other ways it would be desolated. It is strange how much you can remember about places like that once you allow your mind to return into the grooves which lead back. You remember one thing, and that suddenly reminds you of another thing. I guess I remembered clearest of all the early mornings, when the lake was cool and motionless, remembered how the bedroom smelled of the lumber it was made of and of the wet woods whose scent entered through the screen. The partitions in the camp were thin and did not extend clear to the top of the rooms, and as I was always the first up I would dress softly so as not to wake the others, and sneak out into the sweet outdoors and start out in the canoe, keeping close along the shore in the long shadows of the pines. I remembered being very careful never to rub my paddle against the gunwale for fear of disturbing the stillness of the cathedral.

The lake had never been what you would call a wild lake. There were cottages sprinkled around the shores, and it was in farming country although the shores of the lake were quite heavily wooded. Some of the cottages were owned by nearby farmers, and you would live at the shore and eat your meals at the farmhouse. That's what our family did. But although it wasn't wild, it was a fairly large and undisturbed lake and there were places in it which, to a child at least, seemed infinitely remote and primeval.

I was right about the tar: it led to within half a mile of the shore. But when I got back there, with my boy, and we settled into a camp near a farmhouse and into the kind of summertime I had known, I could tell that it was going to be pretty much the same as it had been before — I knew it, lying in bed the first morning, smelling the bedroom, and hearing the boy sneak quietly out and go off along the shore in a boat. I began to sustain the illusion that he was I, and therefore, by simple transposition, that I was my father. This sensation persisted, kept cropping up all the time we were there. It was not an entirely new feeling, but in this setting it grew much stronger. I seemed to be living a dual existence. I would be in the middle of some simple act, I would be picking up a bait box or laying down a table fork, or I would be saying something, and suddenly it would be not I but my father who was saying the words or making the gesture. It gave me a creepy sensation.

We went fishing the first morning. I felt the same damp moss covering the worms in the bait can, and saw the dragonfly alight on the top of my rod as it hovered a few inches from the surface of the water. It was the arrival of this fly that convinced me beyond any doubt that everything was as it always had been, that the years were a mirage and there had been no years. The small waves were the same, chucking the rowboat under the chin as we fished at anchor, and the boat was the same boat, the same color green and the ribs broken in the same places, and under the floor-boards the same fresh-water leavings and débris — the dead helgramite,[1] the wisps of moss, the rusty discarded fishhook, the dried blood from yesterday's catch. We stared silently at the tips of our rods, at the dragonflies that came and went. I lowered the tip of mine into the water, tentatively, pensively dislodging the fly, which darted two feet away, poised, darted two feet back, and came to rest again a little farther up the rod. There had been no years between the ducking of this dragonfly and the other one — the one that was part of memory. I looked at the boy, who was silently watching his fly, and it was my hands that held his rod, my eyes watching. I felt dizzy and didn't know which rod I was at the end of.

We caught two bass, hauling them in briskly as though they were mackerel, pulling them over the side of the boat in a businesslike manner without any landing net, and stunning them with a blow on the back of the head. When we got back for a swim before lunch, the lake was exactly where we had left it, the same number of inches from the dock, and there was only the merest suggestion of a breeze. This seemed an utterly enchanted sea, this lake you could leave to its own devices for a few hours and come back to, and find that it had not stirred, this constant and trustworthy body of water. In the shallows, the dark, watersoaked sticks and twigs, smooth and old, were undulating in clusters on the bottom against the clean ribbed sand, and the track of the mussel was plain. A school of minnows swam by, each minnow with its small individual shadow, doubling the attendance, so clear and sharp in the sunlight. Some of the other campers were in swimming, along the shore, one of them with a cake of soap, and the water felt thin and clear and unsubstantial. Over the years there had been this person with the cake of soap, this cultist, and here he was. There had been no years.

Up to the farmhouse to dinner through the teeming, dusty field, the road under our sneakers was only a two-track road. The middle track was missing, the one with the marks of the hooves and the splotches of dried, flaky manure. There had always been three tracks to choose from in choosing which track to walk in; now the choice was narrowed down to two. For a moment I missed terribly the middle alternative. But the way led past the tennis court, and something about the way it lay there in the sun reassured me; the tape had loosened along the backline, the alleys were green with plantains and other weeds, and the net (installed in June and removed in September) sagged in the dry noon, and the whole place steamed

1. helgramite: more commonly spelled "hellgrammite," the larva of the dobson fly, used for bait.

with midday heat and hunger and emptiness. There was a choice of pie for dessert, and one was blueberry and one was apple, and the waitresses were the same country girls, there having been no passage of time, only the illusion of it as in a dropped curtain — the waitresses were still fifteen; their hair had been washed, that was the only difference — they had been to the movies and seen the pretty girls with the clean hair.

Summertime, oh summertime, pattern of life indelible, the fadeproof lake, the woods unshatterable, the pasture with the sweetfern and the juniper forever and ever, summer without end; this was the background, and the life along the shore was the design, the cottages with their innocent and tranquil design, their tiny docks with the flagpole and the American flag floating against the white clouds in the blue sky, the little paths over the roots of the trees leading from camp to camp and the paths leading back to the outhouses and the can of lime for sprinkling, and at the souvenir counters at the store the miniature birch-bark canoes and the post cards that showed things looking a little better than they looked. This was the American family at play, escaping the city heat, wondering whether the newcomers in the camp at the head of the cove were "common" or "nice," wondering whether it was true that the people who drove up for Sunday dinner at the farmhouse were turned away because there wasn't enough chicken.

It seemed to me, as I kept remembering all this, that those times and those summers had been infinitely precious and worth saving. There had been jollity and peace and goodness. The arriving (at the beginning of August) had been so big a business in itself, at the railway station the farm wagon drawn up, the first smell of the pine-laden air, the first glimpse of the smiling farmer, and the great importance of the trunks and your father's enormous authority in such matters, and the feel of the wagon under you for the long ten-mile haul, and at the top of the last long hill catching the first view of the lake after eleven months of not seeing this cherished body of water. The shouts and cries of the other campers when they saw you, and the trunks to be unpacked, to give up their rich burden. (Arriving was less exciting nowadays, when you sneaked up in your car and parked it under a tree near the camp and took out the bags and in five minutes it was all over, no fuss, no loud wonderful fuss about trunks.)

Peace and goodness and jollity. The only thing that was wrong now, really, was the sound of the place, an unfamiliar nervous sound of the outboard motors. This was the note that jarred, the one thing that would somtimes break the illusion and set the years moving. In those other summertimes all motors were inboard; and when they were at a little distance, the noise they made was a sedative, an ingredient of summer sleep. They were one-cylinder and two-cylinder engines, and some were make-and-break and some were jump-spark, but they all made a sleepy sound across the lake. The one-lungers throbbed and fluttered, and the twin-cylinder ones purred and purred, and that was a quiet sound too. But now the campers all had outboards. In the daytime, in the hot mornings, these motors made a petulant, irritable sound; at night, in the still evening when the afterglow lit the water, they whined about one's ears like mosquitoes. My boy loved our rented outboard, and his great desire was to achieve singlehanded mastery over it, and authority, and he soon learned the trick of choking it a little (but not too much), and the adjustment of the needle valve. Watching him I would remember the things you could do with the old one-cylinder engine with the heavy flywheel, how you could have it eating out of your hand if you got really close to it spiritually. Motor boats in those days didn't have clutches, and you would make a landing by shutting off the motor at the proper time and coasting in with a ready rudder. But there was a way of reversing them, if you learned the trick, by cutting the switch and putting it on again exactly on the final dying revolution of the flywheel, so that it would kick back against compression and begin reversing. Approaching a dock in a strong following breeze, it was difficult to slow up sufficiently by the ordinary coasting method, and if a boy felt he had complete mastery over his motor, he was tempted to keep it running beyond its time and then reverse it a few feet from the dock. It took a cool nerve, because if you threw the switch a twentieth of a second too soon you would catch the flywheel when it still had speed enough to go up past center, and the boat would leap ahead, charging bull-fashion at the dock.

We had a good week at the camp. The bass were biting well and the sun shone endlessly, day after day. We would be tired at night and lie down in the accumulated heat of the little bedrooms after the long hot day and the breeze would stir almost imperceptibly outside and the smell of the swamp drift in through the rusty screens. Sleep would come easily and in the morning the red squirrel would be on the roof, tapping out his gay routine. I kept remembering everything, lying in bed in the mornings — the small steam boat that had a long rounded stern like the lip of a Ubangi, and how quietly she ran on the moonlight sails, when the older boys played their mandolins and the girls sang and we ate doughnuts dipped in sugar, and how sweet the music was on the water in the shining night, and what it had felt like to think about girls then. After breakfast we would go up to the store and the things were in the same place — the minnows in a bottle, the plugs and spinners disarranged and pawed over by the youngsters from the boys' camp, the fig newtons and the Beeman's gum. Outside, the road was tarred and cars stood in front of the store. Inside, all was just as it had always been, except there was more Coca-Cola and not so much Moxie and root beer and birch beer and sarsaparilla. We would walk out with a bottle of pop apiece and sometimes the pop would backfire up our noses and hurt. We explored the streams, quietly, where the turtles slid off the sunny logs and dug their way into the soft bottom; and we lay on the town wharf and fed worms to the tame bass. Everywhere we went I had trouble making out which was I, the one walking at my side, the one walking in my pants.

One afternoon while we were there at that lake a thunderstorm came up. It was like the revival of an old melodrama that I had seen long ago with childish awe. The second-act climax of the drama of the electrical disturbance over a lake in America had not changed in any important respect. This was the big scene, still the big scene. The whole thing was so familiar, the first feeling of oppression and heat and a general air around camp of not wanting to go very far away. In midafternoon (it was all the same) a curious darkening of the sky, and a lull in everything that had made life tick; and then the way the boats suddenly swung the other way at their moorings with the coming of a breeze out of the new quarter, and the premonitory rumble. Then the kettle drum, then the snare, then the bass drum and cymbals, then crackling light against the dark, and the gods grinning and licking their chops in the hills. Afterward the calm, the rain steadily rustling in the calm lake, the return of light and hope and spirits, and the campers running out in joy and relief to go swimming in the rain, their bright cries perpetuating the deathless joke about how they were getting simply drenched, and the children screaming with delight at the new sensation of bathing in the rain, and the joke about getting drenched linking the generations in a strong indestructible chain. And the comedian who waded in carrying an umbrella.

When the others went swimming my son said he was going in too. He pulled his dripping trunks from the line where they had hung all through the shower, and wrung them out. Languidly, and with no thought of going in, I watched him, his hard little body, skinny and bare, saw him wince slightly as he pulled up around his vitals the small, soggy, icy garment. As he buckled the swollen belt suddenly my groin felt the chill of death.

Questions

1. Why is the road to the farmhouse now only a two-track road? Why is the hair of the waitresses now clean? What other details have changed in the lake area since the essayist's boyhood? What hasn't changed?
2. "As he buckled the swollen belt suddenly my groin felt the chill of death." How does this last sentence of the essay join two ideas which we then see have been somehow present in it from the beginning? What are those two ideas and how have they been developed?
3. White describes the lake and camp (then and now) for the large part as serene and idyllic. Yet here and there certain melancholy details appear, reminding us of the imperfection of the human condition. What are they?
4. To what extent does the author tell us about his son as a particular personality? To what extent does he tell us about himself as an individual? What conclusions about the intent of the essay do your answers suggest to you?

General Discussion Questions

1. How and why may a person's attitude towards the social or "class" context of his childhood change as he grows older?
2. What things or places, concretely called to mind, are important to the three essayists in this section? What similarities and differences do you find in comparing their selective remembrances?

8

Man and Nature

"In harmony with Nature?" Restless fool,
Who with such heat dost preach what ere to thee,
When true, the last impossibility . . .
To be like Nature strong, like Nature cool!

Know, man hath all which Nature hath, but more,
And in that *more* lie all his hopes of good.
Nature is cruel, man is sick of blood;
Nature is stubborn, man would fain adore;

Nature is fickle, man hath need of rest;
Nature forgives no debt, and fears no grave;
Man would be mild, and with safe conscience blest.

Man must begin, know this, where Nature ends;
Nature and man can never be fast friends.
Fool! if thou canst not pass her, rest her slave.

MATTHEW ARNOLD

Foreword to *Confessions of a Wood-Chopping Man*

Hugh MacLennan, a Canadian novelist, teacher, outdoorsman, and classical scholar, obviously maintains an immediate and personal relationship with Nature. What he finds in the woods is clarified, not complicated, by his bookishness. Like all really great teachers and really educated men, he finds significant things to perceive in all of his experience.

One of MacLennan's own favorite essayists, the great scholar-politician Francis Bacon, wrote about studies that they "serve for delight, for ornament, and for ability. Their chief use for delight is in privateness and retiring; for ornament, is in discourse; and for ability, is in the judgment and disposition of affairs." We feel that Hugh MacLennan has applied this famous justification for the academic to his "study" in the discipline of Nature. As you read the essay, consider the author's specific attention to the considerations of "delight," "ornament," and "ability."

Confessions of a Wood-chopping Man

by Hugh MacLennan (1907-)

Pleasure, profit and beauty from a single afternoon's exercise — what more could a puritan ask, especially when the profit will not be reaped till next year, and the beauty harvested for years to come. As for the pleasure, merely to be alive on an Indian summer afternoon in my part of the country is as close to heaven as my imagination extends.

After the first frost has turned ferns to brown dust and the birds have flocked south, the woods around my house in the country are filled with the living presence of silence. My feet crunch outrageously in the dry undergrowth as I make my way to the heart of the grove. My jeans are stiff with ancient sweat and my jersey is out at the elbows, the red paint has long ago been rubbed off the bow of my Swedish saw and my axe blade, several ounces lighter than when I bought it nine years ago, is honed sharp enough to sever a hair on my forearm. Looking up to the sky through the leaf patterns I shame my environment by the academic thought that this scene is the equal of Sainte-Chapelle,[1] but the comparison lasts only a few seconds. A hardwood copse in the Eastern Townships of Quebec in Indian summer can be compared to nothing else on this earth, being itself an absolute. By some recurring good fortune I am here; I am here with the axe, the saw, the wedge and the determination to alter the landscape a little.

1. Sainte-Chapelle: 13th century cathedral in Paris.

It is a moment that involves every aspect of the slow change in my whole view of life over the past decade and a half.

I was born and raised in a part of Canada where nobody is able to change the landscape. Along the Atlantic coast of Nova Scotia you grow up with the conviction that everything in nature here is as it is forever, and that man, living with the shifting immutability of the ocean and the unshifting immutability of granite rocks, can never dominate his fate, never play artist with nature, but must take life and the world as he finds them. The glacier that set the mould of the Nova Scotia coast (and the coast set the mould of the Nova Scotian character) so denuded the rocks of topsoil that for evermore only a spruce will thrive there. From childhood I accepted the belief that summer, spring and fall are much the same. One is grateful for a spruce if it is the only tree one really knows, but since any spruce is much the same as any other, and since no spruce ever changes its colours, the trees of my childhood helped the granite and the ocean to confirm me in the belief that nature can neither be altered nor improved.

It took me a good many years to respond to the soft luxuriance of the Eastern Townships, where the eye, the ear and the sense of smell are played upon gently and with subtle variations. It took me no time at all, however, to learn that here the landscape can and must be altered from time to time because it is continually altering itself to your disadvantage. A house in the country for summer living must be tied to the earth by close plantings of shrubs and trees, to give protection from the winds and to take away its aspect of being a brash intruder. But a maple sapling grows eight feet a year in this rich, rainy land, and a small fir that looks like an incipient Christmas tree when you transplant it soon becomes a dense screen breeding swarms of blackflies. Where there was one butternut there is soon a grove, and within a decade the pasture in which your house was built has been taken over by a stand of maples, oaks, poplars, wild cherries, honey locusts, old appletrees, hornbeams, birches, beeches and even some stray pines. Their roots are now under your cottage, their branches are joined over your roof, and they have made your home as dark as an animal's den.

The year I bought my house, I cut away every cedar, pine and spruce that crowded it. This was an act with a double meaning for me. I intended to let the sun filter down through the branches of the great hardwoods farther back, and I also needed a symbol of emancipation from the stern acceptance of my youth, I suppose.

"You'll feel naked without some kind of protection, won't you?" said a neighbour. "Now there's only the garden and the lawn between you and the road."

He meant that *he* would; I felt as though cobwebs had been swept from a dirty window. What good to keep other people from looking in, if at the same time I was prevented from looking out? Anyway I live high on a hill away from the village, on a dirt road that leads to nowhere, and the passers-by are few and friendly. Since my land slopes at a twenty-five degree angle and the road is below the house, I can overlook any activity on the road and let my eye take in a view that extends for ten miles over a deep lake indented with bays that lap the feet of thrusting hills. I can look across wind-blown farms and red pine headlands and the shining roofs of new cattle barns.

I began to cut in order to get sun and air into the house and I continued to cut in order to get sun and air into the surrounding woods. The second year I was mildly surprised to discover that the wood I cut had saved me many dollars. Then I bought a lot across the road and down the hill to protect our view. But the view gradually disappeared behind a wall of rapidly growing trees. They were a fine mixture of greens in summer and an unbelievable blend of colours in the fall, but living with them in front of me was like living behind a seventy-foot hedge.

So, over the years, those rapidly growing trees have given a pattern to my life in much the same way that his rotating wheat fields pattern the life of the farmer. Come the fall and I must get to work on them.

I have a neighbour who thinks it a crime to cut any oak, but what do you do if you have two oaks within six feet of one another? I run my hand over the smooth, olive-green trunk and feel the hard muscles inside the bark. An oak, especially a young one, feels human when your hand strokes it. But more than any tree in the forest, the oak needs room to grow. Its roots spread wide and lie close to the surface of the earth. I look up at this pair and see that they have grown like basketball players, tall, thin and not much good for anything else but growing tall and thin. Their lowest branches are at least twenty-five feet above the ground, since it was always dark in here before I got busy cutting out the saplings, and the trees had to thrust high in order to reach the life-giving sun. I feel the trunks of both and decide that the spindlier one must go, to give the other a chance to fulfil the destiny of an oak.

So I go down on both knees, set the saw at the trunk of the victim and get to work. In such a close-grained tree the opening made by the slim saw blade is almost invisible once the saw has buried itself in the trunk. White dust spurts out, to become brown as the blade reaches the darker heart of the tree. Then comes the crack — hard, solid, vibrating up the entire length of the trunk and echoing through the silent copse. There is a shiver, a twitch in the pinky-brown plumage, a moment of hesitation. As I stand up and watch, one hand on the trunk, the tree nods in the direction I had intended it to fall, then goes down in a swooshing, stately plunge. There is a flash of scarlet as a maple is brushed on the way down. Inevitably the oak comes to rest at an angle, its cascading upper branches caught by the interlocking branches of neighbouring trees.

In the new silence I consider my next move. A fallen tree, even one as modest as this, creates a sizable wreckage. I think of Mr. Gladstone,[2] who used to slay giant oaks, Royal Navy oaks, to relieve his emotions. When Disraeli[3] was extraordinarily wily or the Queen[4] ordinarily rude, another oak on the estate of the Grand Old Man was doomed to fall. And then there was the labour of cleaning up the mess, a job that I know from experience must have taken days. So far as I can discover from my reading, the Prime Minister gave little thought to this aspect of forestry. He was able to sate his aggressions and stalk off, sweaty under the armpits but with his Victorian waistcoat still in place, while humbler men took over the long task of trimming the oak, sawing its trunk into logs, splitting them and trundling them into the woodshed. Humbler men without the need to sublimate a libido must have stacked and burned Mr. Gladstone's slash.

Perhaps the psychiatrist who lives below me on his own tree-enclosed acreage, hearing the crash of my falling oak, thinks I am ridding myself of aggressions, too. He may even think I am slaying a father-image. But no matter what he thinks, my oak has merely been severed at the base, it has not been transformed into cordwood.

It was cold last night. It was colder still at six this morning when I peered out at the thermometer and saw that the mercury stood at twenty-seven degrees. When I got out of bed at eight and built a fire there was still rime on the lawn. The day was fine and clear, but it was so cold my fireplace consumed ten logs before one o'clock. This year a short cord sells at seven dollars, a long cord at anything from fifteen to twenty depending on what kind of wood it contains. No matter what my woodpile represents to a psychologist, it gives me an intense pleasure to use it for warmth, even though (as the countrywoman remarked yesterday when she came in to clean the house) it takes a lot of sweat to build a woodpile.

I think, sometimes, that Mr. Gladstone missed the best part of tree-cutting. Each fallen tree presents it own problems, and the man who walks off and leaves them is as bad a tree-butcher as the one who murders a copse

---

2. Mr. Gladstone: William Ewart Gladstone (1809-98), Prime Minister four different times.
3. Disraeli: Benjamin Disraeli (1804-81), Prime Minister twice; political opponent of Gladstone.
4. Queen: Queen Victoria (1819-1901), Queen of England, 1837-1901.

with a power saw. This oak of mine is entangled with two other trees and of course the simplest thing to do is cut them both down so that all three are prone. But the tree supporting the oak on the left is a rowan, a fugitive from an old garden, probably, and under no circumstances, under absolutely none, will I cut a rowan tree in my own woods. The other is a rock maple, a tree which still fills me with wonder and joy because it was scarce in Nova Scotia and in England almost non-existent. I always have a twinge of conscience when I cut down a maple. But here the maples grow like weeds and this particular one is so close to the rowan it will rob it of nutriment as both try to grow. So the maple goes, and the crack of its fall echoes over the hill.

Still the oak is suspended; when the maple went, its weight was taken by more stuff beyond. There is nothing for it but to cut the oak down to size in the only way left. I start sawing the trunk in eight-foot lengths, each cut about four and a half feet above the ground, which is as high as I can drive the saw. With the entire tree exerting hundreds of pounds of pressure on the saw blade, I must use the wedge. And this means that for the rest of the afternoon these two tree, the oak and the maple, are going to keep me busy.

Towards sunset the logs are piled and split and fragrant, the slash dragged off into a great angular pile to dry and await my pleasure on a future moist day. I come out of the copse and look to see what effect my work has made on the landscape. A little, and the beginning of a lot, because a splendid butternut has now been uncovered and must be given its chance. With that poplar out of the way the sun will slant deeply into the copse and I will have the beginnings of a woodland nave. A forest without sun is like a church without God; I reflect that the thought is corny, but I don't care. Disposing of the poplar will put no burden on my conscience. Along with a ragged spruce, it exists to be destroyed, for if the axe doesn't get to it the insects will, and after the insects will come the flickers and the pileated woodpeckers. Tomorrow afternoon's work is now planned, and it, in turn, will lead to the work of the day after and the day after that. Carving out the raw material of a forest to create a civilized wood is like making a picture or writing a book. One vista suggests another and there is no absolute end to it in a country like ours. But when the season's cutting is over after Thanksgiving, and I go muscle-bound back to the city, I feel as Melville did when he finished *Moby Dick,* as pure as the lamb.

Questions

1. MacLennan begins with the claim that a "single afternoon's" wood-chopping provides him with "pleasure, profit, and beauty," As his essay continues, what do the specific terms of each of these general benefits turn out to be?
2. MacLennan indicates in this essay that he feels differently about cutting oak, maple, and rowan, and cutting spruce and poplar. What reasons lie behind his distinctions?
3. What differences does MacLennan note between trees and landscapes in the Nova Scotia of his boyhood and in the Eastern Townships where he lives now? How does he relate these differences to changes in his own attitudes towards life in general?
4. One of MacLennan's neighbors thinks it a crime to cut any oak. What is MacLennan's response to this position? What differing general moral attitudes are illustrated by the two men's feelings about oak-cutting?
5. MacLennan alludes to neighbors other than the anti-oak-cutting man (although perhaps they are different voices of the same man), as well as to the famous oak-cutting prime minister of England, William Gladstone. How does he use the attitudes and behavior of each of these to clarify his own attitudes?

Foreword to *Wolf*

This episode between man and dog is the opening portion of a much longer essay, "The Angry Winter," which is in Loren Eiseley's book, *The Unexpected Universe*. The author is an anthropologist and historian of science. What he captures in this fragment is a sense of certain mysteries, enigmas of time and being, that involve man and beast alike. Though Eiseley knows, too, the comforts and assurances that man can find in nature, he is also aware of its disquieting elements. Here we see how, on a winter's night, a man and his dog can find themselves in an eerie confrontation, each haunted somehow by the unimaginably remote past of his species.

Those who read about this experience will be interested to know the dedication of *The Unexpected Universe:*

To Wolf,
who sleeps forever
with an ice age bone
across his heart,
the last gift
of one
who loved him

Wolf

by Loren Eiseley (1907-   )

A time comes when creatures whose destinies have crossed somewhere in the remote past are forced to appraise each other as though they were total strangers. I had been huddled beside the fire one winter night, with the wind prowling outside and shaking the windows. The big shepherd dog on the hearth before me occasionally glanced up affectionately, sighed, and slept. I was working, actually, amidst the debris of a far greater winter. On my desk lay the lance points of ice age hunters and the heavy leg bone of a fossil bison. No remnants of flesh attached to these relics. The deed lay more than ten thousand years remote. It was represented here by naked flint and by bone so mineralized it rang when struck. As I worked on in my little circle of light, I absently laid the bone beside me on the floor. The hour had crept toward midnight. A grating noise, a heavy rasping of big teeth diverted me. I looked down.

The dog had risen. That rock-hard fragment of a vanished beast was in his jaws and he was mouthing it with a fierce intensity I had never seen exhibited by him before.

"Wolf," I exclaimed, and stretched out my hand. The dog backed up but did not yield. A low and steady rumbling began to rise in his chest, something out of a long-gone midnight. There was nothing in that bone to taste, but ancient shapes were moving in his mind and determining his utterance. Only fools gave up bones. He was warning me.

"Wolf," I chided again.

As I advanced, his teeth showed and his mouth wrinkled to strike. The rumbling rose to a direct snarl. His flat head swayed low and wickedly as a reptile's above the floor. I was the most loved object in his universe, but the past was fully alive in him now. Its shadows were whispering in his mind. I knew he was not bluffing. If I made another step he would strike.

Yet his eyes were strained and desperate. "Do not," something pleaded in the back of them, some affectionate thing that had followed at my heel all the days of his mortal life, "do not force me. I am what I am and cannot be otherwise because of the shadows. Do not reach out. You are a man, and my very god. I love you, but do not put out your hand. It is midnight. We are in another time, in the snow."

"The *other* time," the steady rumbling continued while I paused, "the other time in the snow, the big, the final, the terrible snow, when the shape of this thing I hold spelled life. I will not give it up. I cannot. The shadows will not permit me. Do not put out your hand."

I stood silent, looking into his eyes, and heard his whisper through. Slowly I drew back in understanding. The snarl diminished, ceased. As I retreated, the bone slumped to the floor. He placed a paw upon it, warningly.

And were there no shadows in my own mind, I wondered. Had I not for a moment, in the grip of that savage utterance, been about to respond, to hurl myself upon him over an invisible haunch ten thousand years removed? Even to me the shadows had whispered — to me, the scholar in his study.

"Wolf," I said, but this time, holding a familiar leash, I spoke from the door indifferently. "A walk in the snow." Instantly from his eyes that other visitant receded. The bone was left lying. He came eagerly to my side, accepting the leash and taking it in his mouth as always.

A blizzard was raging when we went out, but he paid no heed. On his thick fur the driving snow was soon clinging heavily. He frolicked a little — though usually he was a grave dog — making up to me for something still receding in his mind. I felt the snowflakes fall upon my face, and stood thinking of another time, and another time still, until I was moving from midnight to midnight under ever more remote and vaster snows. Wolf came to my side with a little whimper. It was he who was civilized now. "Come back to the fire," he nudged gently, "or you will be lost." Automatically I took the leash he offered. He led me safely home and into the house.

"We have been very far away," I told him solemnly. "I think there is something in us that we had both better try to forget." Sprawled on the rug, Wolf made no response except to thump his tail feebly out of courtesy. Already he was mostly asleep and dreaming. By the movement of his feet

I could see he was running far upon some errand in which I played no part.

Softly I picked up his bone — our bone, rather — and replaced it high on a shelf in my cabinet. As I snapped off the light the white glow from the window seemed to augment itself and shine with a deep, glacial blue. As far as I could see, nothing moved in the long aisles of my neighbor's woods. There was no visible track, and certainly no sound from the living. The snow continued to fall steadily, but the wind, and the shadows it had brought, had vanished.

Questions

Eiseley imagines Wolf inarticulately communicating the thought, "I am what I am and cannot be otherwise because of the shadows." Explain your understanding of this. Is it at all true of the man, also? Could it be true of you, of every man? Would it be quite the same thing in man and dog? If not, how might it differ while yet having some element in common?

Foreword to *The Individual and the Species*

Joseph Wood Krutch (pronounced Krooch) had a distinguished career as a professor and drama critic. Following his retirement and a move to the desert country of Arizona, he began a new, and ultimately more important career, as a naturalist and reflective essayist on man and nature. Always of concern to him, as in the following essay from *The Best Nature Writing of Joseph Wood Krutch* was the subtle question of how man is both a creature in, and of, nature and yet unmistakably an exception to generalizations about all the rest of nature.

Perhaps one point toward the close of the essay might require some modification, or restatement, in the light of current studies of population factors among both man and all other living creatures. Krutch speaks of "nature's insatiable appetite for more and more of every kind of creature, at no matter what cost either to other species or to the individuals of any one species." That is by no means altogether true, for in an untampered-with environment, most, if not all, wild animal species show a tendency to check their numbers by instinctive controls of their own, plus interaction with other species in the total ecology. Man is the creature who often blunders in and upsets this balance for other species and who also shows insufficient awareness of the perils to himself of his own sheer numbers.

The Individual and the Species

by Joseph Wood Krutch (1893-1970)

A few mornings ago I rescued a bat from a swimming pool. The man who owned the pool — but did not own the bat — asked me why. That question I do not expect ever to be able to answer, but it involves a good deal. If even I myself could understand it, I would know what it is that seems to distinguish man from the rest of nature, and why, despite all she has to teach him, there is also something he would like to teach her if he could.

Nature books always explain — for the benefit of utilitarians — that bats are economically important because they destroy many insects. For the benefit of those more interested in the marvelous than in the profitable, they also usually say something about the bat's wonderful invention of a kind of sonar by the aid of which he can fly in the blackest night without colliding with even so artificial an obstruction as a piano wire strung across his path. But before lifting my particular bat out of the swimming pool, I did not calculate his economic importance and I did not rapidly review in my mind the question whether or not his scientific achievement entitled him to life.

Still less could I pretend that he was a rare specimen or that one bat more or less would have any perceptible effect on the balance of nature. There were plenty of others just like him right here where I live and throughout this whole area. Almost every night I have seen several of his fellows swooping down to the swimming pool for a drink before starting off for an evening of economically useful activity. A few weeks before I had, as a matter of fact, seen near Carlsbad, New Mexico, several hundred thousand of this very species in a single flight. That had seemed like enough bats to satisfy one for a normal lifetime. Yet here I was, not only fishing a single individual from the water, but tending him anxiously to see whether or not he could recover from an ordeal which had obviously been almost too much for him.

Probably he had fallen in because he had miscalculated in the course of the difficult maneuver involved in getting a drink on the wing. Probably, therefore, he had been in the water a good many hours and would not have lasted much longer. But he looked as though he wanted to live and I, inexplicably, also hoped that he would. And that would seem to imply some sort of kindliness more detached, more irrational, and more completely gratuitous than any nature herself is capable of. "So careful of the type she seems, so careless of the single life."[1]

At Carlsbad, so it seemed to me, I had seen bats as nature sees them. Here by the swimming pool, I had seen an individual bat as only man can see him. It was a neat coincidence which arranged the two experiences so close together, and I shall always think of them in that way.

Even I find it difficult to love, in my special human way, as many bats as I saw at Carlsbad. Nature is content to love them in her way and makes no attempt here to love them in the way that even I would fail at. She loves bats in general and as a species. For that reason she can never get enough of them. But as long as there are plenty in the world, she is unconcerned with any particular bat. She gives him his chance (or sometimes his lack of it) and if he does not, or cannot, take it, others will. A margin of failure is to be expected. The greatest good of the greatest number is a ruling principle so absolute that it is not even tempered with regret over those who happen not to be included within the greatest number.

Thus nature discovered, long before the sociologists did, the statistical criterion. Bureaucratic states which accept averages and curves of distribution as realities against which there is no appeal represent a sort of "return to nature" very different from what that phrase is ordinarily taken to imply. Insofar as the great dictators can be assumed to be in any sense sincere when they profess a concern with the welfare of their people or even with that of mankind, their concern is like nature's — indifferent to everything except the statistically measurable result. If they really love

1. from *In Memoriam* by Tennyson.

men, then they love them only as nature loves bats. She never devised anything so prompt and effective as the gas chamber, but her methods are sometimes almost equally unscrupulous. For she also has her methods — not always pretty ones — of getting rid of what she considers the superfluous. She seems to agree, in principle, with those who maintain that any decisive concern with a mere individual is unscientific, sentimental, and ultimately incompatible with the greatest good of the greatest number.

But one bat in a swimming pool is not the same thing as two or three hundred thousand at Carlsbad. Because there is only one of him and only one of me, some sort of relationship, impossible in the presence of myriads, springs up between us. I no longer take toward him the attitude of nature or the dictator. I become a man again, aware of feelings which are commonly called humane but for which I prefer the stronger word, human.

It was the barking of two young police dogs taking a natural, unsentimental interest in an individual in distress which first called my attention to what I still think of as "my" bat, though I am sure nothing in nature prepared him to believe that I would assume any responsibility for his welfare. At first, I did not know what he was because a fish out of water looks no less inexplicable than a bat in it. The enormous wings attached to this tiny mouse body had helped, no doubt, to keep him afloat, but they were preposterously unmanageable in a dense, resistant medium. The little hooks on his arms by means of which he climbs clumsily on a rough surface were useless on the vertical, tiled sides of the pool. When I lifted him out with a flat wire net, he lay inertly sprawled, his strange body so disorganized as to have lost all functional significance, like a wrecked airplane on a mountainside which does not look as though it had ever been able to take to the air.

A slight shiver which shook his body when I leaned over him was the only sign of life. The situation did not look promising, for I knew that a live bat is very much alive, with a heart which sometimes beats more than seven times as fast as mine. Since he obviously needed — if he was not too far gone to need anything — to be dry and to be warm I spread him on top of a wall in the full sun to which he had never, perhaps, been exposed before. Every now and then the tremor recurred; and as his fur dried, I began to be aware of a heart beating furiously. Possibly, I began to say, he may survive. When I bent closer, he raised his head and hissed in my face, exposing a gleaming set of little white teeth before he collapsed exhausted again.

By now his leathery wings were dry and his fur hardly more than damp. But he still seemed incapable of any except the feeblest movements. I thought that at best it would be hours before he would be able to fly. I put a stone beside him to cast a semishadow and was turning away when I caught sight of something out of the corner of my eye. I looked, just in time to see him raise himself suddenly onto his bony elbows and take off. He half-circled the pool to get his bearings and, flying strongly now, he disappeared from my sight over the desert, not permanently the worse, I hope, for a near escape from the death which would not have been very important so far as the total welfare of the bat community is concerned. Inevitably, I have wondered whether he has since been among the bats I see drinking at the pool at evening. Or has he, perhaps, found some body of water with less unpleasant associations?

But why had I done more than, like the dogs, peer at him with curiosity? Why had I felt sad when I thought he would never recover, really joyful when I saw him fly away? He is not economically important, however much his tribe may be. If he had drowned, there would have been others left to catch insects as well as to demonstrate for the benefit of science the bat's sonar. Who am I that I should exhibit a concern which, apparently, the Great Mother of bats (and of men) does not share. What did I accomplish for bats, for myself, or for humanity at large when I fished my bat from the water?

These are not rhetorical questions. They probably have several answers, but there is one of which I am especially aware. What I had done was to keep alive an attitude, an emotion, or better yet a strong passion, of which only the faint beginnings are observable in any creature except man and which, moreover, appear in danger of extinction because of two powerful enemies. This sort of concern with a mere individual is scorned alike by the frank apostles of violent unreason and by those proponents of the greatest good for the greatest number who insist upon being what they call scientific rather than what they call sentimental.

It was nature which loved the race, and it was man who added to that a love for the individual as such. Perhaps those two things, though not really incompatible under all circumstances, become so when one accepts also nature's passion for mere numbers. Perhaps, in other words, there really is something incompatible between the value which we put on the individual and nature's insatiable appetite for more and more of every kind of creature, at no matter what cost either to other species or to the individuals of any one species. Perhaps we have retained too much of her immoderate desire for multiplication while developing our own concern for the individual, whom we think of as rare or irreplaceable. Perhaps, in other words, it is easiest to love both man and men when there are not too many (or even not too obviously enough) of the last. Perhaps men should not be too common if they are to have value.

One thing is certain. However many of us there may be or come to be, no man and no group of men should have too much power over too many of us. It makes such men or such groups feel too much as though they were nature herself. So careful of the type they are — or claim to be; so careless of the single life they so indubitably become.

Questions

1. What is the difference between "bats as nature sees them" and as a man such as Krutch sees them? (Or Audubon, or Thoreau, or Eiseley, or many others, but not *all* men.)
2. Discuss the link between nature's "ruling principle" of the greatest good for the greatest number and political theory in human affairs. Is the best human society the most "natural" society in that sense?
3. State in your own words Krutch's philosophical conclusion from his encounter with this bat.

General Discussion Questions

1. Each of the essayists in this section is obviously knowledgeable of his subject. Yet there are limits to their knowledge, made quite evident in each essay. The natural area is ultimately an eternally mysterious one. What limits of knowledge are suggested in these essays? What do the three writers, individually and collectively, have to say or imply about the unknown in Nature?
2. Is it really surprising that some intelligent people have gone on reco d as having no preference for "nature" over the works of man? Is it possible that a number of others have actually held this heretical opinion without saying so? Perhaps, even in the essays of the nature-loving writers represented here, you can find things which a fourth essayist might use to recommend the "artificial" life over the "natural" one, or indoors over outdoors. Try it.

Author and Title Index

Boxing With the Naked Eye, 24
Brownsville, 180
Charles II, 55
Chesterton, G. K.
  On the Classics, 169
Confessions of a Wood-Chopping Man, 195
"Danny Deever," 18
Davis, O. B.
  The Presence of Mine Enemies, 14
DuBois, W. E. B.
  Of Mr. Booker T. Washington and Others, 60
Eiseley, Loren
  Wolf, 201
Fable, 103
Fadiman, Clifton
  Faulkner, Extra-Special, Double-Distilled 137
Faulkner, Extra-Special, Double-Distilled, 137
The Fight, 34
Fuller, Edmund
  The Lord of the Hobbits: J. R. R. Tolkien, 120
Golding, William
  Fable, 103
A Hanging, 8
Hazlitt, William
  The Fight, 34
  On Patriotism – A Fragment, 86
How Impractical are the Humanities?, 157
The Idea of Patriotism, 79
The Individual and the Species, 204
Kazin, Alfred
  Brownsville, 180
Kipling, Rudyard
  "Danny Deever," 18
Krutch, Joseph Wood
  The Individual and the Species, 204
Liebling, A. J.
  Boxing With the Naked Eye, 24
The Lord of the Hobbits: J. R. R. Tolkien, 120
Macaulay, Thomas Babington
  Charles II, 55
MacLennan, Hugh
  Confessions of a Wood-Chopping Man, 195
McKenna, Richard
  New Eyes for Old, 145
A Memory of Father, 175
Mencken, H. L.
  The Politician, 72
Of Mr. Booker T. Washington and Others, 60
New Eyes for Old, 145
Once More to the Lake, 185
On Patriotism – A Fragment, 86
On the Classics, 169
Orwell, George
  A Hanging, 8
The Politician, 72
The Presence of Mine Enemies, 14
Priestley, J. B.
  Wrong Ism, 92
Redding, J. Saunders
  A Memory of Father, 175
Rowse, A. L.
  The Idea of Patriotism, 79
Salomon, Louis B.
  How Impractical are the Humanities?, 157
Twain, Mark
  The War Prayer, 97
The War Prayer, 97
White, E. B.
  Once More to the Lake, 185
Wolf, 201
Wrong Ism, 92